Paula Gooder was a lecturer in biblical studies at Ripon College Cuddesdon and then at the Queen's Foundation for Ecumenical Theological Studies for a total of twelve years before beginning to work freelance as a writer and lecturer in biblical studies. She is a visiting lecturer at King's College, London, an honorary lecturer at the University of Birmingham, a senior research scholar at the Queen's Foundation, Birmingham, and Canon Theologian of Birmingham Cathedral. A published author, her previous books include *Only the Third Heaven? 2 Corinthians 12.1–10 and Heavenly Ascent* (T&T Clark, 2006) and *Exploring New Testament Greek: A Way In* (co-authored with Peter Kevern, SCM Press, 2004).

For
Christopher C. Rowland,
whose passion for biblical interpretation is so infectious

SEARCHING FOR MEANING

An introduction to interpreting the New Testament

PAULA GOODER

SPCK

WJK WESTMINSTER
JOHN KNOX PRESS
LOUISVILLE · KENTUCKY

Copyright © 2008, 2009 Paula Gooder

First published in 2008 in Great Britain by
Society for Promoting Christian Knowledge
36 Causton Street
London SW1P 4ST

Published in 2009 in the United States of America by
Westminster John Knox Press
100 Witherspoon Street
Louisville, KY 40202

08 09 10 11 12 13 14 15 16 17 — 10 9 8 7 6 5 4 3 2 1

British Library Cataloguing-in-Publication Data
A catalogue record for this book is available from the British Library.

ISBN 978-0-281-05835-8 (U.K. edition)

United States Library of Congress Cataloging-in-Publication Data is on file
at the Library of Congress, Washington, D.C.

ISBN 978-0-664-23194-1 (U.S. edition)

Typeset by Graphicraft Ltd, Hong Kong
Printed in Great Britain at Ashford Colour Press

Produced on paper from sustainable forests

Contents

* *Contributed to the chapter.*

Contributors

A. K. M. Adam has taught New Testament and Early Church History at Seabury-Western Theological Seminary, Princeton Theological Seminary and Eckerd College, and has served parishes in New Haven, Tampa and Evanston. He has written and edited numerous books and articles, including *What is Postmodern Biblical Criticism?*; *Making Sense of New Testament Theology*; *A Grammar of New Testament Greek*; *A Handbook of Postmodern Biblical Interpretation* and *Postmodern Interpretations of the Bible: A Reader*; and most recently *Faithful Interpretation* and (as co-author) *Reading Scripture with the Church*. He is presently working on a book that builds on his hermeneutical studies to present a theological and ethical exposition of Matthew's Gospel.

George Aichele is a member of the Bible and Culture Collective, and author and editor of books and articles on semiotics and the Bible, the Bible as fantasy, and the Bible in popular culture. Some of the best known of his publications are *Those Outside: Non-Canonical Readings of the Canonical Gospels* (with Richard Walsh); *The Control of Biblical Meaning: Canon as Semiotic Mechanism*; *Sign, Text, Scripture: Semiotics and the Bible*; and *Jesus Framed*. He recently retired as professor at Adrian College (Michigan, USA).

Bruce Chilton is Bernard Iddings Bell Professor of Religion at Bard College, where he directs the the Institute of Advanced Theology. He has taught in Europe at the Universities of Cambridge, Sheffield and Münster, and in the United States at Yale University and Bard College. His most recent books are *Rabbi Jesus: An Intimate Biography*; *Redeeming Time: The Wisdom of Ancient Jewish and Christian Festal Calendars*; *Rabbi Paul: An Intellectual Biography*; *Mary Magdalene: A Biography*; and – as General Editor – *The Cambridge Companion to the Bible*.

James D. G. Dunn is Emeritus Lightfoot Professor of Divinity at the University of Durham (UK), where he taught from 1982 (previously at the University of Nottingham). He has authored over twenty monographs, including *Baptism in the Holy Spirit*; *Jesus and the Spirit*; *Unity and Diversity in the New Testament*; *Christology in the Making*; *Jesus, Paul and the Law*; *The Partings of the Ways*; *The Theology of Paul the Apostle*; *Jesus Remembered*; *The New Perspective on Paul* and *A New Perspective on*

Jesus, and commentaries on Romans, Galatians, Colossians and Philemon, and Acts.

Kathy Ehrensperger is Senior Lecturer in New Testament Studies at the University of Wales, Lampeter. She earned her degree in theology from the University of Basel, Switzerland and her Ph.D. from the University of Wales. She is the author of *That We May Be Mutually Encouraged: Feminism and the New Perspective in Pauline Studies*; *Paul and the Dynamics of Power: Communication and Interaction in the Early Christ-Movement*; and is co-editor of *Reformation Readings of Romans* (with R. Ward Holder) as well as having contributed numerous articles in journals and edited books.

J. Keith Elliott was Professor of New Testament Textual Criticism in the Department of Theology and Religious Studies at the University of Leeds until his retirement at the end of 2007. He is the editor of *The Apocryphal New Testament* and author of several books on textual criticism, including *A Bibliography of Greek New Testament Manuscripts*. He is book reviews editor for *Novum Testamentum* and President of its Editorial Board. He is Secretary of the International Greek New Testament Project, currently assembling a full critical apparatus to the Fourth Gospel.

Craig A. Evans received his Ph.D. from Claremont Graduate University and is the Payzant Distinguished Professor of New Testament at Acadia Divinity College in Wolfville, Nova Scotia, Canada. He has authored and edited many books on Jesus and the Gospels, such as *Fabricating Jesus: How Modern Scholars Distort the Gospels*; *Jesus and the Ossuaries*; and *Who was Jesus? A Jewish–Christian Dialogue* (with Paul Copan), and served as an advisor in the National Geographic Society's Gospel of Judas project. Evans has also appeared as an expert in several television documentaries and news programmes.

Robert M. Fowler is Chairperson and Professor in the Department of Religion, Baldwin-Wallace College, Berea, Ohio. He is author of *Let the Reader Understand: Reader-Response Criticism and the Gospel of Mark* and *Loaves and Fishes: The Function of the Feeding Stories in the Gospel of Mark*. He is co-author of *The Postmodern Bible* and a co-editor of *New Paradigms for Bible Study: The Bible in the Third Millennium*.

Mark Goodacre is an Associate Professor in New Testament at the Department of Religion, Duke University, North Carolina, USA. He earned his MA, M.Phil. and D.Phil. at the University of Oxford and was Senior

Lecturer at the University of Birmingham until 2005. His research interests include the Synoptic Gospels, the historical Jesus and the Gospel of Thomas. He is editor of the Library of New Testament Studies book series (formally JSNTS) and the author of several books including *The Synoptic Problem: A Way Through the Maze* and *The Case Against Q: Studies in Markan Priority and the Synoptic Problem*. He is well known for his award-winning internet site, *The New Testament Gateway* <www.ntgateway.com>, the web directory of academic New Testament resources. Goodacre appears regularly on television and radio to talk about religious matters, especially the New Testament.

Teresa J. Hornsby is Associate Professor of Religion and Director of the Women and Gender Studies Program at Drury University. She earned an undergraduate degree in religious studies at the University of Tennessee, a Master of Theological Studies at Harvard Divinity School, and a doctoral degree at Vanderbilt University. She has published articles, essays and reviews in numerous biblical journals and books, and is the author of *Sex Texts from the Bible: Selections Annotated & Explained* (SkyLight Illuminations).

David G. Horrell is Professor of New Testament Studies at the University of Exeter, UK. He is currently leading a project, funded by the Arts and Humanities Research Council of the UK, on Uses of the Bible in Environmental Ethics. His other research focuses on Paul, Pauline ethics, 1 Peter, and social-scientific approaches to the New Testament. Major publications include *The Social Ethos of the Corinthian Correspondence*; *Social-Scientific Approaches to New Testament Interpretation*; *An Introduction to the Study of Paul*; and *Solidarity and Difference: A Contemporary Reading of Paul's Ethics*.

Peter Kevern has worked on Bible translation in the Highlands of Papua New Guinea and co-authored (with Paula Gooder) *Exploring New Testament Greek: A Way In*. He is Director of Studies at the Queen's Foundation for Ecumenical Theological Education in Birmingham, UK, and is currently researching the relationship between writing and religion.

Tat-siong Benny Liew is Associate Professor of New Testament at the Pacific School of Religion, Berkeley, California. Alongside New Testament studies, Dr Liew's scholarly interests include literary theory, postcolonial studies, gender/sexuality studies and ethnic studies (particularly Asian American history and literature). He is the author of *Politics of Parousia: Reading Mark Inter(con)textually*; *What Is Asian American Biblical Hermeneutics?*

Reading the New Testament and numerous articles in journals and books. He was the guest editor of the *Semeia* volume on *The Bible in Asian America*.

Elizabeth Struthers Malbon is Professor of Religious Studies in the Department of Interdisciplinary Studies at Virginia Tech, and is an SBL and SNTS member. She is the author of four books: *Narrative Space and Mythic Meaning in Mark*; *The Iconography of the Sarcophagus of Junius Bassus: NEOFITVS IIT AD DEVM*; *In the Company of Jesus: Characters in Mark's Gospel*; and *Hearing Mark: A Listener's Guide*, and co-editor of three other books. She has also authored over thirty articles and book chapters, mostly on Markan narrative criticism.

Bruce J. Malina is Professor of Biblical Studies at Creighton University, where he has taught since 1969. He has studied in the USA and abroad (Rome and Jerusalem) and has degrees in philosophy, theology and biblical studies. He received an honorary doctorate from the University of St Andrews in Scotland (1995). He is the author of numerous books including a Social Science Commentary on each of the books of the New Testament (with Richard L. Rohrbaugh); *The New Testament World: Insights from Cultural Anthropology*; *Christian Origins and Cultural Anthropology*; *Windows on the World of Jesus*; *The New Jerusalem in the Book of Revelation*; *The Social Gospel of Jesus* and *Timothy: Paul's Chief Associate*.

Ched Myers is an activist theologian who has worked in social change movements for three decades. With a degree in New Testament Studies, he is a popular educator who animates Scripture and issues of faith-based peace and justice. He has authored a half-dozen books, including *Binding the Strong Man: A Political Reading of Mark's Story of Jesus* and *The Biblical Vision of Sabbath Economics*, and over a hundred articles. He is a co-founder of the Word and World School, the Sabbath Economics Collaborative, and the Bartimaeus Institute.

Daniel Patte is Professor of Religious Studies and Professor of New Testament and Early Christianity at Vanderbilt University. He is interested in hermeneutics and in theories of communication, structuralism and semiotics. He is the author of a wide range of books including *Early Jewish Hermeneutics in Palestine*; *The Ethics of Biblical Interpretation: A Reevaluation*; *Structural Exegesis for New Testament Critics*; *Paul's Faith and the Power of the Gospel: A Structural Introduction to the Pauline Letters*;

The Gospel According to Matthew: A Structural Commentary on Matthew's Faith and is co-editor of a number of others including *Reading Israel in Romans* (Romans Through History and Culture Series) with Cristina Grenholm, and the *Global Bible Commentary* with J. Severino Croatto, Nicole Wilkinson Duran and Teresa Okure.

Emerson B. Powery is Professor of Biblical Studies at Messiah College in Grantham, Pennsylvania. He was the recipient of Lee University's Excellence in Scholarship Award in 2004 and was the 2006–7 President of the Society of Biblical Literature (SE Region/SECSOR). He is the author of *Jesus Reads Scripture* and co-editor of *True to Our Native Land: An African American New Testament Commentary* and *The Spirit and the Mind: Essays in Informed Pentecostalism*, and has written numerous articles on hermeneutics and biblical interpretation. His current research projects include a commentary on the Gospel of Mark and the function of biblical texts within the nineteenth-century 'slave narrative' tradition.

Christopher Rowland has been Dean Ireland Professor of the Exegesis of Holy Scripture, in the University of Oxford, since 1991. For the last decade he has been involved in editing the pioneering series of commentaries on biblical reception history published by Blackwell. His interests include the study of apocalypticism, and he has recently completed a study of the great English visionary and poet, William Blake, and his biblical interpretation. He is the author of *The Open Heaven*; *Christian Origins*; *Revelation* (Blackwell Biblical Commentaries) and *Wheels Within Wheels: William Blake and the Ezekiel's Merkabah in Text and Image*.

James A. Sanders was Professor of Intertestamental and Biblical Studies at the Claremont School of Theology from 1977 to 1997, while concurrently Professor of Religion at the Claremont Graduate University. After formal retirement in 1997 he has acted as visiting professor at Union Theological Seminary/Columbia University in New York City (1997–8) and at Jewish Theological Seminary in New York City in the spring of 2001. Sanders was made 'founder and president emeritus' of the Ancient Biblical Manuscript Center in Claremont by its Board of Trustees in September 2003. He has been presented with three volumes of essays (Festschriften) published in his honour and has authored or edited thirty books, and over 280 scholarly articles. He co-authored and co-edited *The Canon Debate* and with Dominique Barthélemy of the Université de Fribourg he is co-editor of the (so far) four volumes of *Critique textuelle de l'Ancien Testament*.

R. S. Sugirtharajah is Professor of Biblical Hermeneutics at the University of Birmingham, UK. His research interests include postcolonial theory and biblical studies; the Bible and popular culture; Asian, African, Caribbean, Pacific and Latin American biblical interpretations and theologies; and Diasporic hermeneutic and theologies. He is the author of a large number of books, including *Asian Biblical Hermeneutics and Postcolonialism: Contesting the Interpretations*; *The Bible and Empire: Postcolonial Explorations*; *The Bible and the Third World: Precolonial, Colonial and Postcolonial Encounters*; *Postcolonial Criticism and Biblical Interpretation*; *Postcolonial Reconfigurations: An Alternative Way of Reading the Bible and Doing Theology* as well as the editor of a number of works both alone and with others.

Gerald O. West teaches Old Testament and Biblical Hermeneutics in the School of Religion and Theology, University of KwaZulu-Natal, South Africa. He is also the Director of the Ujamaa Centre for Community Development and Research, which is a collaborative project between socially engaged biblical scholars, organic intellectuals, and ordinary 'readers' of the Bible in communities of the poor, working-class and marginalized. Among Gerald West's recent publications are *The Academy of the Poor: Towards a Dialogical Reading of the Bible*; and an edited volume, together with Musa Dube, *The Bible in Africa: Transactions, Trajectories and Trends*.

Ben Witherington III is Amos Professor of NT for Doctoral Studies at Asbury Theological Seminary in Wilmore, Kentucky. He has also taught at Ashland Theological Seminary, Vanderbilt University, Duke Divinity School and Gordon-Conwell. He has written over thirty books, including *The Jesus Quest* and *The Paul Quest*. He is the author of a series of socio-rhetorical commentaries; one of his most recent was on Philemon, Colossians and Ephesians. He has also recently produced an introduction to New Testament Rhetoric entitled *New Testament Rhetoric: A Handbook*.

Acknowledgements

My greatest debt of gratitude for this volume goes to the 23 experts who have been willing to wrestle their vast knowledge of their area into a brief 800- to 1,000-word introduction. Such a task is not an easy one, and they have been gracious and generous with their time in presenting the wealth of their wisdom in terms as simple as possible. They are responsible only for the section of each chapter that bears their name (i.e. the section headed 'How did the theory develop and what are its main features?'). I have written the rest of the chapter and any errors that might be found in those sections are entirely my own.

Thanks also are due to Rebecca Mulhearn at SPCK, who has been an outstanding editor of this volume, always willing to help with queries from small to great, offering encouragement when needed, and ensuring that I kept going on what has turned out to be a mammoth task.

Thanks also to my husband, Peter, and daughters, Susannah and Ruth, who have borne with good grace my regular early-morning and late-night forays to my study as I attempted to complete this volume.

Introduction

If you browse along the shelves of a New Testament section in any bookshop or library you will encounter a dizzying array of technical descriptions of their methods, such as redaction criticism, structuralism and liberation hermeneutics. You might well ask yourself what on earth they all mean. The study of New Testament today relies on a basic understanding of an ever expanding range of ways of interpreting the biblical text. Someone who is new to the area, or who has done it before but cannot quite remember the distinction between, for example, form and redaction criticism, or rhetorical and narrative criticism, needs a simple guide to enable them to understand the basic presuppositions that lie behind the major studies that are written on the New Testament.

The problem with such guides is that they can teeter on the edge of being like a telephone directory: full of useful information that you know you will need, but deadly boring to read. Describing an interpretation in abstract terms can give you a certain amount of information but it is only when you see it in practice that you begin to understand why it is different from other approaches and what difference using this technique can make to interpretations of the text. This volume seeks to combine theoretical descriptions of the principles that lie behind each particular technique, and brief historical overviews of how the interpretation has reached the form it has, with a practical demonstration of one way in which it could be applied to a biblical text.

Each chapter that follows is laid out in a set way with a brief answer to the question 'What is this criticism?', followed by a historical and theoretical introduction written by a leading expert in the area which lays out the principle of the interpretation alongside the major trends of its development. This is followed by the landmark publications in the area to give a sense of which books have been particularly influential in the development of the method and then a practical example of what this method of interpretation might look like when applied to a biblical text. A short list of books relating to each chapter, to which you might turn if you want to explore the area further, is included at the end of the book.

Breadth over depth

The aim of this volume is to present a brief introduction to a wide range of interpretations. In volumes such as this there is a need to make a decision between breadth (attempting to cover as wide a range of approaches as possible) and depth (giving a detailed analysis of the interpretations explored). Here I have made a clear decision in favour of breadth over depth. The chapters exist simply as tasters of the respective approaches; anyone who wishes to be able to use the interpretations described would need to follow up the references that point to further reading. This volume presents a 'smorgasbord' of New Testament interpretations but does not aim for in-depth analysis.

The problem of presenting a broad variety of interpretations is that the presence of a range of methods can imply exhaustiveness, in other words that this volume contains all the criticisms that one would encounter in New Testament studies. A glance at the table of contents demonstrates that this is clearly not the case. The problem is that the state of current New Testament studies would mean that a volume that aimed for anything like exhaustiveness would need to be at least double if not triple the size of this volume. Anyone who is charged with compiling an indicative but not exhaustive list of interpretations will make personal choices about what to include and what to leave out. This list represents my own personal choice governed by the methods that have been particularly influential on me and are shaped by my own context and also by a desire to include some important criticisms, such as textual criticism, which are often omitted from collections such as this.

Three particular choices may need further explanation. One choice made fairly early on, but which I now regret, is the omission from this volume of *mujerista* or Hispanic criticism. The reason for this is my own context in Britain, where such interpretation is less influential; now that the volume has an intended audience on both sides of the Atlantic, this gap seems larger than it did at the start of the project. A second choice, which may seem unusual, is to include both liberation criticism and sociopolitical criticism; some people will regard these as so similar to each other as to make it unnecessary to include both. The reason for doing so was a desire to give a full and proper voice to a technique that arose among the poorest communities of the world (liberation criticism), while at the same time recognizing that a similar approach was important and has been influential in industrialized countries (sociopolitical criticism); if the approaches are merged together the result is often that the interpretations of the poorest communities are drowned out by those from industrialized countries. The third and final choice that needs further explanation is the inclusion of ecological criticism. In many ways this criticism is still in its infancy and does not quite fit alongside the much more established criticisms of this volume. Its inclusion represents my own personal belief in its importance, as well as an interest to discover whether or not it will flourish and claim a full place alongside the many other criticisms included here.

Choice of practical examples in each chapter

When I began working on this volume, I had the idea that I might use a single text as the practical example for all the chapters. It quickly became clear that this was a terrible idea and that by the twenty-third chapter the text would have been thoroughly spoiled for anyone who had managed to get that far. As a result I decided to choose a range of texts from throughout the New Testament so that a broad sweep of material would have been covered by the end of the book. This proved to be much more complex than I had anticipated and illustrates something important about the nature of different interpretations of the New Testament.

By far and away the most common texts interpreted are Gospel passages. After that, hardly surprisingly, Pauline texts are the next most commonly explored, followed by Acts, Revelation and Hebrews. Despite my best intentions I failed to include anything from the Catholic epistles (those epistles that bear the name of their supposed author, such as 1 and 2 Peter), with the exception of the general inclusion of 1 Peter in the example on the Household codes (see Chapter 20, 'Black criticism'). I regret, therefore, that the practical examples are a little unbalanced with 11 examples from the Synoptic Gospels, two from John, five from Paul, and one each from Acts, the Pastoral Epistles, Hebrews and Revelation, with the one on the Household codes which refers more generally to Ephesians, Colossians and 1 Peter. Nevertheless this spread of interpretations illustrates well the rough proportions of interpretations of different parts of the Bible; in other words there are many more different interpretations of the Gospels than of Paul's epistles. This is not to say that more is written on the Gospels than on Paul's epistles – that would clearly be untrue – but that the Gospels lend themselves to interpretations other than historical criticism more easily than other parts of the New Testament.

It should also be noted here that the practical interpretations of the passages all represent an approach or approaches that have already been done in an interpretation. Again, when I began this volume I had thought that it might have been possible to provide my own practical example using each method, but that quickly proved an impossible aspiration since it would have required assuming an assured expertise in 23 different areas, which, apart from its difficulty, would also have been over-ambitious. Instead I have chosen to present a range of other people's interpretations of passages. Some are landmark historic pieces; some have exercised great influence in a field; but others are simply good examples of the approach.

Another difference between the practical illustrations is that some of them combine a range of models to show how a number of scholars have interpreted a single text using the same method, while others contain a single example. Again it is worth noting that it was much easier to represent a range of interpretations of a single text for the methods in Parts 1 and 2 than it was for the methods in Part 3. The criticisms in Part 3 rely largely on the particular perspective of the author interpreting a given passage; it is therefore harder to place a range of interpretations together in a single practical model without skewing or diluting that author's perspective.

The order of the book

One of the greatest challenges in writing and compiling a book like this is to decide in what order the chapters ought to be placed. The implication of a linear table of contents is that the first chapter begins in one place with the final one representing a position far away from it at the opposite end of the spectrum; thus ecological criticism in Chapter 23 may appear to be the criticism that is furthest from the historical criticism of the first chapter. Again this is not the intention. The order of this volume has been shaped by a common typology, or classification, of New Testament interpretation, which sees methods of interpretation as focusing on one of three areas:

1 Behind the text, or the concern to recreate and understand the events that lie behind any given text.
2 Within the text, or the concern to understand the actual words of the text regardless of the events that inspired them or the reader who is reading them.
3 In front of the text, or the concern to understand the way in which the context of the modern reader affects interpretation.

This typology has influenced the outline of this book, though in an attempt to avoid the monochrome suggestion that all 'behind the text' readings look at the same point of history, I have described it more as a journey from event to reader. The idea is that there is, in fact, a very long journey from event to reader which must be acknowledged in interpretation. Thus a reader who seeks to engage with the New Testament needs to be aware of the different layers of interpretation that address the different parts of the journey from event to reader.

The first part of the book ('From event to text') explores the journey taken from the original event to the text reaching its final written form. The second part ('Text') sets out the criticisms which seek to understand better the final form of the text, and the third part ('From text to reader') examines the relationship between the text and its readers. One of the important things to recognize is that, in common with most typologies, this typology of biblical interpretation does not work completely. It is a helpful starting place to begin to disentangle the many different types of interpretation that exist – a book that simply presented 23 different interpretations in no particular order would be of little use to anyone – but ultimately it breaks down.

The problem is that typologies such as this are still driven by historical critical concerns and not by the concerns of the more **postmodern** approaches. This typology (and particularly the concept of a journey from event to reader) works perfectly well in Part 1, where historical critical concerns are laid out. It is all right in Part 2 but collapses in on itself in Part 3. The problem is that redaction criticism and feminist criticism are not comparable: redaction criticism is a tool for interpreting the text; feminist criticism is a **standpoint** which uses a range of other tools, sometimes including redaction criticism. Consequently feminist criticism often uses forms of interpretation laid out in Part 1 and Part 2, as well as other standpoints found in Part 3. It is possible, for example, to find socio-rhetorical feminist interpretations (those that use social-scientific criticism and rhetorical criticism to critique a text from a feminist perspective) or postcolonial Asian criticism that might combine postcolonial concerns with an Asian context and use tools drawn from redaction criticism, reception history and narrative criticism. Someone who wishes to use this book to understand some of the most recent criticisms will need to use it cumulatively, identifying the multiple strands present in any given interpretation.

If anything can define 'new' interpretations of the New Testament it is pluriformity, or, in other words, an active interest in combining multiple views and methods in order to engage with the text more fully. As a result Part 3 should not be regarded as opposed in any way to Parts 1 and 2;

most of the methods in this part employ some form of the methods found in the first two parts. There is just one key difference: the more traditional manifestations of the criticisms described in Part 1 often believe in arriving at the truth through objectivity; whereas the criticisms described in Part 3 interpret the text subjectively. In other words they adopt a 'standpoint' from which they interpret the text. For this reason many of the interpretations in Part 3 are known as standpoint criticisms: criticisms which function out of a conscious and clearly articulated subjectivity (see the introduction to Part 3, though, for the problems inherent in using this word).

The aim of this volume is not to persuade you that any one method of interpretation is better or worse than any other. It seeks to introduce you to the broad and ever-widening discipline of New Testament interpretation, to guide you through the maze of the different approaches and to give you a sense of what each is like. The different methods included here represent New Testament interpretation as it is currently practised in academic institutions. There are obvious and natural overlaps between academic New Testament interpretation and New Testament interpretation as practised in faith-based communities, but there are also differences. Not all of the methods explored in this volume would be employed in faith-based communities, and some would not be acceptable to all such communities. However, this volume seeks to describe how the New Testament is interpreted; it does not seek to adjudicate on the virtues of such interpretation. This kind of evaluation is one you will need to make for yourself.

Another question that you will need to answer is whether you think the 'original' meaning of the text as intended by the author is recoverable, and, if recoverable, better than any other meaning that can be discovered within the New Testament. This is the crucial question around which New Testament interpreters divide:

- some say it is recoverable and is the only true meaning;
- others say the original meaning is recoverable but other meanings are important as well;
- others still that it is not recoverable but the original meaning remains the most desirable one and the search for the original meaning is what is important;
- others again say that the original meaning is not recoverable because all interpretations are subjective and so the original meaning should not even be sought.

These are only some of the wide range of possible decisions you could make. The introductory guide offered in this book to the different possible methods of biblical interpretation is designed to provide you with a guide to the major issues that will allow you to explore these questions for yourself and to decide where you place yourself in the debate on what the text meant vs. what it means. This book is introductory in the extreme but seeks to open your eyes to the issues involved in interpreting the New Testament and to what has already been achieved in New Testament interpretation, and also to encourage you to continue this search for meaning.

Part 1
FROM EVENT TO TEXT

Introduction

The criticisms laid out in this part of the book have as their primary interest the different points along the journey from event to text. If, for example, we imagine the journey of a story from the life of Jesus to the Gospel in which we now read it, the criticisms of this first section each explore a different part of that journey.

- Historical criticism and social-scientific criticism (Chapters 1 and 2) seek to understand the world of the New Testament better, looking both at the original event (that is, the life of Jesus and the earliest Christian communities) and at the communities into which the texts were written (those for whom the texts were originally written).
- Form criticism (Chapter 3) identifies the units of oral tradition in which the original stories about Jesus travelled around the earliest communities.
- Source criticism (Chapter 4) attempts to uncover the written sources that lie behind the Gospel texts that we now have.
- Redaction criticism (Chapter 5) explores the role of the Gospel writers as editors of the written sources they had to hand.

This first section, then, lays out the methods of interpretation which seek to uncover the different layers of a story's journey as it moves from the event when it first happened to the written text of the Gospels.

It may surprise some people that the Quest of the Historical Jesus is not included here, since it epitomizes, for many, the attempt to strip back these different layers of Gospel tradition. The reason for its lack of inclusion is because it is not a method per se, so much as a goal in the use of the methods described. One purpose, though not the only one, of employing these techniques is to discover more about the historical Jesus, but these techniques are also used to discover many other things about the formation of the New Testament texts and the communities in which they arose.

1

Historical criticism

What is historical criticism?

Historical criticism (sometimes also called higher criticism) does not constitute a particular method of study, but includes a range of techniques to increase our understanding of the social and cultural world of the New Testament and further our understanding of the New Testament itself.

How did the theory develop and what are its main features?
Bruce Chilton

During the sixteenth century Western European scholars began to study the New Testament in Greek, rather than in Latin. At the same time they came to recognize that, in addition to being written in a foreign language, the New Testament represents the product of ancient, non-European cultures, reflecting conceptions of reality radically different from our own. Historical criticism developed by grappling with those basic difficulties in interpreting the New Testament; for the past two centuries, this critical approach has yielded diverse but valuable results.

Although its roots lie back in the sixteenth century, historical criticism as we now know it drew strongly on the work of **Enlightenment** thinkers such as John Locke and David Hume, who stressed the importance of using the intellect to understand the biblical narratives. Eighteenth-century interest in philology brought with it sensitivity to the importance of cultural environment in exegesis, as Adolf Deissmann showed in his brilliant discussion (Deissmann, 1901). Alongside this linguistic interest, there was also a concern to understand why texts emerged and developed as they did.

Discovery of the importance of the social setting of the New Testament brought about a split between a **Hellenistic** and an apocalyptic interpretation of Jesus and his movement. Hellenistic interpretation, most clearly instanced in Deist thought, saw Jesus and his movement as extensions of classical culture, and championed the portrayal of Christianity as a form of natural philosophy (see Jefferson, 1904). The apocalyptic interpretation insisted that the New Testament's preaching was trenchantly otherworldly, a prediction of the end of this age in an apocalypse that would usher in a new, divine order (see Schweitzer, 1906).

While both of these perspectives have much to offer, attempts to reduce Jesus and his movement to one or the other are misleading. Hellenism as a culture, and Greek as a language, did indeed embrace the Mediterranean basin of the first century, but the Hellenistic environment included many microclimates: different languages, cultures, customs and religions were a fact of life during the period. Both anthropology and archaeology have greatly enhanced appreciation of these microclimates and of their significance for interpretation. Jesus, to begin with, was born into the culture of Galilean Judaism, and he moved through three distinctive socio-economic worlds: peasant, town-based and urban. Historical criticism can enhance our understanding by paying close attention to the setting of the texts and understanding each passage in the light of its social, historic and economic background.

Although historical inference makes it possible to discern differing social settings in which Jesus was active, the Gospels themselves were composed in Greek, a generation and more after Jesus' death, as Rudolf Bultmann showed in the most influential account of the development of the Gospels ever written (see Bultmann, 1921). Nonetheless, more ancient sources – nearer to the time of Jesus and sometimes in his own language, Aramaic – were incorporated within the Gospels. 'Q' in its earliest form was a mishnah of Jesus, such as the disciples or rabbis of the time memorized in order to preserve teaching. In addition, teachers such as Peter, James (the brother of Jesus) and Barnabas made contributions to the understanding of Jesus' teaching, and their influences have been discerned within the Gospels, in sources that were generated within their distinctive microclimates.

Paul was a product of Diaspora Judaism, rather than of Galilee or Judaea, but refinement in describing his setting is no less vital for exegesis than in the case of Jesus. Born in Tarsus, Paul grew up with the local custom that women veiled so fully that, according to the statement of a contemporary philosopher, they could not walk in the street without someone to guide them (Dio Chrysostom, *Discourses* 33.48). This cultural reflex came back to Paul when he wrote to congregations in Corinth (1 Cor. 11.5–6). But Tarsus was also a centre of Stoicism, and Paul adapted a Stoic metaphor, speaking of the 'body of Christ' (1 Cor. 12.12–31a) while his contemporary Seneca called the emperor the spirit that animates the body politic (*De Clementia* 1.3.5). At the same time, Paul in his correspondence with the Corinthians claimed personally to have received the most profound revelations that a human being was able to access (2 Cor. 12.1–4), whether in the context of Judaic or of Stoic thought.

Historical critical readings of the New Testament seek to illuminate the text by exploring the world in which the text came into being. It is important to recognize, however, that it also takes account of the differing settings in which the documents and their constituent sources were generated. Meeting that challenge provides a clearer sense of the evolution of the texts and offers insights into the evaluation of their meanings.

B. C.

What are the landmark publications on historical criticism?

Historical criticism is such a central pillar of New Testament scholarship that it is almost impossible to choose a few landmark publications. These five reflect the emphases in the article above.

Johann Salomo Semler (1779) *Beantwortung der Fragmente eines Ungenannten insbesondere vom Zweck Jesu und seiner Jünger*. Halle: Verlag des Erziehungsinstituts.

Semler was one of the first scholars to apply critical thinking to questions about the history and origins of the New Testament.

Thomas Jefferson (1820) *The Life and Morals of Jesus of Nazareth* (otherwise known as *The Jefferson Bible*).

This book was finished in 1820 but only published after Jefferson's death in 1904. His aim in producing this book was to return to the 'pure principles' of what Jesus had said.

Adolf Deissmann (1895) *Bibelstudien: Beiträge, Zumeist aus den Papyri und Inschriften, zur Geschichte der Sprache, des Schrifttums und der Religion des hellenistischen Judentums und des Urchristentums*. Marburg: N. G. Elwert.

Translated into English as (1901) *Bible Studies. Contributions chiefly from papyri and inscriptions to the history of the language, the literature, and the religion of Hellenistic Judaism and primitive Christianity*. Edinburgh: T&T Clark. In this book, Deissmann built on the work of other scholars by developing a view of the language of the New Testament that took account, not only of literary evidence, but of the growing data from papyri and inscriptions.

Albert Schweitzer (1906) *Von Reimarus zu Wrede. Eine Geschichte der Leben-Jesu-Forschung*. Tübingen: J. C. B. Mohr.

Translated into English as (1954) *The Quest of the Historical Jesus*. London: Adam and Charles Black. In this book Schweitzer surveyed how

Jesus had been understood by nineteenth-century scholars and showed how influenced they had been by their own cultures and values. He then went on to argue that Jesus must be understood in the light of apocalyptic expectations.

Rudolf Bultmann (1921) *Die Geschichte der synoptischen Tradition.* Göttingen: Vandenhoeck & Ruprecht.

Translated into English as (1963) *History of the Synoptic Tradition.* Oxford and New York: Blackwell and Harper & Row. In this book Bultmann explored the traditional material used by the Gospel writers and tried to reconstruct how it had reached the form that it has.

Historical criticism in practice

As Bruce Chilton's article makes clear, exploring the background of the New Testament enables us to understand further the meaning of the text and can give depth and texture to our reading of the biblical narrative. It can fill out some of the details that we might otherwise miss and can help us to comprehend a little of the lives of the people about whom we read, such as what their concerns were, how they viewed the world and how they might have understood some of the things that were said. The problem, again as Chilton intimates, is that no one person's life would have been the same as anyone else's. One person might have been heavily influenced by Greek thought, whereas another person might be entirely resistant to it. It is also very difficult, if not impossible, to be exhaustive; it is hard to look at all potential pieces of background at one time.

Jesus eats with tax collectors and sinners: Matthew 9.9–13

In Matthew's story about Jesus eating with the tax collectors and sinners in 9.9–13, two groups stand out: the tax collectors and sinners, and the Pharisees. This passage raises the question of why the Pharisees were so opposed to the tax collectors and, in particular, why they were against Jesus eating with them. An exploration into tax collectors and Pharisees in the first century can help to shed some light on this passage.

The episode contains the account of the calling of Matthew, whom many scholars suppose to be the same person as 'Levi Son of Alphaeus', who, in Mark 2.14–17, was called while sitting at a tax booth. Tax collectors were widely despised and were often listed alongside other undesirables: for example, Cicero, in his treatise *De inventione*, listed tax-gatherers alongside usurers since they both gained people's ill-will.

For many years, the Romans followed a system that they had inherited from the Greek city-states called 'tax farming'. This system allowed tax collectors (known in Latin as *publicani* and hence called publicans in the King James Version) to buy the right to collect taxes from the empire. They would pay in advance for the amount that needed to be collected but how they went about collecting it was left up to the individual. As a result, the tax farmers often extorted much more than they had paid and were particularly exploitative in the Roman provinces (see Hopkins, 2002, 204).

By the first century, however, these practices had changed, largely due to the influence of Julius Caesar, who established officials to collect taxes directly. At the time of Jesus, taxes were collected by officials in the pay of the Romans in Judaea and in the pay of Herod Antipas in Galilee. This did not make them any less hated but scholars are not agreed about exactly why they were so hated.

Jeremias argued that it was because it was well known that they made themselves rich by dishonesty (see Jeremias, 1969, 310). The problem is that this theory seems to point back to the old tax farming system which allowed corruption in tax collecting, whereas the system during the time of Jesus was more directly controlled. Nevertheless, the story of Zacchaeus suggests that as a tax collector he had in fact defrauded people (Luke 19.8). Against this theory, E. P. Sanders argues that the real problem with the tax collectors was that they were collaborators with the hated ruling power, whether that be the Romans in Judaea or Herod Antipas in Galilee.

It is likely that the truth lies somewhere between these two positions. Memories are long, especially in financial matters, and the distrust of the previous tax farming system would not have faded away overnight. Furthermore, even if only a few tax collectors in the new system were corrupt, this reputation would quickly spread to all, especially if they were in a job that was already widely despised. Add to this the charge of collaborating with the detested rulers and the hatred for the tax collectors is understandable.

Before we leave the tax collectors, however, we need to ask why it is that sinners are so often included with them as an epithet in the Gospels (Matt. 9.10–11; 11.19; Mark 2.15; Luke 5.30; 7.34; 15.1). The odd feature about this epithet is that it appears to assume that 'sinners' was some kind of job title similar to 'tax collectors' (see Hooker, 1993, 95). As a result it has caused considerable interest about what it might have meant.

Jeremias was influential in proposing the view that sinners was another word for the Hebrew phrase **'am ha'aretz**, which literally translated means 'people of the land'. This implies that the 'sin' is connected to impurity. So the sinners are simply the ordinary people whose impurity should have prevented a righteous person eating with them. The connection between the tax collectors and sinners, then, was that they were both unclean (see Jeremias, 1971, 108–13).

Sanders vigorously opposed Jeremias's view, arguing that there is no evidence that the Pharisees ever equated the ordinary people with sinners. Instead, he understands the sinners to be traitors, who deliberately and regularly went against God's law. As a result Sanders's argument is that the significance of the criticism against Jesus is nothing to do with impurity but with the fact that in eating with the tax collectors and sinners he was de facto offering them a place in the kingdom without requiring them to repent (see E. P. Sanders, 1985, 179–88).

Various scholars today would say that Sanders went too far in his argument and that he ignored various pieces of Gospel evidence in order to support his case. Yet his view has had a great impact on the way in which the sinners are viewed, and many scholars would now accept that the significance of the criticism of Jesus here is not about him eating with the impure but with those outcasts whose acts have caused them to be labelled 'wicked'.

The Pharisees

Alongside discussions about the nature of the tax collectors and sinners, there has been extensive discussion about who the Pharisees were and what their concerns were. Popular belief about the Pharisees is that they were part of the ruling class of Palestine who were overly concerned with the following of the law and who travelled around Palestine imposing this view on all those they met. Recent research into the Pharisees has demonstrated that this popular view is incorrect, but no agreement has, as yet, been reached about precisely who this important but enigmatic group were in first-century Palestine.

One of our greatest problems for understanding the Pharisees is that the positive picture of them in Josephus does not match the negative picture of them in the Gospels. Josephus portrays them as a voluntary group of Jews, with a particular interest in following the law to the best of their ability, who at various points attempted to exert political pressure on the ruling powers. Sometimes they were successful and at other times they were not. They were based in Jerusalem and were very popular with the ordinary people. In a society influenced by Hellenistic culture and in which people were becoming increasingly disillusioned by their leaders, the Pharisees sought to call people back to their covenant with God, to following the law properly and to a society based on divine principles. In fact the clash between Jesus and the Pharisees may have come, not because they were entirely different, but because they were quite similar. Both wanted to transform God's people, it is just that they wanted to do it in different ways.

Anything more about this group remains a mystery. By the time of Jesus it seems as though they had become much less influential politically. We know that they were interested in certain matters of belief such as life after death and divine providence, as well as in the proper following of the law through their observation of the 'second' or 'oral' law which they believed had been given to Moses on Mount Sinai at the same time as the Torah and had been handed down from generation to generation ever since. They were also particularly concerned about issues of purity in everyday life. Discussion about what we can know of who the Pharisees really were continues apace with scholarship and there is still no consensus on the subject. One of the best and most recent treatments of the Pharisees is Chilton and Neusner's book exploring the historical Pharisees (see Chilton and Neusner, 2007).

Conclusions

When we explore a passage such as Matthew 9.9–13 it is hard to work out precisely why the Pharisees were so irate about Jesus eating with tax collectors and sinners. As well as the suggestion that they were impure (see Jeremias, 1971, 108–13) or wicked (see E. P. Sanders, 1985, 179–88) it is possible that the Pharisees regarded Jesus as one of their own and did not like him mixing with people of whom they did not approve (see, for example, Klausner and Danby, 1925, 274). Yet, whichever one of these options is correct – and it may have been for a combination of reasons – we have gained a clearer understanding of the underlying issues. Such issues would have been obvious to those who originally heard the gospel, but it is easy for a twenty-first-century reader to miss how scandalous and provocative Jesus was being.

Evaluation of historical criticism

The example above highlights both the advantages and the disadvantages of historical criticism. It shows that while we are able to understand a little more about the world in which Jesus lived it is extremely difficult to piece together the evidence in such a way that we have any certainties about this world. Just as in this small passage there are a range of views on what was so wrong with tax collectors, who the sinners were and why the Pharisees objected to them, so also in almost every area of New Testament scholarship there are competing views about how to interpret the first-century evidence. This does not annul the attempt but it does issue a word of caution about relying too heavily on conclusions about which scholars cannot always agree.

Historical criticism forms the foundation for much contemporary New Testament criticism, and as such its impact has been huge. Many techniques of New Testament study have grown out of it, and indeed the umbrella term 'historical criticism' encompasses the rest of the critical methods discussed in this part of the book. Yet the all-encompassing nature of historical criticism is also one of its major weaknesses: there is no method that is consistently and rigorously applied and its detractors can therefore accuse it of being vague and unscholarly. Indeed, what is represented here is only one of a large number of possible descriptions of historical criticism; each scholar who described it would probably describe it differently. Yet however it is described, you are unlikely to read many New Testament commentaries or scholarly works that do not employ historical criticism in one form or another.

2
Social science criticism

What is social science criticism?

Social science (social-scientific) criticism attempts to understand New Testament writings using the perspectives of social history and the methods of social or cultural anthropology.

How did the theory develop and what are its main features?
Bruce J. Malina

Social science criticism is rooted in the insight that the people who wrote the documents in the Bible, as well as the people whom they describe, are all foreigners to the **modern**, Western world. The scholarly attempt to understand foreigners on their own terms emerged in the discipline of social and cultural anthropology (in Britain and America respectively) largely in the second half of the twentieth century. The application of Mediterranean anthropology to biblical documents towards the end of the twentieth century resulted in what might be called historical anthropology (see Craffert, 2007). The historical dimension is intended to filter out the anachronistic features that contemporary readers bring to their reading, while the anthropological component attempts a comparative understanding of those ancient foreigners to overcome a reader's ethnocentrism.

Biblical writers and their audiences were all Mediterraneans, from the north-eastern shore of the Mediterranean. Thus a first step to understanding social science criticism is to realize that all those features that have emerged in Mediterranean societies over the past two millennia simply did not exist for biblical peoples: science and scientism, technology and technologism, the industrial revolution, Romanticism and individualism, the **Enlightenment** and rationalism, a sense of history, the separation of church and state and of bank and state, universities, Talmudic Jewishness formed in the fifth century and the Khazar (Ashkenazi) conversion in the ninth century, Christendom with political Christianity – all of these perspectives intrude upon any proper understanding of biblical peoples. Further, as Mediterranean peoples, their social systems, cultural values and behaviours and person types are all alien to contemporary Western readers.

The way to access those social systems is by beginning with a comparative understanding of modern Mediterranean peoples and their values, for example villagers in Italy, Greece, Lebanon, Palestine and Egypt (not Israelis, since they are a non-Semitic, central European people of Turkic origin). The values and behaviours of people traditional to the region are fairly stable, while social structures apart from kinship have often undergone 'modernization'.

From the study of those people we learn of central themes such as honour, envy, patronage, challenge-riposte, need for revenge or satisfaction, ingroup focus, and the like. Using these themes as mental lenses and filtering out later historical accretions, one can read the biblical documents to discover whether and how the same central themes worked in the lives of the biblical people. Upon discovering those themes, one needs to define them adequately so as to compare them with the prevalent cultural themes in our own societies. The result is a comparative scheme that enables us to understand ourselves and to understand the biblical writers on their own terms with modern historical and cultural features removed. Briefly, then, this is what social-scientific methods are about.

Along with social history and cultural anthropology, this sort of historical anthropology has other components deriving from sociolinguistics, social psychology and, at times, macrosociology. Sociolinguistics, the study of language in use, is premised on the principle that all meanings expressed in language derive from the speaker's or writer's social system. Meanings in language are expressed in wordings (words, language, syntax) that, in turn, are concretely expressed in squigglings and soundings (written and/or spoken language). Wording is patterned squigglings (in writing) or soundings (in speech), used to express social system meanings. To study biblical languages (Hebrew, Aramaic, Greek) without learning the social system meanings of the biblical writers and their original audience is simply to learn how to express English meanings in biblical wordings and syntax.

Social psychology deals with individual persons in their cultural context. Persons are enculturated to understand themselves along a spectrum from collectivistic to individualistic. In antiquity, people were collectivistic; the group had precedence over individuals, and group integrity was the paramount value. In antiquity there were also pseudo-individualists, persons who acted like modern individualistic persons. However, in antiquity, those pseudo-individualists were at the very top or the very bottom of the social ladder. Elite collectivistic persons act narcissistically, concerned only about themselves, expecting all the world to serve them; collectivistic throwaway people, making up the dregs of society, have no one to connect with, hence must do what they individually and shamelessly do to survive (see Rohrbaugh, 2007).

Macrosociology provides a developmental pattern of social institutions. For example, since separation of religion and government occurred only in the eighteenth century, one may rightly presume that before that time, religion was embedded in government. The same was true of economics. In antiquity there was political religion and political economy – just as there was kinship or domestic religion and kinship or domestic economy. To talk of the religions or the economies of antiquity as though they had the same structures, values and functions as they do today would be anachronistic. For example, the group recruited by Jesus was a political religious group; Paul's groups of brothers and sisters formed fictive kinship groups, with religion expressed in domestic structures and values.

Over the past several decades, the social history approach begun in the early twentieth century and the social science approach begun in the latter half of the twentieth century have become confused. Although the two approaches disagree over terminology and methods, both social historians and social science interpreters aim to understand the historical Jesus and early Jesus groups. In practice the difference between the two is the social historian's tendency to evade as far as possible the theoretical issues, whereas social-scientific interpreters rely largely on explicit social-scientific models as a means of interpretation.

B. J. M.

What are the landmark publications on social science criticism?

Adolf Deissmann (1910) *Licht vom Osten*. Tübingen: Mohr.

Translated into English as (1910) *Light from the Ancient East*. London: Hodder & Stoughton. This book explored the social world of the first Christians and gave rise to a large number of similar studies on the subject.

John G. Gager (1975) *Kingdom and Community: The Social World of Early Christianity*. Englewood Cliffs: Prentice-Hall.

This was, perhaps, the first book to use social-scientific models from sociology to understand the New Testament. In it Gager used Festinger's theory of cognitive dissonance to understand revelation and the early Jesus group's concerns about the delayed coming of the Messiah. This book has been criticized for depending too much on Festinger's theory, which itself has been criticized by sociologists.

Gerd Theissen (1978) *The First Followers of Jesus: A Sociological Analysis of the Earliest Christianity*. London: SCM.

This volume had the title in the USA of (1978) *The Sociology of Early Palestinian Christianity*. Philadelphia: Fortress. In it Theissen drew on the social philosophy of scholars such as Max Weber as well as Freudian psychology to understand the early 'Christian' movement.

Wayne Meeks (1983) *The First Urban Christians*. New Haven: Yale University Press.

In this very influential book, Meeks builds up an accurate and careful historical portrayal of what the social world of the Pauline communities might have looked like.

Bruce Malina and Richard Rohrbaugh (1998–ongoing) Social Science Commentary series. Minneapolis: Fortress Press.

This important series seeks to provide a social science commentary on the whole of the New Testament.

Social science criticism in practice

As Malina's article points out, there are a variety of social-scientific approaches to the New Testament. Malina distinguishes social-historical approaches from social-scientific, though not all scholars in this field would make a similar distinction, and some would regard what Malina calls 'social history' as a full part of the social-scientific method (see Horrell, 1999, 3–28). It is true to say, however, that social-scientific approaches do rely more fully on methods drawn from another discipline, such as social anthropology.

Insiders and outsiders at the Lord's Supper: 1 Corinthians 10.14–22 and 11.17–34

One of the New Testament writings in which social science criticism has played the greatest part in interpretation is 1 Corinthians. One of the reasons for this is that there is much that can be known about the Corinthian context at the time of Paul, and this can help to illuminate the situation into which Paul was writing. Paul's discussion of the Lord's Supper has been of particular importance within social science scholarship because it raises questions about the social relationships that existed within that Jesus-group founded by Paul and the divisions that arose as a result of the way Paul's gospel was understood by the Corinthians.

The Lord's Supper and ritual (1 Cor. 10.14–22)

One feature of importance to social-scientific study of 1 Corinthians is the significance of participating in the Lord's Supper. Paul's discussion of the significance of what was going on identified clearly that it was the sharing of the bread and wine that 'embodied concretely their common membership of the group' (see Horrell, 1996, 88). Thus it was the action of taking part in the Lord's Supper which shaped the unity of the body of Christ; perhaps even more important than this was that this unity called for exclusivity. Meeks notes that one of the oddest features of the Christian community was that it was exclusive; membership of it required withdrawal from the membership of other groups ('You cannot drink the cup of the Lord and the cup of demons. You cannot partake of the table of the Lord and the table of demons', 10.21). Thus the act which established the unity of the community also established the boundaries that separated it from groups outside.

A feature of general importance in social-scientific interpretation is that of purity and boundary-marking. All human groups mark off their own group (of varying dimensions) from other groups. This is what Malina identifies as the ingroup/outgroup dimension. He argues that ancient Israel marked itself off from all other groups (called Gentiles) and that Paul maintained that those whom God had chosen to accept this gospel were expected to have the same concern for ingroup boundaries (exclusivity) as did the Israelite societies from which they came. There was a ritual of line-crossing, from the outgroup to the new Jesus ingroup, called the rite of baptism. Rites are rituals which deal with the crossing of social lines. Further, baptism was a ritual of status transformation, like the ritual of marriage. Those in the ingroup were now 'new creatures in Christ', and must act as such, just as those married become 'one flesh', hence new creatures. Moreover, those within the ingroup had a ritual of celebrating their being in Christ. Rituals celebrating ingroup membership and unity are called ceremonies (see Malina and Pilch, 2006, 102–14).

Malina argues that the Jesus-group ceremony, called the Table of the Lord, involved multiple meanings:

- It was performed in memory of the founding ancestor of the Jesus group himself ('Do this in remembrance of me', 11.24). In this sense, Jesus groups formed fictive kin groups of brothers and sisters whose domestic religion was a form of ancestrism.
- The ceremony was in imitation of the prophetic symbolic action performed by Jesus at his last meal.

17

- It was to be carried out until the Lord soon comes ('you proclaim the Lord's death until he comes', 11.25).
- Of course such an ingroup ceremony was exclusive to Jesus-group members who awaited the coming of the Lord soon ('hope'), requiring those group members to demonstrate mutual social support ('love') and to trust in the God of Israel ('faith') while breaking with all other groups ('You cannot drink the cup of the Lord and the cup of demons. You cannot partake of the table of the Lord and the table of demons', 10.21).

Thus the effective memory of the resurrected Lord Jesus, the unity of the body of Christ, the separation from the behaviours of wider society and support for ingroup values were all reinforced by participation in the ritual ceremony of the Lord's Supper (see Malina and Pilch, 2006, 102–14).

Corinthian table fellowship and social status (1 Cor. 11.17–34)

1 Corinthians 11.17–34 makes it clear to us that the 'Lord's Supper' took place within the context of a meal for the gathered group. Such a meal would have been commonplace in the ancient world. Worship at Greek temples often took the form of a meal and, as Meeks points out, there are numerous examples of invitations to dine 'at the couch' of gods such as Helios (see Meeks, 1983, 158). Equally important would have been a meal which took place within elective associations (of which there were three major types: those formed around a household, around a common trade and around the cult of a deity), in which people from across a social spectrum would gather together and gain a sense of respect as a result of the gathering. Although it is quite clear that Jesus groups were not, in fact, the same as these kinds of associations, it is highly probable that they did follow the unusual social rules of elective associations when they gathered.

The rules governing associations meant that people ate according to their social status. This was an essential characteristic of most Graeco-Roman banquets. Even in elite houses the dining room (called the triclinium) was only able to seat between eight and 20 people. The protocol was to have the host and the most honoured guests eat the finest food in the dining room itself, while the less important guests ate other food elsewhere in the house (see Theissen, 1982, 96). Witherington draws on Lucian's description of the Saturnalia to underline the usual state of affairs. At the Saturnalia, the normal rules governing banquets were overturned for a day and poorer guests were expected to be treated well. Lucian gives examples such as that the poorer guests should not just be given the bones to eat, or the leftover bits of cake and should not have to ask seven times for their wine to be refilled (see Witherington, 1995, 241–2). It is this kind of setting that gives a possible background for Paul's criticism of the Corinthians that when they came together, 'each of you goes ahead with your own supper, and one goes hungry and another becomes drunk' (1 Cor. 11.21).

Gerd Theissen was particularly influential in proposing a social historical view of the situation in which it was this kind of social behaviour that gave rise to the divisions in Corinth. He argues that the major divisions in the Corinthian community were caused by a split between the wealthy and the poor of the community. The well-to-do hosts of the gathering were acting according to prevailing societal norms and began eating before the rest of the group, consuming their own food, which they kept to themselves. It was quite normal that they showed little concern for their poorer neighbours. Paul does not ask them to share with the poor, but suggests that they should eat at home before the gathering (see Theissen, 1982, 145–74). Theissen's proposal has given rise to a number of explanations about the social make-up of, and relationships in, the Corinthian community and how this affected the issues addressed by Paul in 1 Corinthians, particularly table fellowship.

Conclusions

The passages about the Lord's Supper in 1 Corinthians are a good illustration of how social science readings of the New Testament can further our understanding. Although social science criticism techniques could be used to learn about various other aspects of these passages, two features in particular stand out. The first affects social relationships. A careful reading of the ancient Corinthian social system, including expectations of common meals, allows a probable reconstruction of the issues that lie behind Paul's reprimand in 1 Corinthians 11.17–34. The historical and cultural background of Corinth suggests that it would be natural during banquets for there to be a strict hierarchy of guests according to social status; a transfer of these expectations into gatherings for the Lord's Supper gave rise to some of the problems that we can see Paul addressing in 1 Corinthians 11.17–34.

A somewhat different social-scientific reading of the Lord's Supper, based around 1 Corinthians 10.14–22, focuses not so much on the reconstruction of historical expectations as on the social function of the Lord's Supper as a ceremony intended to maintain ingroup adhesions ('love') and social identity (over against other Israelites and non-Israelites).

Evaluation of social science criticism

In practice social science criticism overlaps in many ways the historical criticism explored in the previous chapter. The significant difference between the two is that social science approaches seek to utilize the methods available to them from other disciplines such as social and cultural anthropology, whereas historical criticism restricts itself more to historical tools. It is important to recognize that social science criticism is a very broad approach and encompasses a wide range of disciplines; the exploration in this chapter focuses on the work of Bruce Malina, but a focus on the work of another scholar might have produced somewhat different results.

It is the reliance of social science criticism on interdisciplinary techniques that is both its greatest strength and its greatest weakness. The value of drawing on well established methods of cultural and societal investigation is that the methods adopted in social science criticism are clear, well established and able to be utilized carefully and efficiently. Furthermore, there is a body of material that lies outside of New Testament scholarship against which it is possible to check the methods to ensure that they are being used as effectively as possible.

The disadvantage of social science criticism is a problem common to all interdisciplinary approaches. It is a great challenge to weave together the scholarship of two unconnected disciplines. It is all too easy for a study to be published in, for example, social anthropology, which appears to have insights to offer to New Testament scholarship. This study can then be used to understand the New Testament and can develop into a well established mode of reading a New Testament passage, while at the same time in the area of social anthropology subsequent examination of the study demonstrates its flaws. The challenge to the social-scientific critic is to stay abreast of the scholarship both in the original discipline in so far as it is relevant and in New Testament studies and to weave together the two approaches in such a way that pays constant attention to both. For individuals to do valuable interdisciplinary work, constant interactions with credible colleagues from other disciplines is most useful. When this is done successfully the value of the criticism is great; when this does not happen the criticism becomes flawed.

3

Form criticism

What is form criticism?

Form criticism is the study and classification of the literary patterns and typical features of texts (for example, controversy stories, miracle stories) often with the aim of gaining an insight into the context which shaped them.

How did the theory develop and what are its main features?
James D. G. Dunn

In 1919 Martin Dibelius coined the term *Formgeschichte*, indicating his interest in the 'history of the form', which is, in other words, the way in which the literary features of a text have changed and developed over time as it is passed on in oral tradition (Dibelius, 1919). The English term 'form criticism' is not a translation of the German, but indicates a mode of critical study of New Testament material analogous to but different from the more traditional source criticism.

Form criticism resulted from the recognition that both the letters and the Gospels contain many units which were evidently pre-formed, taken over and incorporated or adapted by the writer. In the New Testament letters, these 'forms' are typically confessional statements (for example, 'God raised Jesus from the dead', 'Jesus is Lord'), poems or hymns (such as John 1.1–18; Phil. 2.6–11), or catechetical patterns (vice-lists, household rules, and so on). But the main impact of form criticism has been on the study of the Gospels, particularly the tradition which makes up the Synoptic Gospels.

The principal pioneer here was Rudolf Bultmann, who in the 1920s built on the work of two predecessors: Julius Wellhausen and K. L. Schmidt (see Bultmann, 1921). Wellhausen had demonstrated that in each of the Synoptic Gospels one can distinguish between old tradition and the editorial work of the evangelist (see Wellhausen, 1905); and Schmidt had gone on to examine the connecting links which join the separate episodes in Mark's Gospel, noting in particular that almost all references to time and place in Mark's Gospel belong to these connecting links provided by the evangelist (see Schmidt, 1919). When the editorial material is set on one side what remains is a series of single units, without indications of time or place. Bultmann examined these forms and classified them; particularly important classifications were controversy stories, dominical sayings, parables, and miracle stories.

The value of form criticism is that it enabled researchers into the history of the traditions regarding Jesus to penetrate behind the earliest written sources. If the earliest Gospel (Mark) could be shown to have incorporated earlier material, then a focus on these earlier forms took the researcher back another step. The same logic could apply analogously to the Q document inferred by most to be the other earliest written source for the Synoptic tradition. The forms gave evidence of how the Jesus tradition was being handled in the 40s and 50s, and therefore gave evidence regarding the interests and concerns of the early Christian communities which thus handled and shaped these traditions.

That the earliest stages of the Gospel tradition must have been oral has commonly been recognized through the last two hundred years, and form criticism helped focus attention on the oral period and the character of the Jesus tradition during that phase. Progress, however, was undermined by several dubious assumptions which became the basis for further research into the history of the Synoptic tradition.

1 The early form critics assumed a process which began with a '*pure* form', and envisaged a natural progression of the forms from purity and simplicity to greater complexity. Bultmann also assumed a *literary* model to explain the course of transmission, where recovery of the *original* version could be achieved by stripping away the later (**Hellenistic**) layers which now obscure the earlier Palestinian layers.
2 A widespread assumption has been that the earliest stage in the process consisted of individual units and fragments of tradition. Any clustering of material was a sign of later editing.
3 It became a prominent assumption that each layer of tradition could be associated with one or more particular communities. In the latter half of the twentieth century it became commonplace to talk about 'the Q community', with different editions of Q indicating different stages in the Q community's history.

Closer study of how an oral community and oral tradition function, however, has called into question such assumptions. Oral tradition is characterized by 'variation within the same', where the same story or body of teaching can be retold in an almost endless variety of performances.

Consequently, in oral tradition there is no 'original', since each presentation of a familiar story or teaching important to a community will be different in detail and emphasis. So the quest for an 'original' version as though only that were 'authentic' is wrong-headed from the start. Similarly wrong-headed is the assumption that at the earliest stage of transmission there would be only individual sayings. From the first, Jesus' own disciples would have been able to recall sequences of events and teaching which they had witnessed (notably the last week prior to Jesus' execution), and teachers in oral communities would naturally group teaching material in various ways as suited different occasions. And the implication of references to tradition in the New Testament letters is that knowledge of Jesus tradition was widespread across the diversity of first-generation churches.

The probability, then, is that the character of the Synoptic tradition, same in substance but different in detail and emphasis, reflects the way in which the traditions of Jesus' mission were circulated and used from the beginning.

J. D. G. D.

What are the landmark publications on form criticism?

Julius Wellhausen (1905) *Einleitung in die drei ersten Evangelien*. Berlin: G. Reimer.

One of the first books to argue that it was possible to distinguish 'old tradition' from the editorial work of the evangelists.

K. L. Schmidt (1919) *Der Rahmen der Geschichte Jesu: literarkritische Untersuchungen zur ältesten Jesus überlieferung*. Berlin: Trowitzsch.

In this book Schmidt pointed out the significance of the gaps between the units of tradition. He famously likened the Gospels to a string of pearls and maintained that if the string was broken and rearranged in a different order the pearls would remain unaltered.

Martin Dibelius (1919) *Die Formgeschichte des Evangeliums*. Tübingen: Mohr (Siebeck).

Translated into English as (1934) *From Tradition to Gospel*. London: Nicholson and Watson; (1965) New York: Scribner. In this book Dibelius coined the word *Formgeschichte* (history of the form) and analysed the Gospel traditions from the perspective of oral tradition.

Rudolf Bultmann (1921) *Die Geschichte der synoptischen Tradition*. Göttingen: Vandenhoeck & Ruprecht.

Translated into English as (1963) *The History of the Synoptic Tradition*. New York: Harper & Row. This book classified the Gospel stories into different forms.

C. F. D. Moule (1962) *The Birth of the New Testament*. London: A&C Black.
Moule picked up the scholarship of people like Bultmann and sought to identify the circumstances that gave rise to the writing of the New Testament.

Form criticism in practice

One of the passages which has profited greatly from a form critical analysis is the Lord's Prayer. One of the reasons for this is the fact that the prayer does not appear in Mark's Gospel but does appear in different forms in Matthew's and Luke's Gospels. Using the methods of form criticism is one of several ways to begin exploring why these differences might have occurred.

The Lord's Prayer: Matthew 6.7–15 and Luke 11.1–4

The differences between the Matthean and the Lukan accounts here are striking. The context is different, the opening words of the prayer differ as indeed do a number of crucial phrases. In brief, the Matthean account of the Lord's Prayer is much longer than the Lukan one and is found within a different context in the Gospel. Laying out Matthew 6.7–15 and Luke 11.1–4 side by side clearly shows their differences:

Matthew 6.7–15	Luke 11.1–4
[7] 'When you are praying, do not heap up empty phrases as the Gentiles do; for they think that they will be heard because of their many words. [8] Do not be like them, for your Father knows what you need before you ask him.	[1] He was praying in a certain place, and after he had finished, one of his disciples said to him, 'Lord, teach us to pray, as John taught his disciples.' [2] He said to them,

24

9 'Pray then in this way: Our
<u>Father</u> in heaven, <u>hallowed be
your name</u>. 10 <u>Your kingdom
come</u>. Your will be done, on
earth as it is in heaven.
11 <u>Give us</u> this <u>day our daily
bread</u>.
12 <u>And forgive us</u> our debts,
<u>as we also have forgiven</u> our
debtors.
13 <u>And do not bring us to the
time of trial</u>, but rescue us
from the evil one. 14 For if you
forgive others their trespasses,
your heavenly Father will also
forgive you; 15 but if you do not
forgive others, neither will your
Father forgive your trespasses.

'When you pray, say:
<u>Father, hallowed be your name</u>.
<u>Your kingdom come</u>.

3 <u>Give us</u> each day <u>our daily
bread</u>.
4 <u>And forgive us</u> our sins, for
<u>we</u> ourselves <u>forgive</u> everyone
<u>indebted to us</u>.
<u>And do not bring us to the
time of trial</u>.'

Scholars have disagreed about how these differences arose. For example, drawing on source criticism, Streeter argued that both Matthew and Luke derived the prayer from Q (Streeter, 1924, 277–8). Whereas Goulder, drawing on redaction criticism, maintained that the substance of the prayer was derived from Jesus' own teaching on prayer but that Matthew formalized it as we now have it and Luke edited it to fit into his Gospel (Goulder, 1963, 45). However, neither of these explanations is entirely persuasive as Streeter does not give sufficient evidence to explain why, if the original source is the same, the versions are so different; and Goulder does not account for why Matthew and Luke would feel so confident to alter in such a radical way dominical teaching on prayer.

A third possible explanation for the differences, which draws on form criticism, locates the texts in liturgical use. In other words, the variations arose as the prayer was prayed regularly in the course of worship.

The Lord's Prayer in the Didache

One of the crucial pieces of evidence to support this view is *Didache* 8.3. In this early Christian document the Lord's Prayer occurs in a form similar to but not identical with Matthew's Lord's Prayer. It ends with the command to pray this way three times a day: a command which highlights the regular liturgical use of the prayer. Crossan notes that the *Didache*'s version of the prayer has most of what is in Matthew but differs in its opening line: it has 'Father in heaven' in the singular but not 'Our Father' as in Matthew. This he takes as an indication that it is an 'independent rendition of the same prayer known to Matthew himself' (Crossan, 1991, 293). The implication of this being that the prayer existed in the worship of early Christian communities in slightly different forms.

The Lord's Prayer and Gethsemane

Although the Lord's Prayer is not included in Mark's Gospel, various scholars have noted that it has strong similarities with the content of Jesus' prayer in Mark 14.32–42 (and parallels). Three phrases stand out here. Jesus begins his prayer in Mark 14.36 with 'Abba, Father' (compare with 'Father' at the start of the Lord's Prayer in both Gospels); Mark's account contains the phrase 'not what I want but what you want' (compare with 'Your will be done' in Matthew's Gospel) and includes the command to the disciples that they should pray that they may not come to the time of trial (compare with 'do not bring us to the time of trial' in both Matthew and Luke). S. Van Tilborg sees here a strong indication that the Lord's Prayer began its life as a liturgical reflection upon the Gethsemane prayer of Jesus and slowly changed in the worshipping communities of Matthew and Luke until it reached the forms it did in each respective Gospel (see Van Tilborg, 1972, 96).

The development of the prayer within a worshipping context

J. D. G. Dunn also sees this prayer as having a life within a liturgical setting of the early Christian communities and argues that the early Christians were most likely to know this prayer not in a written form but in an oral form. The significance of this is that although liturgy both preserves and adapts tradition, it does the latter only gradually. In other words prayers do change with usage in liturgy but these changes are slow. In Dunn's view the differences between the Matthean and Lukan Lord's Prayer reflect differing liturgical contexts. Consequently he believes that Matthew 6.7–15 reflects a context shaped by formal congregational usage in that the start of the prayer 'Our Father in heaven' has a more formal air, as does the doxology at the end 'for yours is the kingdom . . .'. Furthermore the other additions like 'Your will be done on earth as it is in heaven' and 'but rescue us from the evil one' seem to be explanatory. In contrast, Luke's 'give us *each day* our daily bread' suggests a context in which the prayer is said daily (see Dunn, 2003, 227–8).

Conclusions

One of the complexities of Gospel study is that at a certain level the debate has to be based on sensible conjecture. The question of why we have three different forms of the Lord's Prayer in Matthew, Luke and the *Didache* and no Lord's Prayer in Mark, but a dominical prayer in Gethsemane that contains some of the same themes, is an occasion which calls for this kind of informed guesswork. Somewhat inevitably different scholars produce different answers, but form criticism has provided an interesting solution to the problem. The proposal that the slight differences between the versions are due to differing liturgical usage is attractive, and provides a good explanation for these differences. It draws attention to the fact that most early Christians would have known this prayer not because it was written down but because they used it regularly in worship. As such the theory has much to commend it.

Evaluation of form criticism

Form criticism was a method of New Testament interpretation that, at its height, shaped much New Testament scholarship. Its concentration on the set forms of texts, on typical characteristics of these forms and on the differences that exist between versions has been valuable. However, as Dunn points out, in his introduction to form criticism above, the value of the technique has been undermined by numerous questionable assumptions, such as that it is possible to discover an original text or that individual sayings would have been transmitted alone. Recent work by scholars such as Bauckham on the role of eyewitnesses in Gospel tradition further challenges the principles of form criticism, though it remains to be seen how influential his theory will be within the field.

The practical example of the Lord's Prayer given above indicates that, if the caveats about form criticism are accepted and the method is used with caution, it has a continued value for New Testament interpretation. The detailed work demanded by form criticism clarifies certain aspects of the texts and can suggest a context in which they might have developed. Although the influence of form criticism upon New Testament interpretation has waned in the past twenty to thirty years, careful use of the method can still provide valuable insights which illuminate and enrich our understanding of the New Testament.

4

Source criticism

What is source criticism?

Source criticism is the attempt to discover the sources used by an author in the construction of a text.

How did the theory develop and what are its main features?
Craig A. Evans

Source criticism of the Synoptic Gospels has been almost exclusively concerned with the resolution of the **Synoptic problem**, that is, how to account for the literary relationship that clearly lies behind the Gospels of Matthew, Mark and Luke. It can scarcely be doubted that there is some sort of literary relationship between them, but the question of how to account for it is open to many answers. One of the earliest explanations was offered by Augustine, who in his *Harmony of the Gospels* (1.2.4) thought Mark was an abbreviation of Matthew and that Luke made use of Mark; this illustrates a belief in Matthean priority which was, in all probability, the assumption of the early Church, from the second century onwards.

In the eighteenth century Henry Owen and J. J. Griesbach defended Matthean priority, but contended that Luke had made use of Matthew and that Mark had combined and abridged both Matthew and Luke (Owen, 1764; Griesbach, 1789–90). The Griesbach hypothesis held sway for about a century, eventually giving way to the views of H. J. Holtzmann and B. H. Streeter, in which Mark (or an earlier form of canonical Mark) and a source of sayings (that is, the hypothetical 'Q') were understood to be the principal sources of Matthew and Luke (Holtzmann, 1863; Streeter, 1924). In the wake of Streeter's work the two-source (or two-document) hypothesis began to dominate Synoptic scholarship.

In 1964 W. R. Farmer challenged the dominant two-source hypothesis and, along with a few others, argued for a return to the Griesbach hypothesis (Farmer, 1964). But their assault on the two-source hypothesis has been unsuccessful for many reasons, among them the following:

1 Mark's literary style lacks the polish and sophistication that one regularly encounters in Matthew and Luke. One must wonder, if the Griesbach hypothesis is correct, why the Markan evangelist time after time rewrote his Matthean and Lukan sources in a cruder and less polished form.

2 In comparing the Synoptics one observes that sometimes Mark's version of a story is potentially embarrassing. Jesus and the disciples are sometimes portrayed in a manner that appears either undignified or possibly at variance with Christian belief. We see this when Mark 1.12 says Jesus was 'cast out' (*ekballein*) by the Spirit into the wilderness. With greater dignity Matthew 4.1 reads 'was led up' (*anagein*) by the Spirit and Luke 4.1 reads 'was led' (*agein*) by the Spirit. It is difficult to explain why the Markan evangelist would substitute *ekballein* for *anagein* and *agein*, especially knowing that *ekballein* will be used many times in reference to the casting out of unclean spirits (for example, Matt. 7.22; Luke 11.18). Accordingly it is easier to see Matthew and Luke as revisions of Mark.

3 Where there is no Markan parallel, Matthean and Lukan divergence is greatest. For example, Mark offers no infancy narrative. Not surprisingly, Matthew and Luke, having no Markan source as a guide, go their divergent ways in their respective infancy narratives. This phenomenon is explained best in reference to Markan priority.

4 Another indication of Markan priority lies in the observation that in some instances, due to omission of Markan details, Matthew and Luke have created difficulties. We see this in Matthew's editing of the story of the request of James and John to sit on Jesus' right and left hand when he comes in glory (Mark 10.35–40). Matthew puts the request on the lips of the brothers' mother (Matt. 20.20–21), yet Jesus (as in Mark's version) replies in the second plural: 'You do not know [*oidate*] what you are asking [*aiteisthe*]' (Matt. 20.22). In editing Mark's account of Pilate's presentation of Jesus before the crowd (Mark 15.6–15), Luke omits reference to Pilate's custom of releasing a prisoner at Passover time. It is therefore not clear why the crowd shouts for the release of Barabbas in Luke 23.18.

5 The small amount of material that is unique to Mark also supports Markan priority. This material consists of 1.1; 2.27; 3.20–21; 4.26–29; 7.2–4, 32–37; 8.22–26; 9.29, 48–49; 13.33–37; 14.51–52. It is much easier to view this material as omitted by Matthew and Luke when they used Mark than as added by the Markan evangelist when he used Matthew and Luke.

6 The final consideration that adds weight to the probability of Markan priority has to do with the results of the respective hypotheses. The conclusion that Mark was the source for Matthew and Luke has resulted in major advances in form criticism, redaction criticism and the newer literary criticisms in vogue today.

Traditionally Markan priority has encouraged acceptance of the hypothetical sayings source Q, which the Matthean and Lukan evangelists used in addition to Mark itself. However, serious objections have been raised against the existence of Q. Austin Farrer and most recently Mark Goodacre have argued that Mark was written first (for all the reasons given above), that Matthew made use of Mark and that Luke made use of both Mark and Matthew (see Farrer, 1955; Goodacre, 2002). E. P. Sanders and M. Davies agree and concluded that 'Matthew used Mark and Luke used them both' (Sanders and Davies, 1989, 117). According to this view, there is no need to hypothesize the existence of Q, a document for which there is no attestation.

However, many Gospel scholars still regard the Q hypothesis as the best explanation of the non-Markan material shared by Matthew and Luke. Overlapping Markan and Q tradition, as well as scribal harmonization, may well explain the Matthew–Luke agreements over against Mark, which some think tell against the existence of Q or against the priority of Mark.

C. A. E.

What are the landmark publications on source criticism?

Henry Owen (1764) *Observations on the Four Gospels*. London: T. Payne.

Johan Jakob Griesbach (1789–90) *Commentatio qua Marci Evangelium totum e Matthaei et Lucae commentariis decerptum esse monstratur*, 2 vols. Jena: C. Heinrich Cuno.

Griesbach's major work was translated into English as (1978) 'A Demonstration that Mark was Written after Matthew and Luke', in *J. J. Griesbach: Synoptic and Text-Critical Studies*. Cambridge and New York: Cambridge University Press, 103–35. Both Owen and Griesbach argued that Matthew was written first, and was used first by Luke, then by Mark.

H. J. Holtzmann (1863) *Die synoptischen Evangelien: Ihr Ursprung und geschichtliche Charakter*. Leipzig: Engelmann.

This book was the first to raise serious questions about the Griesbach hypothesis.

B. H. Streeter (1924) *The Four Gospels: A Study of Origins.* London: Macmillan.

Streeter's volume popularized the two-source hypothesis and was influential in establishing it as the major view on the Synoptic problem.

A. M. Farrer (1955) 'On Dispensing with Q', in D. E. Nineham, ed., *Studies in the Gospels: Essays in Memory of R. H. Lightfoot.* Oxford: Blackwell, 55–88.

A robust rebuttal of the need for Q in the Synoptic problem; instead Mark is seen as the major source for Matthew and Luke.

Source criticism in practice

One of the greatest problems in attempting to select a Gospel passage to explore in order to illustrate source criticism is that the issues raised depend upon which passage is being explored. So it would be possible to pick a passage that demonstrated a simple reliance of Matthew and Luke on Mark (such as Mark 8.34—9.1 with parallels in Matt. 16.24–28 and Luke 9.23–27) but ignored the more complex questions of what happens when Matthew and Luke agree with each other against Mark (for example, Mark 1.12–13 with parallels in Matt. 4.1–11 and Luke 4.1–13).

The mission of the twelve: Mark 6.7–13 with parallels in Matthew 10.1–14 and Luke 9.1–6

The passage chosen for study below illustrates neither the most complex of relationships between Gospels, nor the most simple. As such, then, it portrays some of the classic issues that arise when studying the Synoptic problem but does not require too much involvement with complex detail.

Matthew 10.1–14

1 Then Jesus summoned his twelve disciples and gave them authority over unclean spirits, to cast them out, and to cure every disease and every sickness.

2 These are the names of the twelve apostles: first, Simon, also known as Peter, and his brother Andrew; James son of Zebedee, and his brother John; 3 Philip and Bartholomew; Thomas and Matthew the tax collector; James son of Alphaeus, and Thaddaeus; 4 Simon the Cananaean, and Judas Iscariot, the one who betrayed him. 5 These twelve Jesus sent out with the following instructions: 'Go nowhere among the Gentiles, and enter no town of the Samaritans, 6 but go rather to the lost sheep of the house of Israel.

7 As you go, proclaim the good news, "The kingdom of heaven has come near." 8 Cure the sick, raise the dead, cleanse the lepers, cast out demons. You received without payment; give without payment. 9 Take no gold, or silver, or copper in

Mark 6.7–13

7 He called the twelve and began to send them out two by two, and gave them authority over the unclean spirits.

compare with Mark 6.12

Luke 9.1–6

1 Then Jesus called the twelve together and gave them power and authority over all demons and to cure diseases,

2 and he sent them out to proclaim the kingdom of God and to heal.

your belts, 10 no bag for your journey, or two tunics, or sandals, or a staff; for labourers deserve their food.

11 Whatever town or village you enter, find out who in it is worthy, and stay there until you leave.

12 As you enter the house, greet it. 13 If the house is worthy, let your peace come upon it; but if it is not worthy, let your peace return to you.

14 If anyone will not welcome you or listen to your words, shake off the dust from your feet as you leave that house or town.'

8 He ordered them to take nothing for their journey except a staff; no bread, no bag, no money in their belts; 9 but to wear sandals and not to put on two tunics. 10 He said to them, 'Wherever you enter a house, stay there until you leave the place.

11 If any place will not welcome you and they refuse to hear you, as you leave, shake off the dust that is on your feet as a testimony against them.'

12 So they went out and proclaimed that all should repent. 13 They cast out many demons, and anointed with oil many who were sick and cured them.

3 He said to them, 'Take nothing for your journey, no staff, nor bag, nor bread, nor money [silver] – not even an extra tunic. 4 Whatever house you enter, stay there, and leave from there.

5 Wherever they do not welcome you, as you are leaving that town shake the dust off your feet as a testimony against them.'

6 They departed and went through the villages, bringing the good news and curing diseases everywhere.

Agreements between the texts

The first thing to notice is the agreements between the three versions of the account. The bare bones of the narrative are the same in all three accounts. Jesus called the twelve to him and gave them authority to cast out demons (Mark 6.7; Matt. 10.1; Luke 9.1), he commanded them to take nothing with them (Mark 6.8–9; Matt. 10.9–10; Luke 9.3) and only to stay where they are welcome (Mark 6.11; Matt. 10.11–14; Luke 9.4–5). Also noteworthy is the fact that the content of what they preached included in Mark 6.12–13 is to be found in Matthew 10.7 as the command of what they are to preach.

The factors that make this passage significant from a source critical perspective, however, are not the parallels between Matthew, Mark and Luke but between Matthew and Luke alone. This passage contains a number of features that are found in Matthew and Luke but not in Mark. Sanders and Davies identify these as including the following overlaps (see Sanders and Davies, 1989, 95):

- In Mark 6.7 the disciples are sent out with authority over the unclean spirits but Matthew (10.6) and Luke (9.1) also include the healing of diseases.
- Mark 6.8 says that the disciples may take a staff but Matthew 10.10 and Luke 9.3 say they may not.
- Both Matthew 10.9 and Luke 9.3 specifically forbid the taking of silver (Matthew uses the word *argurion* and Luke the word *arguros* but note that the NRSV obscures this by translating the Lukan word as money) whereas Mark uses the word *chalkos*, meaning 'money' (6.8).
- Both Matthew and Luke have 'whatever' house or town you enter.
- In Luke 9.5 Jesus commands the disciples to leave the *town* if they are unwelcome; whereas in verse 4 Luke only mentions entering a *house*. Matthew, however, talks about entering a town and leaving a house or town (Matt. 10.11, 14).

Whose account is the basis for the others?

These overlaps between Matthew and Luke alert us to the fact that a simple solution of Matthew and Luke copying Mark independently will not suffice in this instance; we are plunged into the heart of the Synoptic problem. Indeed Davies and Allison comment that it is passages like this that mean that 'the Synoptic problem is in fact a problem' (Davies and Allison, 1991, 163).

The Griesbach hypothesis explanation. One explanation for the longer Matthean version of the narrative is, in accordance with the Griesbach hypothesis, that Matthew is the basis of this text and that Luke and Mark have abbreviated it. Davies and Allison consider that the evidence provided in these parallel passages does nothing to undermine a possible Griesbach hypothesis. However, they, along with the majority of scholars, opt for the two-source hypothesis (see Davies and Allison, 1991, 163–4).

The two-source hypothesis solution. By far the most common solution offered to this conundrum is the two-source hypothesis. This maintains that in this passage there are two basic sources that contain a mission account: Mark, whose account provides the bones of the story and from whom the main details were drawn, and Q, which contains additional material. This kind of passage is known as 'Mark–Q overlap', where the two different sources are believed to have the same, or a similar, story with slightly different details, and it is thought that they were both used as a source for Matthew and Luke's version of the account.

In his commentary on Luke, C. E. Evans takes the majority view that while Matthew has conflated Mark and Q's versions into a single account (Matt. 10.1–14), Luke has largely copied Mark's account in 9.1–6 but with what Evans calls just a few 'reminiscences of Q' thrown in (see C. E. Evans, 1990, 394). I. H. Marshall holds the same view and points to Luke 10.1–12 in his account of the sending of the seventy (as opposed to the twelve) as the location for most of the Q account of the mission of the disciples. In fact Marshall maintains that although presented by Luke as two separate events, it is likely that the sending of the twelve and the sending of the seventy were the same event but drawn by Luke from two different sources: Mark and Q (see I. H. Marshall, 1978, 349–50).

What this means here is that in Matthew the framework of the narrative has been drawn from Mark but that details such as being sent to heal diseases, being forbidden to take a staff and the reference to entering and leaving a town are drawn from Q. The reason that Luke also has these details is because he too has reminiscences of Q but has reused the majority of this material again in 10.1–12.

The Mark-without-Q solution. The third possible view on this text, presented strongly by Mark Goodacre and following Michael Goulder's work, is that the reason for the similarity between Matthew and Luke here is that Luke copied Matthew as well as Mark. An important point is that Luke mentions leaving the town (9.5) when he has not mentioned entering it. Goodacre points out that it is a part of Luke's narrative style that he exhibits 'fatigue' when using Mark and often forgets what he has or has not included from the original. Goodacre points to this omission in Luke 9 as evidence that Luke has also tired of his use of Matthew's Gospel and has made a similar mistake here (see Goodacre, 1998, 55–6).

Conclusions

The story of the sending of the twelve illustrates amply the problem that lies behind the 'Synoptic problem'. It is clear that there is a literary relationship between Matthew, Mark and Luke but it is equally clear that a very simple model that explains this relationship simply will not work. There are numerous theories to explain the literary connections that have given rise to the story in the three versions that we have in Matthew 10.1–14, Mark 6.7–13 and Luke 9. 1–6, but the three most influential are that Matthew contains the original version (the Griesbach hypothesis), that the differences reflect two different versions of the story in Mark and Q (the two-source hypothesis) or that Luke has both Mark and Matthew as his source (Mark-without-Q hypothesis). All respond to the issues in the text in a different way but by far the most accepted of these theories is the two-source hypothesis.

Evaluation of source criticism

The clue to understanding the value and frustrations of source criticism is that the theories that exist to explain the relationships between the Gospels have the word 'hypothesis' after them. Source criticism consists of a number of competing hypotheses. None of them can tell us exactly what happened. Instead they provide a theory to explain how the relationship might have worked.

The major value of source criticism, and the reason that it continues in popularity despite the uncertainty of its results, is that it attempts to answer the questions that we all ask when we read the Gospels side by side, namely 'Why are so many of the accounts so similar?' and 'What kind of relationship exists between Matthew, Mark and Luke?' The obvious disadvantage of the criticism is that its findings are so disputed. Although the majority of scholars remain convinced by the two-source hypothesis, the alternative views, particularly Mark without Q, are persuasive in their arguments.

It is also important to recognize that source criticism is not so much a tool that is valuable for understanding individual passages; instead it is a tool for understanding the relationship between whole Gospels. This is an occasion where small detail sheds light on the big picture. The value of the study of an individual passage such as was done above is not so that we can make our minds up about the relationship between Matthew, Mark and Luke in the story of the sending of the twelve, but so that we can derive information which we can add to a much bigger pool of information drawn from the study of all the Synoptic passages, and from that begin to draw conclusions about the nature of the relationship between the three Gospels.

5

Redaction criticism

What is redaction criticism?

Redaction criticism is the study of the way in which the Gospel writers 'redacted' (edited) their source material.

How did the theory develop and what are its main features?
Mark Goodacre

The term 'redaction criticism' comes from the German *Redactions-geschichte* (literally 'the history of editing') and was pioneered by German New Testament critics in the 1950s. 'Redaction' refers to the process of editing, moulding and crafting traditions. The analysis of this redaction aims to discover the Synoptic evangelists' literary and theological agendas and, in the process, to learn more about the communities from which they came.

Hans Conzelmann's *Die Mitte der Zeit* (1954), 'The Middle of Time', unimaginatively translated into English as *The Theology of St Luke*, focused on differences between Luke, Mark and the hypothetical source 'Q'. He claimed that Luke's eschatology differed radically from that of his sources; the delay of the parousia had caused Luke to rethink eschatology and now Luke no longer expected an imminent end. As a result Luke wrote a work of salvation-history in which Jesus' life, death and resurrection is no longer conceived as being at the end of time but is instead in the 'middle of time', preceded by the period of Judaism and succeeded by the period of the Church, about which Luke wrote in Acts. Although details of Conzelmann's case have been heavily criticized, especially the idea that Luke depicts a 'Satan free' ministry, his approach has been highly influential, and has paved the way for the intricate analysis of the distinctive features in each Gospel, as scholars search for clues about the viewpoints of their authors.

One particularly influential early exercise in redaction criticism was Günther Bornkamm's article 'The Stilling of the Storm in Matthew', which attempted to show how the changes Matthew makes to Mark in this pericope (a small unit containing a story, Matt. 8.23–27) reflect

Matthew's own situation, in a church in a sea of conflict, praying to Jesus for rescue (Bornkamm, 1948). But redaction criticism is not limited to studies of Matthew and Luke, and one of the most important early studies was Willi Marxsen's *Mark the Evangelist*. Redaction criticism of Mark is inevitably more difficult because we do not, assuming that Mark is the first Gospel, have access to his literary sources. It proceeds, therefore, by looking at repeated, important motifs that occur at key moments in the Gospel, analysing the text for elements that appear more likely to come from the mind of the evangelist than from the traditions he inherits. For Marxsen, the key feature Mark contributed was the repeated emphasis in his Gospel on Galilee, which Marxsen saw as evidence that Mark's community was itself located there, awaiting Jesus' return.

The first redaction critics presupposed, built on and to some extent reacted against the work of form critics and source critics before them. They took for granted that the evangelists were working with oral traditions that were passed on, moulded and embellished in the early Church (form criticism) and they presupposed the dominant solution to the **Synoptic problem**, that Matthew and Luke independently used Mark and Q. Unlike some of their predecessors, however, they imagined the evangelists as authors rather than archivists, creative thinkers rather than unimaginative cut-and-paste people. This revolution in the conceptualizing of the Synoptic authors has continued to the present day and redaction criticism remains a popular scholarly method for historical critics attempting to look behind the Gospel texts. Many historical studies of the Synoptic Gospels are based on careful analysis of the texts, searching for distinctive, redactional elements that might provide clues to the minds of the evangelists and the communities they lived in.

Nevertheless, redaction criticism has limitations, and is not universally popular among New Testament scholars. Its dominance has been challenged by the rise of approaches like narrative criticism which focus on the narrative dynamics of the text at hand without theorizing about authors, their minds and their communities. Its presupposition that the evangelists were writing their Gospels to particular communities has been challenged by Richard Bauckham (1998) and others, who suggest that the Gospels were directed to a broad, non-sectarian Christian audience. Other limitations relate to the tendency of its practitioners to take the **two-source hypothesis** for granted, especially where this relates to the potential circularity of reconstructing the hypothetical source Q by means of redaction criticism. Furthermore, one of the central premises of redaction criticism, the special importance of material distinctive in a given

Gospel, is not watertight since it may often have been the case that the evangelists repeated verbatim material that they found congenial. Such material may not appear in the Synoptics as textual leftovers, clumsily copied from a source document, but as a faithful re-appropriation of material the author wishes to underline.

M. G.

What are the landmark publications on redaction criticism?

George D. Kilpatrick (1946) *The Origin and Purpose of the Gospel according to St Matthew*. Oxford: Clarendon.

Although not a full example of redaction criticism, in this important book Kilpatrick explored the major characteristics of Matthew, including his editorial activity.

Günther Bornkamm (1948) 'Die Sturmstillung im Matthäusevangelium', *Wort und Dienst. Jahrbuch der Theologischen Schule Bethel* 1, 49–54.

Translated into English as (1963) 'The Stilling of the Storm in Matthew', in G. Bornkamm et al., eds, *Tradition and Interpretation in Matthew*. London and Philadelphia: SCM and Westminster Press, 52–7. This short article is widely accepted to be the first and most influential example of redaction criticism in Matthew.

Hans Conzelmann (1954) *Die Mitte Der Zeit: Studien Zur Theologie Des Lukas*, Beiträge Zur Historischen Theologie 17. Tübingen: Mohr.

Translated into English as (1960) *The Theology of St Luke*. London: Faber; (1961) New York: Harper. This book explores Luke's use of his sources and argues that Luke had a different conception of the end times from that of his sources.

Willi Marxsen (1969) *Mark the Evangelist: Studies on the Redaction History of the Gospel*. Nashville: Abingdon.

Here Marxsen looks at what he considers to be Mark's use of his sources and attempts to reconstruct Mark's community.

Redaction criticism in practice

Redaction criticism relies on two main principles:

1 that it is possible to identify how the New Testament authors (normally the evangelists as very little redaction criticism is done outside of the Gospels) have changed the sources that they were using; and

2 that these changes took place because the authors wished to communicate something particular to their audience.

As Goodacre points out above, this has meant that redaction criticism has
been a much more popular technique for understanding the Gospels of
Matthew and Luke than for understanding Mark. The community for which
Matthew's Gospel was written has been of particular interest to scholars,
partly because of the influential essay by Günther Bornkamm referred to
above. Indeed Bornkamm's essay on the Stilling of the Storm in Matthew
has had such continued influence on redaction critics that it is worth exploring in depth.

The stilling of the storm in Matthew: Matthew 8.23–27

Bornkamm begins by setting out the context that Matthew provides
for this passage. He notes that Matthew 4.23 ('Jesus went throughout
Galilee, teaching in their synagogues and proclaiming the good news of
the kingdom and curing every disease and every sickness among the
people') and 9.35 ('Then Jesus went about all the cities and villages,
teaching in their synagogues, and proclaiming the good news of the
kingdom, and curing every disease and every sickness'), being so similar,
mark out a discrete section of the Gospel which can be characterized as
'Messiah of the word' (Chapters 5—7) and 'Messiah of deed' (Chapters
8—9). Further, Bornkamm notes that in Mark the narrative has much
more of the character of a miracle story, with Jesus as a miracle worker
in the centre of it. In Matthew, however, although the overall tone of
'miracle story' remains, added impact is given by the context surrounding the narrative and the additional words used in the narrative itself.

Although in Mark the story of the stilling of the storm is preceded
by Jesus' teaching on parables, in Matthew it is preceded by two discussions about discipleship: the first with a scribe who wishes to follow him
and the second with a disciple who wishes to bury his father first. This
emphasis on discipleship is maintained by the fact that Matthew draws
our attention to the disciples following Jesus into the boat; thus Matthew
is the first interpreter of this story and he understands it as a quasi-
parable about the nature of discipleship. Thus Bornkamm agrees with
church tradition, which stretched back to the time of Tertullian in the
second and third centuries, and which identified the boat, in which
Jesus and his disciples travelled, as the Church.

Bornkamm adds to his case the changes that Matthew has made to the
story at this point. For example in Mark, when the disciples fear that they

are about to drown, they cry out 'Teacher' (Mark 4.38), in Luke they cry out 'Master' (Luke 8.24); only in Matthew do they cry out *Kyrie* or 'Lord' (Matt. 8.25) which contains not only a human title of respect, but also 'a divine predicate of majesty' (Bornkamm, 1963, 55). This Bornkamm interprets as being not only a prayer but also a confession of discipleship. Another feature of Matthew's version of this account is that Jesus reprimands the disciples for their lack of faith before he stills the storm, not after it as he does in the other Gospels. Again, this appears to focus the reader more closely on the nature of discipleship and how to follow Jesus when things are difficult. Jesus expects his disciples to have faith and trust in him even when the situation seems impossible.

For Bornkamm, one of the most crucial changes made by Matthew to this account is the description of the storm in 8.24. In Mark and Luke the storm is described as a 'storm of great wind' (Mark 4.37) and a 'storm of wind' (Luke 8.23). In Matthew, however, the storm is described as a great '*seismos*', which literally means earthquake or storm. It is a very unusual word to use, however, of a storm at sea and is much more commonly used of what will happen at the end times. This may indicate that Matthew has more than simply drowning at sea in mind when he chose this word; it can be associated with the many different afflictions that the disciples will encounter during their lives.

These features lead Bornkamm to conclude that Matthew has worked with this account creatively and theologically so that, as well as being an account of the stilling of the storm, it is now also a reflection on the dangers and glory of discipleship. The passage that immediately precedes this one in Matthew reminds the reader that the Son of Man has nowhere to lay his head, thus Jesus' disciples must also expect danger and hardship like the great storm of the story; at the same time, Jesus' power over the storm was absolute. Thus the story of the stilling of the storm becomes in Matthew's Gospel a 'kerygmatic paradigm of the danger and glory of discipleship' (Bornkamm, 1963, 57).

The stilling of the storm and Christology

Although Bornkamm's article has become a classic example of redaction criticism, it has been criticized. The most important criticism is that Bornkamm's focus on discipleship has led him to miss the significance of Christology within the passage: he misses the key moment when the disciples wonder what sort of a man Jesus is. Feiler, along with various other scholars, has argued that this crucial moment in the story points attention to the parallels between this passage and the story of Jonah. These include overlapping features such as travel by boat, a storm at sea, the main character sleeping during the storm, badly frightened sailors and a miraculous stilling of the storm, as well as verbal parallels such as that between Matthew 8.24 and Jonah 1.4–5 (see Feiler, 1983). Feiler suggests that a clue to the answer to the disciples' key question in Matthew 8.27 ('What sort of a man is this?') is given here, that is to say, he is a man much greater than Jonah. This question is answered more fully in Matthew's second miraculous boat and storm story (Matt. 14.22–33), when Jesus walks on the water and Peter proclaims, 'Truly you are the Son of God' (Matt. 14.33).

Bornkamm's critics, therefore, believe that he has misunderstood the import of the changes made by Matthew to his original sources and that the true emphasis in this passage lies not on the nature of discipleship but on the one being followed, Jesus. Matthew's message in crafting the story as he has, therefore, is that Jesus is able to save his followers from disaster.

Conclusions

The differences between redaction critical interpretations of the stilling of the storm in Matthew focus not so much on method – scholars are agreed that Matthew has changed his account to communicate with his community – as on content: they disagree on what he was trying to say to the community. Thus for Bornkamm the key message of the story is that discipleship will bring with it danger and glory, whereas for Feiler the message is that Jesus, the Son of God, is able to save his disciples from disaster. Davies and Allison offer a helpful evaluation of both positions in that they recognize that Bornkamm has indeed overlooked the christological elements of 8.23–27 but argue that Feiler has overstated them. Thus for them the key question to Matthew's community is not that of the disciples ('What kind of man is this?'), as they already know the answer to this question. The question for them is do they trust Jesus in the storms of life or will they be of little faith? (see Davies and Allison, 1991, 69–70).

Evaluation of redaction criticism

The practical example illustrates well both the advantages and the disadvantages of redaction criticism. The great advantage of the method is the recognition that Matthew, Mark and Luke have an investment in the story that they are writing. They are not scribal automatons who simply copy the sources they have in front of them; they are creative theologians who are using their sources to encourage and inspire their audiences. As a result they have ordered the stories they are using for a reason; they have chosen words carefully and used them to shape their message.

The problem is that it is not always easy to identify what this message is. Redaction critics seek not only to identify differences between the accounts but also to work out the reasons for these differences. The first task is straightforward; the second much more difficult. The reality is that authors shape their sources for a wide variety of reasons; it is very difficult to work out precisely why they make changes at any point. Different critics see different motivations behind the shaping of an account. Even an interpretation as influential as Bornkamm's has received criticism by those who see Matthew's message in a different light.

Despite these difficulties, redaction criticism remains an important tool for understanding the text. The method encourages a careful reading of the passage alongside its parallel passages in Mark and Luke, a detailed exploration of how the passage's context affects its meaning and the message that may be being communicated through the words used and the location of the story. The attempt to understand the communities of the evangelists remains valuable, even though its results are not assured. The key to using this method is due caution and recognition that others may identify a very different message in a passage or even in the whole Gospel.

Part 2
TEXT

Introduction

The focus of the criticisms in Part 2 is the text itself and the many different concerns that arise out of the final form of a text.

The beginning of this part explores two criticisms often not included in volumes such as this:

- Textual criticism (Chapter 6) is a vital part of New Testament interpretation, since it seeks to trace the ways in which the Greek manuscripts of the New Testament shifted and changed as the texts were copied and recopied.
- Translation theory (Chapter 7) acknowledges that many students of the New Testament read the New Testament in English and discusses the factors that make translators make one decision over another in their translations.

From there, Part 2 contemplates the whole canonical text of the Bible before turning to methods which examine how particular units of varying sizes communicate meaning:

- Canonical criticism (Chapter 8) explores the importance of comprehending properly citations, references, allusions and echoes of earlier literature that appear in any given passage.
- Rhetorical criticism (Chapter 9) explores how the rules of rhetoric (either ancient or modern) help us to comprehend texts better.
- Narrative criticism (Chapter 10) is more interested in paying close attention to features such as plot and characterization as a means of understanding how a story communicates its meaning.
- Structural criticism and poststructural criticism (Chapters 11–12) use the specific tools of structuralism and poststructuralism to understand the deep structures of texts and how texts disrupt themselves, respectively.

Although this volume has a chapter on poststructuralism it has no comparable chapter on **postmodernism** and this requires an explanation. Postmodernism is a broad umbrella term used to describe, in general, responses to or reactions against **modernism**. It is not a criticism in its own right so much as a state of mind. Numerous criticisms within this volume can fall under the general category of postmodernism, including structuralism and poststructuralism in this part, and a wide range of the **standpoint criticisms** included in Part 3.

The criticisms in Part 2 adopt widely ranging methods, from tracing different versions of Greek manuscripts (textual criticism) to the ways in which the physical form of a text interferes with its meaning (poststructuralism), but all are concerned to explore the final form of the New Testament text.

6

Textual criticism

What is textual criticism?

Textual criticism (sometimes called lower criticism) seeks to discover, as far as is possible, the original version of the text found in a manuscript and to remove errors or alterations that have been made by scribes when they transcribed the document.

How did the theory develop and what are its main features?
J. Keith Elliott

Since the Reformation the text of the New Testament has been established in the West by using Greek, rather than Latin, manuscripts. In 1516 the first printed Greek New Testament was based on the dozen manuscripts Erasmus had found in Basle. These witnesses – as ancient documents are sometimes called – contain a text typical of medieval, Byzantine manuscripts. Successors to Erasmus's edition, often dubbed the Textus Receptus, lie behind the New Testament of the Authorized Version in English. After Erasmus's day an increasing number of manuscripts became available to scholars. In some instances the text in those newly rediscovered manuscripts differed significantly from the versions that were already known.

In the modern period textual criticism of the Greek New Testament developed under Karl Lachmann (1793–1851): he attempted to get behind the prevailing medieval type of text currently printed and to establish the New Testament text as it would have appeared in the fourth century. In so doing, he toppled the Textus Receptus from its pedestal. This eclipsing of Erasmus's influence and with it the Byzantine text-type was completed after Constantinius Tischendorf's discovery of Codex Sinaiticus, which he discovered in parts at St Catherine's Monastery, Sinai, in 1844 and 1859. The distinctive readings in that manuscript and in Codex Vaticanus, also made available to scholars by the mid-nineteenth century, influenced B. F. Westcott and F. J. A. Hort, who published their *Greek New Testament in the Original Greek* based on the readings found in these two witnesses, which they described as 'neutral'. That edition was published in 1881; its text was responsible for most of the text-critical changes introduced into the English Standard Version.

Over the past hundred years a large quantity of Greek New Testament manuscripts has come to light including witnesses predating the fourth century, thus enabling scholars to reach behind Lachmann's reconstruction. A recognition of the great fluidity of the text in the earliest Christian centuries means that scholars have abandoned the three categories ('Western', 'neutral' and 'Caesarean') that they had previously used to classify and judge manuscripts.

It is now the task of textual critics to identify the earliest recoverable form of each book from the myriad of available variations within the entire manuscript tradition. In many instances editors can agree confidently to print the earliest, even the authorial wording, but there are several places, often theologically sensitive, where opinions differ as to what ought to be printed as the 'original' text. But it is now accepted that it is also the text-critic's task to explain how and why secondary readings, both deliberate and accidental, originated. Deliberate changes made by scribes are now recognized as important because they can reveal fashions in interpretation and demonstrate movements in Christian doctrine and church history as well as developments within the Greek language.

Textual criticism is concerned with assembling and collating manuscript copies; this is a science and is verifiable scholarship. However, the *assessing* of variants between witnesses is the subject of often differing principles; this is the 'art' of the discipline. Among differing principles applied by editors, some still adopt a cult of favouring certain manuscripts whose distinctive readings are privileged; others defend the text found in the majority of manuscripts. However, most modern editors are eclectic in varying degrees, that is, they favour a reading that conforms to the author's demonstrable language, style and usage or first-century theological concerns as long as that reading is, ideally, supported by a representative selection of manuscripts from a range of geographical and chronological backgrounds. The weighting allowed to such manuscript support gives rise to much academic debate, but this encourages as objective an assessment of the alternatives as possible. Nevertheless, modern editions of the Greek New Testament sometimes print a reading with little Greek support – and even, very occasionally, none; and this causes controversy.

Differing textual decisions inevitably influence readers' understanding of a passage. One's judgement on Mark's purposes and indeed his literary pretensions depends on where one's edition of Mark ends (16.8 or 16.20); one's assessment of Mark's Christology differs, depending on whether or not the Gospel includes in its opening verse the designation 'Son of God' of Jesus; our extant manuscripts differ. Similarly, Luke's account of Jesus' words at the Last Supper is textually uncertain, as too are the words of the Lord's Prayer in both Matthew and Luke. A commentary on the parable of the Two Boys in Matthew 21.28–31 will depend on the text used: is the unwilling but subsequently obedient son mentioned first or second and what is the reply to Jesus' question? A sermon on Paul's teaching on resurrection needs to decide what he said at 1 Corinthians 15.51: manuscripts disagree about whether we are all to die or to be changed. The book of Acts is particularly fraught with text-critical problems throughout.

Textual criticism can display all known alternative readings; it can propose principles to aid scholarly appraisal of these alternatives, but, ultimately, it is the editors of a printed Greek New Testament and the translators working from such texts who are responsible for promoting certain meanings and recommending particular interpretations.

J. K. E.

What are the landmark publications on textual criticism?

Desiderius Erasmus (1516) *Novum Instrumentum omne, diligenter ab Erasmo Roterodamo recognitum et emendatum.* Basle: Johann Froben.

The first published Greek New Testament. Successors to this volume became the 'Textus Receptus' on which the King James Version of the Bible was based.

Karl Lachmann (1831) *Novum Testamentum Graece.* Berlin: G. Reimer.

This was the first version of the Greek New Testament to break away from the Textus Receptus and sought to restore some more ancient forms of the text.

Constantinius Tischendorf (1869–72) *Novum Testamentum Graece: ad antiquissimos testes denuo recensuit.* Leipzig: Giesecke & Devrient.

Tischendorf used a vast number of new manuscripts in this important 8th edition of his Greek New Testament.

Eberhard Nestle (1898) *Novum Testamentum Graece: cum apparatu critico.* Stuttgart: Privilegierte Württembergische Bibelanstalt.

This was the first edition of the influential Greek New Testament often called the 'critical text'; it is an eclectic text now agreed by a committee of scholars. The 27th edition of this work is now the major critical version of the text used by New Testament scholars.

Textual criticism in practice

Textual criticism considers all textual variations both large and small. These can range from the change of a single letter in a word to whole passages which are included in some manuscripts and not in others. Of these larger passages, which are not present in all manuscripts, two of the most important are the ending of Mark's Gospel and the story in John's Gospel about the woman who was caught in the act of adultery. The value of looking at one of these longer passages here is that it allows a more extensive discussion than some of the explorations of smaller differences between versions.

The woman caught in adultery: John 7.53—8.11

The story of the woman who was caught in adultery which appears in some manuscripts of John's Gospel is an important example of the impact and significance of textual criticism. This well-loved story is present in the Authorized Version of the Bible, but in many other more modern translations it is bracketed with a note to indicate that it is not present in some of the oldest and most reliable manuscripts. It is still used in the Roman Catholic lectionary during Lent, though not in the version of the Revised Common Lectionary used by many Protestant denominations. It is also used in the Book of Common Prayer lectionary. The story remains influential within Christian tradition and is often cited within discussions of sexual ethics.

The different manuscript versions of the account

The story of the woman caught in adultery (sometimes called the *pericope de adultera*) appears in different places in different manuscripts. While most manuscripts that include the passage have it in 7.53—8.11, others place it after John 7.36 or at the end of John's Gospel (21.25). In certain manuscripts it is in Luke's Gospel, sometimes at the end of the Gospel (24.53), or following Luke 21.38. Still others omit it entirely from the New Testament canon. Indeed it appears only in Greek manuscripts dated to the fifth century and later. Even in those manuscripts that agree about the placing of the text, there are different versions of the narrative and although the rough outline of the story remains the same from manuscript to manuscript, the details of the story vary (Parker, 1997, 96–7).

Although the written version of this passage has had a somewhat varied history, this story, or one like it, seems to have been known relatively early. Eusebius in his *Church History* refers to Papias, a bishop in

Hierapolis in the early second century CE, saying that there was a story about a woman accused *falsely* of many sins who was brought before Jesus in the Gospel of the Hebrews (this Gospel no longer exists and we know of it only through references made in a variety of early sources). Another reference to this account can be found in a commentary on Ecclesiastes written by Didymus the Blind (*c.* 313–98 CE), where he comments that there is a story in 'certain Gospels' which tells of a woman who was condemned (presumably justly) by the Jews for a sin and was about to be stoned. When Jesus saw it, he said 'he who has not sinned let him take a stone and smite her'. These two references tell us not only that the account was known quite early but that it was known in different forms.

It is doubly odd, therefore, that this account is not present in the earliest and most reliable manuscripts. We know that a narrative like this one existed in the earliest period but we have no written evidence of its existence. This picture is compounded by the fact that there are few references to the passage in the commentaries of the Greek fathers before the thirteenth century in the West and the tenth century in the East and there is no evidence that it was known as being a part of John's Gospel until its inclusions in the fifth-century manuscripts of the New Testament.

Thus we have some apparently contradictory evidence about this passage:

- This story – or one very like it – existed early and was known in the early second century by Papias.
- It does not exist in a written form in the earliest and most reliable manuscripts.
- Where it is referred to there is a variety of detail such as that the woman was falsely accused (Papias) or rightly accused (Didymus).

Who is the author of the account?

As Elliott makes clear above, the 'art' of textual criticism lies not in identifying the text-critical evidence but in deciding upon what it means. Although scholars are agreed about what we know about the history of this text, they are not agreed about what that tells us. From the nineteenth century onwards scholars have questioned the Johannine authorship of the passage and it became common among textual critics such as Lachmann to raise questions about whether John was, in fact, its author. For a long time it was widely agreed that John could not be the author of this passage and eminent textual critics like Metzger argued strongly against Johannine authorship of the passage (Metzger, 1971, 219–21). Parker agrees that the evidence points towards this passage not being Johannine and argues from the apparent early existence of the account and the variance between traditions that this story represents a piece of oral tradition. In his view, the sub-apostolic era (that is, the period immediately after the New Testament period) still valued oral tradition highly, but as time went on written texts became more important. Consequently, because this story was so highly valued it was embedded in the Gospels (though in different places) to indicate its authenticity.

Yet another view put forward by Petersen suggests that the form of the story such as is found in John's Gospel may have existed in the early second century. Petersen argues that the *Protevangelium of James*, a mid-second-century Christian book sometimes called the *Infancy Gospel of James*, and which contains a lot of material that contributed to traditions about Mary the mother of Jesus, shows evidence of knowing the form of the story that is found in John. He bases his argument on the inclusion of the phrase 'and neither do I condemn you' in the *Protevangelium*. This evidence is not strong and other scholars would disagree with his evaluation of its significance, but if he is right, Petersen's theory might indicate that the story, as it exists in John's Gospel now, was known in the early second century (W. Petersen, 1997, 191–221). An entirely different view is put forward by Hills, who argues the opposite case that this passage fits well in its context and that it was subsequently omitted from the text because of the Church's prejudice against the apparent leniency towards sexual sin displayed in the passage (Hills, 1984, 150–9).

Conclusions

The differing views of this text illustrate well the complexities of textual criticism. Working from the same evidence some scholars have concluded that the story of the woman taken in adultery is definitely not Johannine; others that it is original to John but that the Church didn't like it. Some have concluded that the story circulated in various different forms due to oral tradition; others that this may be the case but that it existed quite early on in a form that we would recognize today. The same evidence gives rise to widely differing interpretations.

Evaluation of textual criticism

Textual criticism is one of the central pillars of New Testament interpretation, even though most people will not engage in the discipline. Every act of New Testament interpretation begins with a version of the text that has been achieved by the careful and painstaking work of textual critics, sifting the evidence, weighing its significance and deciding whether or not the variant it contains should be included in the main text or marked in the footnotes. Decisions made in textual criticism affect the very words we read in our New Testament.

As has become clear in the practical passage, however, although textual criticism may appear to be one of the most 'scientific' of all New Testament interpretations, its application is as disputed as other areas of New Testament interpretation. Discussions about the most reliable texts are ongoing. Another problematic question is: if something is missing from a text, why is it absent? Arguments from silence are always difficult. Whenever there is a choice between a longer and a shorter text we cannot know for certain which is the original because scribes could both add to and take away from the text which they were transcribing. We will never know whether something is missing because the scribe was unaware of it or because the scribe was aware of it and deliberately omitted it. It is easy to see what exists but harder to decide why, yet the decisions that textual critics make about these issues have a huge impact on the text that we read.

7

Translation theory

What is translation theory?

Translation theory is the study of the principles and procedures that govern a good translation of the Bible.

How did the theory develop and what are its main features?
Peter Kevern

> Pilate also had an inscription written and put on the cross . . . in Hebrew,
> in Latin, and in Greek.   (John 19.19–20)

Christianity was born into a multilingual world, and from the very beginning its message has had to be translated in order to be understood. The Gospel writers themselves often quote from the **Septuagint**, and when they record Aramaic phrases and names, they tend to give the Greek alongside (for example, Matt. 27.33; Mark 5.41; John 9.7). For Luke, the key sign of the coming of the Spirit was that the gospel could be understood in all languages (Acts 2): if it could be understood, it had the power to save.

So it is misleading to think of the New Testament as simply originally written down in Greek and then translated into a number of other languages some time later. Some of its writers were translating from Aramaic, Jesus' native tongue, even as they wrote, and in the polyglot (multilingual) ports of the Mediterranean their work was most likely translated into other languages almost as soon as they had completed it. In the Western tradition, Latin translations of different parts of the New Testament became popular very early on, and by the end of the fourth century Augustine of Hippo is complaining of 'Latin translations out of all number' (Metzger, 1977, 20). Jerome was commissioned to compile a higher-quality translation from the Greek, and although he only managed to translate the Gospels, he set the standards for future translators to aspire to: the best possible manuscripts and a thorough knowledge of both Greek and the language into which it is to be translated. The translation which Jerome began, later known as the Vulgate, became the standard biblical text for the whole of Western Europe until the Reformation in the sixteenth century.

A new wave of biblical translation, inspired by Jerome's example, was an integral part of the Reformation. Erasmus produced a definitive Greek text, and Luther carried out the first real translation into a northern European language (German). William Tyndale followed closely with the first English translation, and the United Bible Societies and some others are now racing to translate the New Testament into all the identifiable languages of the world, so that 'the gospel may be preached to all nations'. Even in the English language, new translations are appearing all the time. Each claims to have a distinctive feature: perhaps a better grasp of Greek; perhaps a better use of English, or at least the English of one particular group of speakers. All claim to be an improvement, but what makes an 'improved' translation?

Modern Bible translators tend to arrange themselves on a spectrum between two extremes: formal equivalence and functional (or dynamic) equivalence. For the devotees of formal equivalence, the important thing is that the meaning of each Greek word is translated as *exactly* as possible into English, even if that means that the text reads in a strange and stumbling way. A good example of this is the King James Version, in which every word that has been added in the English is put in italics, and all the remaining words are supposed to be a direct translation from the Greek. Tyndale, the first and most important contributor to the version eventually adopted by King James, even went so far as to invent English words where no equivalent to the Greek existed – most notably, 'fornication' and 'atonement'. But opponents of this approach would say that there is no point in producing a Bible translation if it is incomprehensible to the average reader, and if you have to make up a whole new language, 'King James English', in order to understand it.

At the other end of the spectrum are the devotees of functional equivalence. They argue that the important thing about the text is its *meaning*, and so they try to find a phrase in English that captures the sense of the Greek – even if the words do not match up very precisely. A good example of this is the Good News Bible (Today's English Version), in which the English is fresh, simple and accessible, if quite different from the Greek in places. Naturally, opponents of this approach criticize it for assuming that we can know the meaning of a text, instead of letting it speak for itself.

In practice, translators always use a mixture of approaches. Even the most 'formal' have sometimes to choose between different readings of a word, or different meanings of an ambiguous phrase. Even the most 'functional' try to stay faithful to the text, and to make their interpretations on the best possible evidence. Perhaps the dilemma is not about 'formal' or 'functional', but about 'equivalence': with the idea that a text in English can ever be 'equivalent' to a text in Greek. Meanings are not entombed in languages, waiting to be chipped out and displayed against a new background, but come to life when the world of the Bible meets the world of the reader. This means that Bible translators 'make' meaning as well as simply passing it from one language to another. They make decisions that shape how the text is heard and received. Language is living, active, ever-changing and ever-fresh: each time we read and speak, we change and revive it, making it our own. The translators make it their own, before we readers make it ours.

P. K.

What are the landmark translations of the Bible?

The Septuagint (third to first century BCE)

The most widely used Greek translation of the Hebrew Bible which also contains some additional texts (for example The Wisdom of Solomon).

The Vulgate (fifth century CE)

A Latin translation of the Bible which brings together a number of Latin translations, some of which are newly translated by Jerome for the Vulgate and others of which were incorporated by him.

Wyclif's Bible (1380–95)

The first, literal translation from the Latin Vulgate into Middle English. For a long time people believed that this was the work of Wyclif, though now it is recognized that numerous people were involved in the translation.

The Luther Bible (1522 and 1534)

A translation of the New Testament from Greek into German by Martin Luther. He completed the New Testament in 1522 and the whole Bible in 1534.

Tyndale's Bible (1526)

The translations of the Bible by William Tyndale: a first incomplete version was published in 1522 and a final one published in 1535 shortly before he died. The translations were based on Hebrew and Greek texts, though with help from other translations like the Vulgate.

The Authorized King James Version (1611)

The translation of the Bible authorized by King James I based on Greek and Hebrew texts and 'authorized' by Act of Parliament for use in the Church of England in 1622.

What are the landmark publications on translation theory?

E. A. Nida and C. R. Taber (1969) *The Theory and Practice of Translation.* Leiden: Brill.

One of the books in which Nida expounded his theory of functional equivalence. The theories found here and in his other major writings have given shape to much modern translation practice.

H. C. Kee (1993) *The Bible in the Twenty-First Century: Symposium Papers.* New York: American Bible Society.

A collection of essays by 17 leading scholars in the field who continued to discuss the means by which one would know that a translation was a 'good' one.

Translation theory in practice

The practice of translation theory focuses on the decisions that are made in the translation of a particular passage or phrase. As Kevern noted above, the primary decisions are between accuracy (formal equivalence) and meaning (functional equivalence). On the surface this appears to be a straightforward choice; a closer look at the decisions that need to be made about a particular passage, however, illustrate that in practice the issue is very much more complex.

Jesus and his mother: John 2.4

John 2.4 is one of those passages where the whole question of how we translate a passage comes to the fore. John 2 contains the famous story of the wedding at Cana. The wedding guests run short of wine and Jesus' mother came to Jesus to tell him so. At this point Jesus responds to his mother in a somewhat surprising way. If we were to adopt the stance of formal equivalence Jesus' response would read: 'Woman, what to you and to me?' The difficulty here is that this does not obviously mean anything. So if we wish to communicate the essence of what Jesus is saying here, we need to decide how to do it. There are two aspects to this question which are confusing. The first is Jesus' address to his mother as 'woman' and the second is the enigmatic phrase 'to me and to you'.

Woman

Jesus regularly addresses women as 'woman' during his ministry. So in the story of the healing of the Syro-Phoenician woman's daughter Jesus says to her, 'Woman, great is your faith! Let it be done for you as you wish' (Matt. 15.28) and in Luke 13.12, when he healed the woman who was bent over and unable to stand upright, he said, 'Woman, you are set free from your ailment.' While it is common, and indeed polite, to address women as 'woman' it is much more unusual for a son to address his mother like this. Jesus addresses his mother in the same way at the end of his ministry when he commends her to John's care from the cross (John 19.26) and consequently this might indicate that Jesus was attempting to distance himself from his family ties by addressing her in this way.

The disagreement among scholars about the force of this address makes the task of functional equivalence even more difficult, and the decisions that people have made about its meaning are reflected in the different translations. Many of the modern translations stick with just 'woman' (see among others the New Revised Standard Version, New American Standard Bible and New Jerusalem Bible). The problem with this, however, is that while it fulfils the criteria of formal equivalence it sounds more impolite and brusque to us than it would have done in the first century CE. As a result the New International Version has made a decision in line with functional equivalence and translated the word 'dear woman' here: adding a word to the Greek but attempting to demonstrate that they believe that Jesus was being affectionate here.

To you and to me

Similar issues apply to the second phrase: to you and to me. This phrase is Semitic in origin and can be found from time to time in the Hebrew Bible. When it is used there it has two primary meanings.

1 It can be used to indicate hostility. So in 1 Kings 17.18 when the widow of Zarephath's son became ill while Elijah was staying with them, the widow said to Elijah, 'what to me and to you', implying that Elijah had something against her that had caused the illness. The phrase is used in this way in Matthew 8.29 when the Gadarene demoniacs come out to ask, 'What to us and to you, have you come to torment us?'
2 It can also be used in a more neutral context. So in 2 Kings 3.13 when the king of Israel wanted Elisha to prophesy for him, Elisha said, 'what to me and to you', meaning we have no relationship, go and find someone else who does. Here the phrase does not imply hostility, merely lack of relationship.

Some people, however, argue that it might also have two other meanings:

3 Another option is that Jesus' indifference is displayed not to his mother but to the event: Jesus sees no reason why it should have anything to do with him.

4 It is possible that this phrase evokes neither hostility nor lack of relationship but a genuine question – what is the nature of our relationship? – to which the answer is given by the fact that Jesus does in fact do as his mother asks.

It be should noted, however, that although 3 and 4 present easier interpretations of the text – as they do not portray Jesus as being hostile or indifferent to his mother – there is not much usage elsewhere in the Bible to support either of these as a translation. Despite this, many translations opt for the third meaning of the word, and understand the phrase to be declaring Jesus' indifference to the situation:

- 'what concern is that to you and to me?' New Revised Standard Version
- 'what does this have to do with me?' English Standard Version
- 'why do you involve me?' New International Version
- 'Is that any of our business, Mother – yours or mine?' The Message
- 'How does that concern you and me?' New Living Translation
- 'That is no concern of mine' Revised English Bible

A few opt to portray Jesus as indifferent to his mother as in 2 above:

- 'what do I have to do with you?' New American Standard Bible
- 'what have you to do with me?' Revised Standard Version
- 'what have I to do with thee?' King James Version

The New King James Version mixes an indifference to the situation with an indifference to his mother (whom in this version Jesus addresses as 'Woman'):

- 'what does your concern have to do with me?'

Only the New Jerusalem Bible opts for the more hostile rendering of the phrase:

- 'what do you want from me?'

What is interesting here is that all the translations with the exception of the ultra-'accurate' Young's Translation ('What – to me and to thee, woman?') have decided to opt for functional equivalence, and the difference of their translations indicates how very difficult it is to understand the phrase and replace it with a good functional equivalent.

Conclusions

This passage illustrates the inaccuracy of setting up the dichotomy of 'formal' and 'functional' equivalence, since nearly all translations use a mixture of both. Even those texts that seek to maintain the highest fidelity to the Greek text are forced from time to time to evoke functional equivalence, as in the decision over how to translate 'what to me and to you'. In the same way many of those that are largely governed by functional equivalence, from time to time use formal equivalence because it is easier: trying to work out the exact level of intimacy or distance involved in calling Jesus' mother 'woman' is so complex that many opt to keep just 'woman', which as we noted above appears much more rude in our context than it would have done in Jesus'.

Evaluation of translation theory

The different translations of this verse demonstrate that it is right to include translation theory in a book on New Testament interpretation. At first glance, translation theory appears to be so different from the rest of the tools in this volume that it stands out as being out of place. On closer examination, however, it becomes clear that translation theory, a little like textual criticism, forms the foundations for much New Testament interpretation. Those who study the New Testament through the medium of a language other than Greek are trusting their interpretations to the interpretative decisions of others. There is, of course, nothing wrong with this; the translations we have available to us in the twenty-first century are based upon the highest level of scholarship. Nevertheless, a translated text is an interpreted text and it is important to be aware of this.

Translation theory highlights that it is impossible to have a completely accurate translation of the Bible. Every translator has to make interpretative decisions as they translate from the original language. It is therefore inadvisable to rely entirely upon a single translation. Instead, those who do not have access to the original Greek of the New Testament should probably study a number of translations before they begin their study of a passage, to ensure that they are aware of some of the decisions that the translators had to make.

8

Canonical criticism

What is canonical criticism?

Canonical criticism is the study of a particular passage in the light of other passages and books of the Bible.

How did the theory develop and what are its main features?
James A. Sanders

Canonical criticism arose in the 1970s and has two major proponents, James Sanders and Brevard Childs. The term was coined by Sanders in his 1972 book *Torah and Canon* to refer to the way in which earlier texts were adapted and used in later contexts. Somewhat confusingly it is also used of Brevard Childs's approach to Scripture, though he himself would describe his method as a 'canonical approach' rather than 'canonical criticism'. The two approaches are actually quite distinct. Sanders is interested in tracing the way in which texts were interpreted at different points throughout Scripture and the conscious method that biblical writers employed when they used other biblical texts. Childs, however, is concerned with the final form of the canon, which he sees as a new literary unit and which, in his view, provides the only evidence available for how traditions were preserved and understood within the community. In summary, we might say that the difference between the two is that Sanders is interested in the 'canonical process', whereas Childs's approach interprets a given New Testament passage in the light of the rest of the biblical canon. These two approaches are so different that it is not possible to represent both here. As a result what follows is an exploration of just one of these approaches: that of James Sanders.

Sanders is concerned with exploring the citations, references, allusions and echoes of earlier literature that appear in any given passage. These provide an insight into the 'canonical process' (J. A. Sanders, 2006) and it is this that can yield quite a different reading from any that focuses only on the form and function of a passage in its New Testament context. The exercise involves giving attention to three critical factors: the citations or references in the passage studied; the ancient historical or political context for which the New Testament passage was written; and the **hermeneutic** by which the writer or author of the passage caused the reference to mean something in the context. All three are important. It is called the 'hermeneutic triangle', as shown in Figure 1.

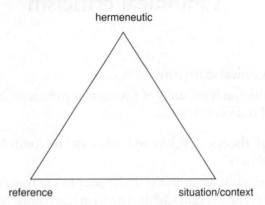

Figure 1 The hermeneutic triangle

First, it is very important to discern as clearly as possible what references or allusions are made in the passage (bottom left angle). Even the most professional and skilled readers sometimes miss allusions in the New Testament simply because they are not familiar with how scriptural references were made in early Jewish literature. Although many versions of the New Testament have notes that indicate what some of the references are, they sometimes miss a crucial allusion or echo that can make a big difference to the passage's meaning.

Second, the reader should be as familiar as possible with the first-century situation that the New Testament writer was addressing (bottom right angle). In the Gospels this should be done on two levels: the level of Jesus and also the level of the author of the Gospel. This is sometimes the most difficult of the three factors to identify, since our knowledge of the first century is not always as firm as we would like it to be, though it has increased considerably over the past several decades of critical New Testament study (see Reed, 2000).

Third, it is very important to try to discern the hermeneutic at play in the application of the biblical reference to the new situation or context. We must try to discern how the author understood the citation or allusion and what authority was sought in making the reference. Although scholars may think that they know what the Hebrew Bible passage meant back in its original context, it is often quite different from the way it was understood in later times, which in turn affects the reasons for it being cited (Sanders, 2006).

A truly thorough study of the *Nachleben* (ongoing life) of a Hebrew Bible passage (or any early literature) means tracing all the places where it was cited or echoed in the literature between inception in the Old Testament passage and the New Testament citation of it. By using the hermeneutic triangle we can ferret out how the cited passage functioned on each occasion it was referred to. In Greek, *hermeneia* means 'understanding', and the critical or careful reader needs to try to discern the understanding each ancient tradent (that is, one who seeks to bring the past, in this case the passage cited, into the present in contemporary terms) had of the passage cited to see why they went to the trouble of calling attention to it.

J. A. S.

What are the landmark publications on canonical criticism?

James A. Sanders (1972) *Torah and Canon*. Philadelphia: Fortress.

James A. Sanders (1984) *Canon and Community: A Guide to Canonical Criticism*, Guides to Biblical Scholarship. Philadelphia: Fortress.

In *Torah and Canon* Sanders coined the termed 'canonical criticism', a concept which he then developed further in *Canon and Community*.

Michael Fishbane (1985) *Biblical Interpretation in Ancient Israel*. Oxford and New York: Oxford University Press.

In this book, though restricted to Hebrew Bible texts, Fishbane traces the way in which biblical writings begin to show evidence of interpreting early biblical texts in ways more readily associated with later Jewish **midrash**.

Robert W. Wall and Eugene E. Lemcio (1992) *The New Testament as Canon: A Reader in Canonical Criticism*. Sheffield: Sheffield Academic Press.

Here Wall and Lemcio pick up the theme of 'intrabiblical dialogue' as a means of understanding the New Testament.

Brevard S. Childs (1984) *The New Testament as Canon: An Introduction*. London: SCM.

This is the crucial book that follows a 'canonical approach' to the Bible.

Canonical criticism in practice
James A. Sanders

Canonical criticism, as constituted by James Sanders, looks at the way in which Hebrew Bible texts have been interpreted and reinterpreted in the different contexts in which they are used. As such we cannot just focus on New Testament passages because the Hebrew Bible and its Greek translations had been used and interpreted long before the New Testament period. Thus, the New Testament usage of the texts is only a small proportion of their overall *Nachleben*.

One of the New Testament passages in which this reading of the texts becomes particularly important is Luke 4.16–30, to which we now turn.

Jesus in the synagogue: Luke 4.16–30

In Luke 4.16–30 Jesus famously read from Isaiah 61, and his choice of reading was probably governed by the fact that Isaiah 61 was the Haftarah reading (a selection from the prophets that is read after the Torah in a synagogue service) the day he was invited to read in the synagogue in Nazareth. Nevertheless, it is important to try to discern Jesus' understanding (or hermeneutic) of Isaiah and in particular of Isaiah 61.1–2a. We need to ask not only what Jews of the first century thought of Isaiah and of this particular passage when they heard Jesus read it that day, but also what we can discern Jesus understood by it when he preached on it after reading it and what it might have meant when Luke's congregation later heard Luke's version of the event.

Before we get to that, let's look at the situation (bottom right angle) of Jews in Palestine and the Graeco-Roman world in the first century. First and foremost they lived under Roman domination and oppression and, due to several revolts by Jews in Palestine and in Egypt against Rome before the time of Jesus, the Roman authorities were wary and vigilant. The situation was tense and the occupation shaped their everyday lives. They needed hope, and they were looking for a messiah who would bring them that relief, but Jesus, as we shall see, had in mind a greater need than they thought they had.

The Jesus level

According to Luke, after Jesus read the passage in Isaiah 61, he had captivated the attention of everyone there: their eyes were fixed on Jesus (Luke 4.20). Why? This is a crucial question for our understanding of the whole passage. This Isaiah passage more than most, perhaps, was in their minds a promise of the relief they needed. A thorough study of the *Nachleben* of Isaiah 61, through early Jewish literature from its inception in Isaiah down to the first century, shows that it was a favourite passage of Jews of the time. It was cited or echoed in eleven passages in the Dead

Sea Scrolls (see J. A. Sanders, 1975). Even given Isaiah's popularity in Early Judaism, this is a large number of occurrences and indicates that Isaiah 61 was more influential than any other Isaianic passage.

As a result, when Jesus sat down after reading the passage, all the people in the synagogue were anxious to hear the message of hope that they were certain he would bring. Then as though to heighten the tension Jesus said, 'Today this Scripture has been fulfilled in your hearing' (4.21). This seems to have animated the crowd even more, since they 'spoke well of him and were amazed at the words of grace that came from his mouth' (4.22). Translations at this point are sometimes misleading saying 'gracious words', leading the reader to think that Jesus was an eloquent speaker. He apparently was a great speaker, but that is not the point of the saying. It is, rather, a clue to the hermeneutic by which the congregation heard what Jesus had said: they understood him to have read the Isaiah passage by a hermeneutic of the grace of God. That means that they thought that he was going to preach to them the message of hope that they longed for. They were amazed that their neighbour Joseph's son had been appointed as the herald of Isaiah 61 to bring good news to the poor (themselves, of course), release to captives (again themselves), sight to the blind and release to prisoners (Isa. 61.1; Luke 4.18; cf. Luke 7.21–23). One can only imagine the joy they felt despite their doubt about a son of the village fulfilling the role of the prophetic voice they wanted so badly to hear.

Jesus' response to the people's challenge, to show them a miracle to prove his credentials in the way he had done in Capernaum (4.23), involves a play on words. Jesus picks up on a crucial word in Isaiah 61.2, 'acceptable' (*dektos* in Greek). There the prophet had said that the herald would proclaim the 'acceptable year' (*eniauton dekton*), which is the year of God's choosing, that is to say, the messiah would appear on God's timetable and not theirs. Jesus then quotes an old proverb that no prophet is 'acceptable' (*dektos*) in his own home town. Such wordplays were common in Greek literature as well as in early Jewish midrash when a word in the passage cited would be picked up and used in the response. In Greek translations of Isaiah the word referred to the Jubilee year, when the messiah would appear, being 'acceptable' to God. Jesus' response in effect said that prophets have to be 'acceptable' to God whether they are to the people or not.

Jesus went on to preach a startling sermon on the familiar Isaiah passage. He interpreted it by citing events recorded in 1 Kings 17 and 2 Kings 5 (Luke 4.25–27). Luke tells us that this enraged the people and made them so mad that they tried to throw him down the hill on which the town was built, which was an act preparatory to stoning someone to death. This raises the question of how the two passages from Kings were understood. The first of these, 1 Kings 17, recounts the first biblical story about the prophet Elijah, who became a major figure in later Jewish expectations of the messiah (see Mal. 4.5). At the time of Jesus, the character of Elijah was connected to the coming of the messiah and popular hope for the future, but 1 Kings 17 tells a different story. It talks of Elijah being pursued by Ahab and Jezebel who sought his life and of God sending Elijah to hide by a brook so that during the drought that had hit the land he would have a little water and be fed by the ravens that God would send to feed him.

Although the modern reader may focus on the question of whether ravens can feed human beings, the real point of the story is that Elijah risked his life to speak God's message, and nobody in Israel tried to help him. His only human helper was a foreign widow (1 Kings 17.8–24), to whom Elijah was sent after the brook dried up. Although she had only a little to feed herself and her son, who was near death, she cared for Elijah and, as a reward for her generosity, Elijah provided 'meal' and oil for the woman and even revived her son. Here the point is not what Elijah did for the woman but that when Elijah was in dire need, God had to send him to a foreign country to get help.

A similar point is made in 2 Kings 5, but with an even sharper edge for the hearers in Nazareth. In that story God had Elisha heal the foreign commander of Syria, Israel's worst enemy. Jesus' use of the passage here appears to be saying that God, who the Jews believed would save them from their Roman oppressors, was also the God of the Romans. Here Jesus, just like the prophets before him, was nudging the leaders and the people to see that there is only one God: the God of all peoples everywhere. They were trying to say, each in their own time, that the hope humans have is in understanding that there is only one God, and that all humans share a common bond because of that. They were hence in their time monotheizers (that is, people who encouraged others to believe in one God), even though most people then were not ready to hear that God is one.

Thus a careful exploration of the passages used by Jesus here helps us to understand why the people felt their hopes were dashed by the sermon and caused them to turn from being his admirers, when they presumed they knew what Jesus would say about the passage from Isaiah, to a lynch mob when they heard what he did say.

The Gospel level

When we turn to the situation into which Luke the evangelist was writing, the picture changes. The readers a few decades later in Luke's time may have heard this Nazareth story not only as encouraging them to see the Romans as humans but also, perhaps, to look down on Jesus' fellow Jews who did not do this. This attitude may have laid the foundation of Christian anti-Semitism and of the radical split of Christian Judaism from its parent faith. Towards the end of the first century Christians felt they needed to appease Romans who were anti-Jewish because Romans had to keep putting down Jewish revolts. In Luke's time Rome had just defeated the biggest Jewish revolt of all in Jerusalem itself (66–73 CE). The only way Christians may have felt they could avert Roman persecution was to disavow their Jewish origins and roots. Thus Jesus' prophetic sermon could become anti-Semitic without changing a word in it. This is because the social and political context had changed alongside the hermeneutic by which the Christians of Luke's community heard it (the right and top angles of the triangle). Jesus' lesson that God is the one God of Jews, Romans and of all peoples could consequently gain a different meaning.

Some scholars think that Luke and other Christians of his time invented accounts such as the Nazareth sermon in order to appease the Romans, but this mode of reading indicates that it was not invented, simply understood differently. Changes in context allow texts to be heard differently; the change in situation of early Christians in the Graeco-Roman world gave them the ears to hear Jesus' prophetic and essentially Jewish message anew. It is unfortunate that intense Roman anti-Jewishness induced Christian anti-Semitism, but the rehearing of the gospel message in persecution firmly established Christian belief in the one God of all. Monotheism became the major belief of all Christian sects and groups that survived the persecutions no matter their other widely varying differences (Pelikan, 1971–89).

Conclusions

Luke 4.16–30 warrants a close reading not only of what it contains but also what this would have sounded like to its audience at different points in history. Using the hermeneutic triangle outlined above, we can begin to recover not only the original messages of the prophets and of Jesus in their own time but also what they meant to subsequent audiences. A canonical critical reading of Luke 4.16–20 reveals something of the hopes of Jesus' original audience and of their outrage when his message suggested that salvation was available to their most hated enemies. It also allows us to appreciate how this original radical message became adapted into one which gave rise to anti-Semitism, within Luke's community.

J. A. S.

Evaluation of canonical criticism

When one is evaluating canonical criticism it is vital to be clear about which form is under examination. One of the most common causes of confusion in this area is to mix up Sanders's 'canonical process' theory with Childs's 'canonical approach'. This chapter has restricted itself to Sanders's 'canonical process' version of canonical criticism, largely because it is more immediately relevant to New Testament interpretation. Although Childs has published a book on the New Testament as canon, most followers of his canonical approach focus on Hebrew Bible texts, not New Testament ones.

The great value of Sanders's approach is that it brings to the fore a recognition that texts do not always mean the same thing to every audience. As contexts change so also does the way in which people understand texts. As a result it is not sufficient to establish what a text meant when it was originally written, or originally heard; this is only one factor in establishing what it means when used again in a later passage. Sanders's approach challenges us to a careful and thoughtful engagement with how texts shift and change their meaning in different contexts and to probe the usage of earlier texts whenever they are cited or alluded to in the New Testament.

The problems of this approach are straightforward. Just as it is difficult to know exactly what an author meant when they first wrote their text, so it is also difficult to know precisely what a text meant at different points in its history. The problem gets worse rather than better as a text is used and reused. Another factor to bear in mind is that Sanders's careful work on canonical criticism has led him to conclude that the overriding hermeneutic at work in the interpretation of texts within the Bible is a desire to monotheize. Not all scholars would accept this, and a different systematic approach to the text might produce another 'overriding theme'.

Nevertheless, canonical criticism provides important tools for paying attention to the original reference, to the different contexts in which the passage has been used and to the hermeneutic at work in its interpretation that can only enhance our appreciation of New Testament passages.

9

Rhetorical criticism

What is rhetorical criticism?

Rhetorical criticism is the study of how texts use either ancient or modern rhetoric (the art of persuasion) to convince their readers of a particular point or position.

How did the theory develop and what are its main features?
Ben Witherington III

Within the field of New Testament studies, rhetorical criticism has been approached by scholars in two rather different ways. The first way, pioneered and championed by Hans Dieter Betz (Betz, 1979) and George Kennedy (Kennedy, 1984) and their students, is more of a historical enterprise and seeks to analyse the New Testament documents on the basis of ancient Graeco-Roman rhetoric, asking and answering the question of how the New Testament authors may or may not have used this art. Here we may speak of how the New Testament authors adopted and adapted ancient rhetoric for their Christian purposes of communication.

The second approach, growing out of modern language theory and epistemology, has been pioneered and championed by Vernon Robbins (Robbins, 1996) and his students. This approach, rather than primarily looking for rhetorical structures embedded in the New Testament texts by their authors, seeks to apply certain modern rhetorical categories to the text (for example, categories such as inner texture – the ways in which the text uses words and language to communicate). Both the terminology and the method, as well as the theory of meaning of this latter approach, have more in common with the 'new' rhetoric of Henrich Lausberg (Lausberg, 1998) and others than with the rhetorical guidelines established by Aristotle, Quintilian and other practitioners of ancient rhetoric. In other words it is more an exercise in modern **hermeneutics** than in the analysis of the use of Graeco-Roman rhetoric by the New Testament authors themselves. The methodological issue here is whether or not the New Testament should be analysed only on the basis of categories the New Testament authors themselves could have known and used.

In my view, both approaches can yield good insights into the biblical text, but the attempt to fuse the methods of old and new rhetoric in fact confuses more people than it enlightens. In particular, I would insist that the primary task is to ask the appropriate historical questions about the New Testament text and what its ancient authors had in mind, which means that only analysis on the basis of Graeco-Roman or Jewish rhetoric is appropriate, since ancient authors were completely innocent and ignorant of modern rhetorical theory and epistemology. As a result, the remainder of this section will explain more particularly rhetorical criticism in the Kennedy and Betz vein.

Most New Testament scholars at this juncture are convinced that micro-rhetoric (that is, rhetorical devices such as rhetorical questions, dramatic hyperbole or personification) can be found in New Testament documents, particularly in Paul's letters, but also elsewhere.

More controversial is whether macro-rhetoric (whether the overall structure of the document reflects rhetorical categories and divisions) is also used in the New Testament. There are six normal divisions of an ancient speech:

1 *exordium*: the introductory section of a discourse;
2 *narratio*: a narrative account of what has happened;
3 *proposition*: a brief summary of what the main thesis of the discourse will be;
4 *probatio*: the main positive arguments on behalf of the speaker's case;
5 *refutatio*: answers to the counter-arguments given by opponents;
6 *peroratio*: an appeal to the emotion of the audience and a summing up.

These six divisions can be found in the three different species of ancient rhetoric: forensic, deliberative and epideictic. These different species of rhetoric served very different functions.

- Forensic rhetoric, used in the law court, consisted of techniques of attack and defence and focused largely on the past.
- Deliberative rhetoric, used in the assembly (when the leaders of a city gathered together to make decisions), included advice and consent and focused on changing beliefs and/or behaviour in the future.
- Epideictic rhetoric, used in the forum (marketplace where business took place) and at funerals, involved praise and blame and focused on the present.

In any given ancient speech, attention was also paid to the issues of 'ethos', 'logos' and 'pathos', which is to say the establishing of rapport with the audience at the outset (ethos), the use of emotion-charged arguments in the middle of the speech (logos), and the appeal to the deeper emotions (pathos) in the final summation.

It is fair to say that New Testament scholars who have undertaken detailed rhetorical analysis of all the New Testament documents have concluded that while micro-rhetoric can be found throughout the New Testament, macro-rhetoric only appears in the letters, homilies and the speech summaries of Acts; particular examples can be found in Paul's letters and the homilies called Hebrews, 1 John and 1 Peter. It is, however, used with some flexibility, and the features of macro-rhetoric are often enfolded within the framework of letters. Thus, for example, the beginning and end of Paul's letters do almost always reflect epistolary conventions, and can certainly be categorized as ancient letters. However, epistolary categories help us very little in analysing the structure of the material outside of the opening and closing elements (prescript, travel plans, opening or closing greetings). In other words, they help us very little with the bulk of the material in the documents traditionally called New Testament letters. Here is where rhetoric has proved much more helpful in unlocking the structural and substantive intricacies of the majority of New Testament documents.

It is much more helpful to ask how texts functioned in a largely oral culture such as existed in the New Testament era, and in particular how sacred texts functioned in such an environment. All the New Testament documents are oral texts. In other words they were designed to be heard, not read silently. They are public documents, and in particular they were meant to be read out loud in worship and other Christian community contexts. Even Paul's letters were not meant to be privately studied. In the first instance they were surrogates for the speeches Paul would have made could he have been present with his audience, and as such they use all the ad hoc characteristics of such purpose-driven ancient speeches. They were intended as timely remarks to affect the belief and behaviour of the various audiences and not as theological or ethical treatises. Rhetorical criticism helps us realize the dynamic and interactive nature of these documents.

B. W.

What are the landmark publications on rhetorical criticism?

Hans Dieter Betz (1979) *Galatians: A Commentary on Paul's Letter to the Churches in Galatia*, Hermeneia: A Critical and Historical Commentary on the Bible. Philadelphia: Fortress.

This commentary expounds in detail Betz's theory that the structure and argument of Galatians can be best understood through the lens of ancient Greek rhetoric.

George A. Kennedy (1984) *New Testament Interpretation through Rhetorical Criticism.* Chapel Hill: University of North Carolina Press.

Here Kennedy picks up Betz's theory and looks at a wide range of New Testament texts from the perspective of ancient Greek rhetoric.

Vernon Robbins (1996) *Exploring the Texture of Texts: A Guide to Socio-Rhetorical Interpretation.* Harrisburg: Trinity Press International.

Robbins's approach to rhetorical criticism is somewhat different from that of Betz and Kennedy, in that he applies modern, not ancient, rhetoric to the New Testament and so seeks to discover more how the New Testament communicates today than how its authors intended it to do so.

Rhetorical criticism in practice

One of the most famous, and influential, attempts to read Galatians from the perspective of Graeco-Roman rhetoric was H. D. Betz's 1979 commentary on Galatians (Betz, 1979). Betz proposed that Galatians is an 'apologetic letter' of a type that was common in the Graeco-Roman world. According to Betz, the purpose of a letter like this was to defend authors against charges levelled at them by opponents. One of the most noteworthy examples of this art was Plato's *Apology*, in which he gave a version of the speech given by Socrates at his trial. This and other famous apologies inspired other later Graeco-Roman orators and writers to shape their arguments in a similar way. Betz proposes that Paul is aware of this kind of writing and wrote Galatians in imitation of this style.

Galatians as an 'apologetic' letter

The connection between Galatians and 'apologetic letters' is much more than content, although it is quite clear that Galatians was written to defend Paul against his opponents; the real connection lies in the structure of the text and the way in which the argument is formed. Betz has identified in Galatians similarities in structure between it and the ancient apologetic letters. Betz splits Galatians into seven major sections, outlined in Table 1 (pp. 76–7) and gives to them Latin titles, which he draws from Quintilian (*Rhetoria ad Herennium*) and Cicero (*De inventione*) to describe their function in the book.

The value of this is that it focuses our attention not only on the meaning of the text but on how the text achieves that meaning. In this particular instance, it demonstrates Paul's major concern in writing to the Christian community at Galatia and draws out the steps that he used to communicate his concern to them. Betz's detailed examination of Galatians through the lens of ancient rhetoric highlights Paul's attempt to draw the Galatians back from insisting that Gentiles must be Jews in order to be 'in Christ' and to remember that it was their belief in Christ and not their Judaism that had shaped them thus far.

The fictional audience of Galatians

Betz's argument that Galatians is an apologetic letter puts it into the category of forensic rhetoric, such as Witherington defined above. The important feature of his argument here, though, is that the forensic setting is a fictional one. Thus, although the 'real audience' was the Galatian Christians, Betz argues that in Paul's mind he was addressing a judge and jury, who were listening to Paul's defence of his position against his accusers, Jewish Christians (see Betz, 1979, 24).

The structure of Galatians

One of the strongest parts of Betz's case is the close fit between certain aspects of an ancient speech and the epistle of Galatians. The easiest way to illustrate this with broad brushstrokes is in tabular form (see Table 1 on pp. 76–7).

Critiques of Betz's theory

Betz's use of ancient rhetoric in understanding the New Testament epistles has been formative for many scholars in shaping a method for understanding Paul's epistles, as well as other New Testament texts (see Anderson, 1996; Classen, 2000; Nanos, 2002). Scholars are widely agreed that Betz's approach to Galatians has made a crucial step forward in our understanding of the epistle. At the same time, however, many are uneasy at the rigid use Betz made of ancient rhetoric; they accept that he is right to use macro-rhetoric to understand Galatians but are critical of the way in which he has done it. Even Betz himself struggles with the rigidity of his own method, and it is intriguing to note that he finds it difficult to tie up what Paul is saying with established rhetorical categories, so much so that at one point he acknowledges the complexity of the task by saying: 'One may say that Paul has been very successful – as a skilled rhetorician would be expected to be – in disguising this argumentative strategy'; in

Table 1 An outline of the argument of Galatians in terms of Graeco-Roman rhetoric drawn from Betz, 1979

Reference in Galatians	Rhetorical label	What it means	Use in Galatians
1.1–5	Epistolary prescript	The introduction, including an identification of the author and the greeting	The introduction of Paul and addressees, the definition of Paul's apostleship and his greeting
1.6–11	Exordium	Laying out the purpose of the discourse by presentation of facts	Paul's main point to the Galatians: they should not desert the gospel that Paul pronounced to them, to which Paul adds an attack on his opponents on the grounds that they are confusing the Galatians
1.12—2.14	Narratio	Statement of facts, intended to persuade the audience	Paul received the gospel directly from Christ and gives the historical evidence for this at his conversion and subsequent events (1.3–24); at the Apostolic council (2.1–10) and at the conflict in Antioch (2.11–14)
2.15–21	Propositio	Summing up of the content of the *narratio* and providing a bridge for the *probatio*	Sets up points of agreement (2.15–16 – a person is justified by faith in Jesus Christ not by works of the law) and disagreement (2.17–18 – the implications of justification by faith for Gentile Christians) and sets up four theses: 1 I died to the law 2 I have been crucified with Christ 3 I no longer live but Christ in me 4 I live in [the] faith in/of the son of God

3.1—4.31	*Probatio*	Presentation of the proofs of the argument	Paul presents six arguments (+ a digression): (a) You received the Spirit by what you believed not by doing the works of the law (3.1–5) (b) An argument from Scripture – the case of Abraham (3.6–14) (c) An argument from common practice – a will (3.15–18) Digression on the nature of Torah (3.19–25) (d) An argument from Christian tradition (3.26—4.11) (e) An argument from friendship (4.12–20) (f) An allegorical argument from Scripture (4.21–30) Summary of whole argument (4.31)
5.1—6.10	*Exhortatio*	A series of encouragements	Paul makes three major points in this section: 1 Do not bow to what others are saying to you, you are free (5.1–12) 2 Because you are free live by the Spirit and not the flesh (5.13–24) 3 Some advice for how to do this (5.25—6.10) Ends with a warning and a summary of the whole section (6.7–10)
6.11-18	Epistolary postscript	Sums up the main point of the argument	Paul adds a PS in his own handwriting and also concludes the letter

other words he was so clever that we can't work out what he thought he was doing (Betz, 1979, 129).

Disagreements with Betz's method take different forms and there are many different suggestions of how to take Betz's original idea forward. For example:

- Kennedy argues that Galatians displays not judicial rhetoric but deliberative. One of Betz's biggest difficulties is the importance of the exhortatio in 5.1—6.10, and as Kennedy points out it is deliberative not judicial rhetoric that depends strongly upon exhortation (Kennedy, 1984, 148–50).
- Longenecker maintains that Betz has not paid sufficient attention to Galatians as a letter. He disagrees with Betz's conclusion that epistolary analysis of Galatians is unnecessary for understanding Galatians and uses this alongside certain rhetorical categories that he sees operating both in ancient rhetoric and in Galatians to interpret the letter (Longenecker, 1990).
- Kern states that Galatians is too different from the handbooks of Aristotle and Cicero to allow Galatians to be an example of ancient rhetoric. Kern's argument is that ancient rhetoric arose in particular social contexts not shared by the epistle to the Galatians and therefore cannot be used to understand the epistle. Galatians, he argues, should be understood against its own social milieu and not against one from 'outside'. He is not opposed to exploring rhetorical devices, simply to imposing a whole system of rhetoric from what he sees to be 'outside' the Pauline context (Kern, 1998).

Conclusions

These criticisms of Betz are a representative sample of a large number of critiques of his theory. All, in their own ways, argue against the rigidity of the monochrome rhetorical structure that Betz imposes on the text. Some, like Kennedy, because they disagree with the particular structure that Betz employed, namely judicial rather than deliberative; others, like Longenecker, do not think that he pays enough attention to other aspects of Galatians and its rhetoric, that is, its epistolary structure; while others still, like Kern, disagree with looking for macro-rhetoric at all and instead restrict rhetorical analysis to micro-rhetoric.

One thing remains clear, however. Even though the details of Betz's theory on Galatians are heavily disputed, the fact that it should be interpreted through the lens of some kind of rhetoric is widely accepted and as such his theory remains influential.

Evaluation of rhetorical criticism

One of the greatest values of rhetorical criticism is that it recognizes that the New Testament documents are, and are intended to be, persuasive documents – they are not unbiased or dispassionate. The purpose of rhetorical criticism (after Betz) is to discover the authorial intent behind the use of rhetoric and, as with many forms of historical criticism, herein lies the problem. It is difficult for modern interpreters to discover precisely what someone writing two millennia ago, in a different culture and with a different worldview, intended. This does not devalue the field in any way; it simply acknowledges that that author's intended use of any one rhetorical field is difficult to identify with any certainty.

On one level, the other rhetorical critical approach, followed by scholars like Robbins, which seeks to discover the rhetorical power of the New Testament using modern rhetorical techniques, appears easier, as it seeks simply to discover how a passage persuades in our modern context, regardless of how its author intended that it would persuade. Nevertheless, despite its complexities, the aim of discovering the rhetorical intention of a text's original author is desirable, even if the results cannot be assured, and the contribution of this form of rhetorical criticism to New Testament studies has been significant. For example, it has encouraged us to see Ephesians as an epideictic homily written not to a specific situation but to a series of Pauline churches, and it has encouraged us to understand Romans as a work of deliberative rhetoric, with its thesis statement plainly laid out at the outset in Romans 1.16–17. It is safe to say that rhetorical criticism of the New Testament has established itself as a viable and vital means of analysing the New Testament in the last 25 years, and promises to yield yet more fruit in the years to come.

10

Narrative criticism

What is narrative criticism?

Narrative criticism interprets New Testament narratives as literary texts, using categories that are applied in interpreting all other forms of literature, for example, plot, characterization, setting, and so forth.

How did the theory develop and what are its main features?
Elizabeth Struthers Malbon

Narrative criticism is heir both to **new criticism** and to structuralism in terms of general literary criticism and to redaction criticism in terms of biblical criticism. Like redaction criticism, narrative criticism focuses on the final version of the text; like new criticism it concentrates on the world internal to the text rather than its external references and relationships; like structuralism it perceives the text as the centre of a communication event between sender (author) and receiver (reader or audience) and as comprised of cultural signs that have meaning only within a system of relationships.

Most importantly, narrative criticism makes literary rather than historical concerns central to its interpretation. This can be seen in the model of the literary critic Seymour Chatman (1978) as it has been expanded by biblical narrative critics (see Figure 2).

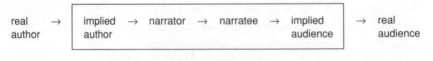

real → implied → narrator → narratee → implied → real
author   author   audience   audience

TEXT or NARRATIVE

Figure 2 How biblical narrative critics have expanded Seymour Chatman's model

Although narrative critics acknowledge that there was a historical author and original audience, their concern is with an 'implied author' and an 'implied audience'. The implied author is a theoretical construction based on the requirements of knowledge and understanding presupposed in a narrative; in other words, the implied author is the one who would be necessary for a particular narrative to be told or written. The implied audience is the one that would be necessary for a particular narrative to be heard or read. The use of the term implied audience instead of Chatman's 'implied reader' is based on growing awareness of the fact that biblical materials originated in an oral context. Narrative critics are wary of what is called the 'intentional fallacy' (overvaluing the presumed motivation of the 'real' author) and the 'affective fallacy' (overvaluing the response of the 'real' audience), but of course they realize that basic information about the cultural context is essential to any interpretation. An implied author can be limited or unlimited, ironic or straightforward, in tension or in agreement with the characters.

Within this model, narrative elements explored generally include characters, settings, plot and rhetoric. Characters are revealed by words and actions, both their own and those of other characters and/or the narrator. They are understood in relation to each other: minor characters may parallel or contrast major characters; 'flat' characters (consistently showing only one trait) may highlight 'round' characters (who are more complex or dynamic). Characters may be aligned with or opposed to each other and/or the narrator in terms of their evaluative points of view. These various aspects of characters affect the implied audience's response in praise, judgement or identification.

Settings are examined by narrative critics not in terms of their external references, historical geography and chronology, but in terms of their internal system of meaning. Places and times are rich in connotational, or associative, values, and these values contribute to the meaning of the narrative. Jesus' appearance 'in the wilderness for forty days' or 'on a high mountain' brings with it a network of biblical connections. Often settings participate in the drama of the narrative, such as when 'the sea' takes on a demonic role. Temporal markers pace the unfolding of the story, from urgency to slow motion, to underline significance.

If settings present the 'when' and 'where' of narrative, and characters the 'who', plot offers the 'what' and 'why'. The narrative critic Norman Petersen (1978b) has distinguished 'narrative world' – all the events mentioned in a narrative in their causal and logical order – and 'plotted time' – the way these events have been selected and arranged in a narrative sequence. Narrative critics investigate that plotted sequence as a source of meaning for the implied audience. The literary theorist Gérard

Genette (1980) has worked out an intricate system for discussing the order, duration and frequency of events in the plotted narrative. Changes in these aspects are ways the implied author has of leading the implied audience through the story to an interpretation. Conflict – physical, ideational, spiritual – is frequently a key element of plot.

Rhetoric, the way the implied author persuades the implied audience to follow and evaluate the story, is the 'how' of narrative. In Chatman's terms, rhetoric is part of the discourse level of narrative in contrast to the story level that includes events, characters and settings, and their inter-action as the plot. The story is where the characters interact, but the dis-course – or better, the story-as-discoursed – is where the implied author and implied audience interact. Repetition, intercalation (inserting some-thing between other things), framing, foreshadowing and echoing, sym-bolism and irony are favourite rhetorical devices in biblical narratives. By these and other ways of telling the story the implied author persuades the implied audience first to understand and then to share and extend the story's levels of meaning. Narrative criticism investigates this dynamic process of communication between implied author and implied audience by means of the characters, settings, plot and rhetoric of narrative.

E. S. M.

What are the landmark publications on narrative criticism?

Seymour Chatman (1978) *Story and Discourse: Narrative Structure in Fiction and Film.* Ithaca: Cornell University Press.

The classic text on the theory of narrative that has influenced many narrative critics in New Testament scholarship.

Norman R. Petersen (1978) *Literary Criticism for New Testament Critics*, Guides to Biblical Scholarship. Philadelphia: Fortress.

One of the earlier attempts to apply the principles of narrative criticism to the study of the New Testament.

David Rhoads and Donald Michie (1982) *Mark as Story: An Introduction to the Narrative of a Gospel.* Minneapolis: Fortress.

This book explores some of the key literary elements of narrative in Mark's story, such as narrator, setting, plot and characters. It has been so influential that it has been completely rewritten as a second edition with an additional author, Joanna Dewey (see 'Further reading' for details).

Robert J. Tannehill (1986–90) *The Narrative Unity of Luke–Acts*, vols 1–2. Minneapolis: Fortress.

An influential and effective exploration of the message of Luke–Acts through the lens of literary criticism.

Narrative criticism in practice

The concerns of narrative criticism encourage us to read the text in larger portions than might normally be the case. Methods of interpretation that focus attention on the minutiae of historical detail require the text to be split into relatively small units; narrative criticism, however, pays more attention to the way in which a story unfolds from event to event and consequently is often better applied to larger sections.

Discipleship and the sea: Mark 4.1—8.26

The central section of Jesus' ministry in Mark's Gospel focuses on the theme of discipleship, most notably on the failure of the twelve to respond adequately to Jesus. Indeed it is intriguing to notice that the episodes that feature the disciples' failure to respond appropriately to, or even comprehend, Jesus occur most often on the sea. Narrative criticism helps us to understand the significance of this juxtaposition.

Implied author and implied audience

One of the most important features of Mark's Gospel is the implied conversation that takes place between the narrator of the story and the reader (and thus between the implied author and implied audience). The role of the narrator in Mark's Gospel is particularly strong. Rhoads, Dewey and Michie point out the way in which the narrator in Mark's Gospel is able to move in the account from place to place in a way a human character could not (Rhoads, Dewey and Michie, 1999, 40–1). So for example in chapter 6 the narrator can move from describing the twelve being sent out by Jesus (6.6b–13), to Herod's hearing of the event (6.14–16), and even back in time from there to describe John the Baptist's beheading (6.17–29). Not only that, but the narrator is also able to perceive the thoughts, feelings and reactions of the characters that he describes. So we are able to know that Herod thought that John had come back to life (6.16) and that Herodias had a grudge against John the Baptist (6.19).

This also means that the narrator can have some kind of relationship with the reader and is therefore able to pause occasionally and explain something about what is going on. Probably the best example in Mark 4.1—8.26 is 7.1–23, which contains the discussion between Jesus and the Pharisees about defilement. At two points in this story the narrator explains something. In 7.3, the narrator points out that Pharisees and Jews do not eat unless they have washed their hands, and in 7.19 that Jesus had by what he said declared all foods clean. It is almost as though the narrator and reader are standing together watching the events unfold and that the narrator turns to the reader from time to time to make sure he or she has understood what is going on.

This is exacerbated in the accounts where the reader is shown something that the other characters in the story are not. Again Rhoads, Dewey and Michie point out the dynamic within Mark between the reader and the disciples, where the reader is given privileged insight into the events of the baptism (Mark 1.9–11) by the narrator (Rhoads, Dewey and Michie, 1999, 42–3). After Jesus was baptized, he, but apparently not the others present, saw the heavens opened and heard a voice coming from heaven declaring him to be God's son. As a result, the reader is aware throughout the first half of the Gospel who Jesus is and how he is regarded by God – the other characters, however, are not. The narrator, then, encourages the reader to wonder whether the disciples are ever going to understand who Jesus is. In 8.29 Peter suddenly does grasp Jesus' identity but seems unable to do so fully because he immediately reprimands Jesus when he talks about the necessity of his death (8.32–33). Again the readers are almost encouraged to roll their eyes at the disciples' slow and partial comprehension of who Jesus is. Perhaps the implied author is suggesting the implied audience should examine the completeness or incompleteness of its own understanding.

The setting

One of the most important differences between narrative criticism and historical critical approaches is the way in which they interpret the different settings of the gospel. For historical critics the important issue is to be able to identify the location of the setting, to be able to see how the characters moved from one point to the next, and to learn as much as possible about that place in the first century. For narrative critics, however, the setting is important because of what it signifies.

Chapters 4—8 of Mark contain a striking number of journeys that Jesus and his disciples take in a boat. The first one takes place in 4.35–41 with the narrative of the stilling of the storm. This is followed in 6.45–54 with Jesus walking on the water past the disciples in a boat and in 8.10–21 with the discussion about the leaven of the Pharisees. These major events are interspersed by smaller narratives that describe Jesus sitting in a boat to teach (4.1) and Jesus crossing back after healing the Gerasene demoniac (5.21). The significance of the sea is that it represents chaos and destruction, as in the creation narratives, the flood and the crossing of the Red Sea (Rhoads, Dewey and Michie, 1999, 70) but also God's power over it (Malbon, 1992, 31). The repetitive motif of the sea, therefore, alerts us to God's power over the chaos of the world and to Jesus' connection to that power. Malbon has further drawn attention to the way in which the sea incidents initiate a series of Jesus' mighty deeds that are resonant with echoes intended to focus attention on an understanding of who Jesus is and what following him entails (Malbon, 1993).

Major characters

It is widely acknowledged that there are three major groups of characters in Mark's Gospel: the authorities, the crowd and the disciples. Each is characterized by its attitude to Jesus. Although there are several groups of Jewish authorities who each act on their own, they are all characterized by their hostility towards Jesus. The crowd, however, follows Jesus open-mouthed with wonder and is constantly described as amazed by what he does. Between the open hostility and blank amazement are the disciples, whose struggle to perceive and comprehend Jesus can be found throughout Mark's narrative. Petersen divided the characters of Mark into two major groups: those who think 'the things of God' and those who think 'the things of people' (N. R. Petersen, 1978a, 105–11). The authorities are always in the latter group, as are the disciples on occasions; whereas Jesus and the narrator are always in the former group of those who think the things of God.

Malbon points out the importance of recognizing another layer of characterization in Mark, which exists beyond the simple positive and negative characteristics of different characters (Malbon, 1992, 28–30). This is the distinction between 'flat' and 'round' characters. So, for example, the authorities are flat and negative. Most of them react badly to Jesus and, with a few notable exceptions such as 'one of the scribes' (12.28), Jairus and Joseph of Arimathea (see discussion in Malbon, 1989, 275–6), are characters that are not developed beyond simple hostility. The disciples, however, are much more complex. They are round characters who veer between being positive (like Peter was at Caesarea Philippi) and negative (again like Peter when he disputed Jesus' statement that he would be killed).

We noted above the importance of the sea in chapters 4—8 of Mark. When we add the round and complex characters of the disciples to the sea motif in these chapters, another emphasis emerges. Journeys in boats seem to be associated with the disciples' difficulty in comprehending Jesus. Those moments of chaos over which Jesus exerts divine power coincide with the disciples' inability to comprehend who he is. This is drawn out in the narrative by Jesus asking the disciples why they are timid (4.40), by the narrator telling us that their hearts were hardened (6.52), and by Jesus' string of questions to the disciples in 8.17–18:

- Do you still not perceive or understand?
- Are your hearts hardened?
- Do you have eyes and fail to see?
- Do you have ears and fail to hear?
- And do you not remember?

All this narration emphasizes the disciples' inability to see that Jesus' command over the chaos of the sea tells the disciples something about who he is – something the implied audience does see.

Minor characters

Alongside these major groups of characters in Mark we find minor characters, who do not fit into any one of the major categories of people whom Jesus meets, but who nevertheless are important within the story. Williams notes that the minor characters in Mark change roles as we progress through the Gospel (J. F. Williams, 1996, 336). In the first half of the Gospel the minor characters come to Jesus to beg for his help; in the second half they become exemplars of true discipleship, but at the end (16.8) the women (who Williams sees as minor characters) flee like the male disciples.

In chapters 4—8 we encounter the minor characters' responses, which differ wildly from the incomprehension of the twelve. Here we meet the Gerasene demoniac, who begs to be allowed to come with Jesus, Jairus (a synagogue ruler and thus an exceptional religious authority), who believes that Jesus can heal his daughter, the woman with a haemorrhage, who touches Jesus' cloak in faith, the Syro-Phoenician woman, who combats Jesus' apparent reluctance to heal her daughter, and the blind man, who is healed first partially and then wholly by Jesus. It is in the minor characters and their responses to Jesus that the reader is encouraged to observe glimpses of true discipleship.

Conclusions

When we read chapters 4—8 through the lens of narrative criticism, we can begin to see how the narrative itself functions both in communicating its message and in drawing the reader into responding to the events described. The asides and revelations made by the narrator both engage the reader and point towards the kind of response that might be made to the narrative. Narrative criticism also draws our attention to 'set scenes', such as the disciples in a boat on the sea, and to 'set characteristics', such as the responses of the three major groups (authorities, crowd and disciples) to Jesus. These set scenes not only identify the message that they convey (for example, the inadequacy of the disciples' response to Jesus) but also cast into greater relief the responses of minor characters who seem to comprehend much more who Jesus is. The theme that emerges from a narrative reading of chapters 4—8 is the call to discipleship, a call whose difficulty is illustrated by the failure of the twelve to respond fully and truly to this call and whose possibilities are suggested by the presence of responses to this call in the most surprising of places, such as a healed demoniac or a Gentile woman.

Evaluation of narrative criticism

The value of narrative critical readings of the text is that they draw attention to the internal features of the story. It is tempting when we read the Bible to use the narrative like a window which we look through to understand more about the historical events that the story describes. Narrative criticism reminds us of the importance of viewing the text more like a picture, of focusing our attention on what is there rather than what is not and of learning to read the significance of various 'set' pieces such as typical scenes, reactions of characters, and so on. This approach highlights the meaning of the story itself rather than what the author might have thought, or how the text might have reached its final form. It is an approach grounded firmly in the meaning of the text and in discovering how the story communicates its meaning.

It is worth noting that narrative criticism is often, though not always, coupled with other interpretative techniques. So David Rhoads' more recent book on Mark and narrative criticism also contains social science analysis of the text (Rhoads, 2004) and Robert Tannehill's influential work on Mark's Gospel combines narrative criticism with reader-response theory (Tannehill, 1977). This indicates that there are some scholars who, though interested in the way in which narrative creates meaning, find this insufficient as the sole mode of interpretation and want to look backwards into history or forwards to the current reader for further illumination. Indeed it is almost a definition of narrative criticism that it will reach beyond itself in interpreting texts. Texts cannot make meaning without an engaged reader, and this opens the door into other methods of interpretation explored elsewhere in this volume.

11

Structural criticism

What is structural criticism?

Structural criticism (also called structuralism) is a form of narrative criticism which pays particular attention to the deep, permanent structures that are common to all stories.

How did the theory develop and what are its main features?
Daniel Patte

The theory of structural criticism has a long history. A brief overview is helpful to understand the diverse ways in which structural criticism breaks down the (biblical) text into potential meaning-producing dimensions, thereby calling attention to the fact that any reading (including scholarly readings) chooses one of these dimensions as most significant, relegating other dimensions into the background. **Semiotics** (in Greek a *semeiotikos* was an interpreter of symptoms and signs), which is one form of structuralism, is the study of communication by means of signs (something that points to something else) and of *sign*ification (the message that is intended).

Plato and Aristotle were interested in communication through signs. Augustine wrote of *signum* (the Latin word for sign or mark) as the universal means of communication and examined the relationship between natural signs (symptoms, for example, in medicine) and human-made signs (language and other cultural artefacts). Augustine pondered consistent symbol systems that presume connections between individual reality, community reality and ultimate reality. In the same way that a metaphor affirms that two unlike 'things' are actually the same despite their seemingly strong incompatibility, Augustine followed Aristotle in maintaining that there is an intrinsic relationship between sign/symptom and the signified; they refer to the same concept for all humans (despite cultural diversity and various modes of expressions), a universalist view still presupposed by the Enlightenment.

Yet, a sign is always also part of a signification process, that is, the process by which meaning emerges. Augustine emphasized that 'a sign is something that shows itself to the senses and something other than itself to the mind'. This triadic or threefold view of signs (the sign, the senses and the mind) provided the framework for semiotic reflections and for its implications in logic and pragmatics from Boethius to Anselm of Canterbury and Abelard, Bacon, John Duns Scotus and following them Charles Sanders Peirce (1839–1914).

Structural semiotics was initiated by Peirce and the linguist Ferdinand de Saussure (1857–1913). For Saussure, a sign is the arbitrary (not intrinsic) relation of a signifier (for example, the four letters and uttered sounds 'tree') and a signified (the mental concept of the reality 'tree'). Saussure affirmed that a semiotic system (for example, a language, or a text) is the arbitrary relation of signifiers and signifieds, which was a direct challenge to the universalist view, and posited that signification is constructed and structured. Thus understanding a text is not a matter of elucidating its abstract conceptual 'content', or the intelligible intention of the author, but the ways in which it 'makes sense' (produces meaning) through its construction as a semiotic system.

Semiotics provides tools for structural criticism by exploring further the implications of the triadic character of sign: a sign is always a sign *of* something *to* some mind. Beyond Peirce, for the linguist Charles W. Morris (Morris, 1938) this triad refers to three aspects of linguistic communication: syntax (the positioning of words in a sentence), semantics (the meaning of words), and pragmatics (how language is used). Saussure's followers, including Louis Hjelmslev (1961), Roland Barthes (1972), Umberto Eco (1976), and A. J. Greimas (Greimas and Courtés, 1986), broadened the application of this triadic view of communication to any semiotic system.

For Greimas, any semiotic system is characterized by three kinds of structure. For instance, if one considers a narrative as a semiotic system one can distinguish the following structures, each of which readily becomes the primary focus of one of the family of critical exegetical methods.

1 The *'narrative syntax'*
   (a) the unfolding of the plot and the overall transformation it involves; the interactions of actants (subject, object, opponent, helper, sender, receiver) (this is a focus of structural exegesis, because it is related to narrative semantics, see below);
   (b) the fleshing out of this fundamental narrative syntax, transforming actants into fully fledged characters in time and space (this is often a focus of narrative criticism).

2 The '*narrative semantics*'
   (a) the basic convictional value system that spontaneously distin-
       guishes between what is euphoric and dysphoric, real and illusory;
   (b) the unfurling of this fundamental semantics into an overall
       semantic universe or meaningful worldview (this is a particular
       focus of structural criticism).
3 The '*discursive structure*' through which the storyteller pragmatically
   addressing an audience (presumably with different expectations about
   what constitutes a realistic narrative unfolding and/or a meaningful
   worldview) seeks:
   (a) to 'make realistic' for this audience the narrative plot and charac-
       ters (an attempt to create verisimilitude by underscoring those
       features of the plots and characters that correspond to the experi-
       ence of the intended audience) (this is often a focus of historical
       criticism);
   (b) to 'make sensible' the value system posited by the narrative by con-
       structing through the analogical imagination a symbolic system –
       including metaphors, figures and symbols that bring together the
       semantic universe posited by the narrative and the presumed
       semantic universe of the audience (as a metaphor brings together
       two semantic fields) (this is a focus of rhetorical and theological
       studies, since it was the concern of Augustine and the scholastics,
       and also of certain structural semiotic criticism).

Beyond its complexity (each structure can be further subdivided), this view
of the overall semiotic structure (found in all semiotic systems) leads to
two essential conclusions for biblical critical studies.

1 As Greimas posited and his followers have demonstrated, the process
   of the reading of a text involves the process of 'textualization' ('making
   sense of the text-on-the-page') by choosing one of its dimensions and
   the corresponding structure as *most significant*. Any given reading does
   not, and should not pretend to, exhaust the meaning of the text. Thus
   each method in biblical criticism appropriately chooses to focus on one
   textual dimension and its structure; and one should not expect from
   each the same conclusions regarding the meaning of the text.
2 Structural criticism, as a set of exegetical methods, chose to focus the
   reading of biblical texts upon structural dimensions that were overlooked
   in biblical studies, namely 'narrative semantics' and 'discursive semantics', and therefore upon religious dimensions of these religious texts.

Thus in my work I have focused on elucidating the 'faith' (system of convictions) of Paul and Matthew whereas others – the Groupe d'Entrevernes, Jean Delorme, Louis Panier, Jean Calloud – focused on elucidating the symbolic sign system.

D. P.

What are the landmark publications on structural criticism?

Charles Sanders Peirce (1998) *The Essential Peirce, Selected Philosophical Writings, Volume 2 (1893–1913)*. Peirce Edition Project, eds. Bloomington and Indianapolis: Indiana University Press.

In his writings, Peirce explored semiotics, among many other things, and devised the system of three categories (the sign, its object and its interpreter) in order to explain how communication works.

Ferdinand de Saussure (1916) *Cours de linguistique générale*. Lausanne: Payot.

Translated into English as (1983) *Course in General Linguistics*. London: Duckworth. Saussure's influential work was published after his death from lecture notes taken by some of his students. It is widely acknowledged to be a seminal work in structuralism.

Claude Lévi-Strauss (1958) *Anthropologie Structurale*. Paris: Plon.

Translated into English as (1963) *Structural Anthropology*. New York: Basic Books. In this, the most popular of his many books, Lévi-Strauss adapted the linguistic theory of Saussure to anthropology and demonstrated that people think about the world in binary opposites. This is illustrated in

Claude Lévi-Strauss (1964) *Le Cru et Le Cuit*. Paris: Plon.

Translated into English as (1969) *The Raw and the Cooked*. New York: Harper & Row.

Daniel Patte (1980) *Religious Dimensions of Biblical Texts: Greimas's Structural Semiotics and Biblical Exegesis*, Society of Biblical Literature Semeia Studies. Atlanta: Scholars Press.

In this book, Patte lays out the theory that lies behind his application of Greimas's structural semiotics to the New Testament. Patte stands out as the scholar who has applied the insights of structuralism most systematically and effectively to a reading of the New Testament.

Structural criticism in practice

The structural criticism outlined above is influenced most heavily by linguistics. Lévi-Strauss, a structural anthropologist, was also influenced by this linguistic work but went on to apply its insights to the study of human behaviour, anthropology, and in particular to myths which he considered to be illustrative of the way that human beings relate to one another and to the world around them. In so doing Lévi-Strauss focuses on what Greimas calls 'narrative semantics'. This view of the way in which myths reveal deep human relationships has also found expression in New Testament interpretation, and it is an example of this kind of approach that we will explore below.

The Aqedah *and Jesus' self-offering: Hebrews*

In his 1992 monograph, John Dunnill helpfully used the method of myth interpretation proposed by Lévi-Strauss to understand more fully the way in which Jewish traditions about the binding of Isaac (the *Aqedah*) and the view of Jesus' atoning death in Hebrews share the same foundational view of what he calls covenant-sacrifice (Dunnill, 1992, 190). The significance of his argument is that the apparent overlap between the *Aqedah* and Jesus' atoning death may come not so much from the influence of one tradition on another (the Jewish on the Christian or the Christian on the Jewish) as it does from a shared view of the world.

The Aqedah *and the atonement*

It has long been accepted *that* there is a connection between Jewish traditions about the binding of Isaac and Christian traditions about Jesus' atonement, though less acceptance about *what* that connection comprises. The story of the binding of Isaac, based on Genesis 22, occurs in many different forms in Jewish literature. The Targums (Aramaic translations and interpretations of the Hebrew Bible) present numerous different accounts of the story. *Targum Pseudo-Jonathan* reports that Isaac was 37 years old when the story took place and recounts a conversation between him and Ishmael in which Isaac claims that he was ready to offer himself to God as a willing sacrifice (*Targum Pseudo-Jonathan* 22.8). Other texts state that Scripture treats Isaac as though he had actually died (*Midrash ha-Gadol* 22.19) and that his willingness to sacrifice himself atones for Israel's sins (*Babylonian Talmud Gittin* 57b). These similarities to the Christian tradition of atonement have caused extensive discussion about the direction of influence (Jewish to Christian, Christian to Jewish or both, that is, that they mutually influenced each other).

The Aqedah *and Jesus' death*

It is at this point that Dunnill uses Lévi-Strauss's theory of the structural form of a myth to explain the connection between the two (Lévi-Strauss, 1968). Lévi-Strauss argued that the words used in a story and even the story-line itself are part of *parole* – individual acts, statements or speeches – whereas the *langue* of a myth contains the collective intelligence of a culture. Thus myths with entirely different words and even story-lines can be seen to be 'about' the same thing, because they address the foundational issues of their culture. Often, the *langue* of myths attempts to resolve the contradictions that exist within the word such as life and death by 'mediating between irreconcilable opposites by creating an area of significant ambiguity in which different rules of logic apply' (Dunnill, 1992, 190).

In Dunnill's opinion the *Aqedah* and the death of Jesus both address the foundational issue of the ambiguity of God in the face of death and the testing of the seed of Abraham. In his view all versions of the *Aqedah* contain two irreconcilable features: God blesses Abraham by giving him a son and then also demands that he sacrifice him. The oppositions focus on the ambivalence of the divine nature which, Hebrew tradition asserts, created both good and evil. Consequently God both protects and destroys, nurtures and annihilates; the same God looks after characters, such as Abraham, promising him that his descendants will live for ever and then demands the life of his only son. Lévi-Strauss's view was that the initial opposition can never be resolved but that the purpose of myths is to present additional, similar oppositions which *can* be resolved – and are – so that a resolution between the initial apparently irreconcilable oppositions seems possible. Structural interpretations of such myths, therefore, seek not only to identify the oppositions but to perceive the means by which they are resolved.

Dunnill argues that the tradition about the binding of Isaac gives rise to an initial set of oppositions which he sets out as:

God gives a son (Blessing)
   Abraham trusts in God's promise
      Isaac is restored and the promise of the 'seed' is reaffirmed
   Abraham gives up his son as a sacrifice
God demands the son (Testing).

(Dunnill, 1992, 194)

The initial opposition between a God who blesses and a God who tests is resolved through Abraham's trust in God's promise and willingness to give up his son. He traces a similar set of oppositions through the Passover:

God the protector of Abraham, Isaac and Jacob vs God the destroyer of the first born is resolved through the covenant meal shared by the Israelites only, and avertive action with the blood of a yearling lamb so that Israel escapes. Dunnill perceives a similar myth-pattern in New Testament beliefs about Jesus' atoning death, which he lays out as:

> God the giver of life and covenant
>   Jesus is faithful to God
>   Jesus gives salvation to those who trust in him
>   Jesus gives his life as atoning sacrifice
> God the destroyer (demands Jesus' death).
> (Dunnill, 1992, 199)

Thus he argues that a structural analysis of New Testament Christology reveals a myth-pattern at work similar to that which lies beneath the Isaac-myth. It is probably worth noting that the use of the word myth here does not connote an 'untruth', as it often does in modern speech, but, along with Lévi-Strauss, an expression of the truths to which a certain culture adheres.

In Hebrews, Dunnill finds this structural pattern even more explicitly than elsewhere in the New Testament. The crucial factor here is the stress that is laid on Jesus as the 'son of Abraham'. So for example in chapter 2.10–18 we see that it is through entering into death that Jesus maintains the release of humanity. What 2.10–18 makes clear is that Jesus shares with humanity their nature as sons of Abraham (v. 16) while at the same time being the son of God (1.2–9). Thus when Jesus is tested in the same way that Abraham was tested (11.17) and in the same way that humanity is constantly being tested (2.18), he reveals his identity as a son of Abraham. Through this identity the binding of Isaac is present in a shared mythic pattern. Just as covenant-sacrifice resolved the ambiguity of God's relationship through Isaac and Abraham's faithfulness, so Jesus' death as a son of Abraham enters into the oppositions of God's ambivalent relationship with humanity and resolves it.

Conclusions

Dunnill's treatment of the book of Hebrews seeks mythic patterns not only in the book itself but across the whole of the Bible. Dunnill argues that Hebrews encapsulates, through its focus on Abraham, resolution of the ambivalence of God's relationship with humanity in the same way that the binding of Isaac did. Thus the connections between the Jewish interpretation of Genesis 22 (the *Aqedah*) and Hebrews' understanding of the atoning death of Jesus may simply be revealing reliance on the same mythic pattern.

The value of this approach is that it attempts to tackle one of the most complex questions that arises both in the story of the binding of Isaac and in the theory of the atoning death of Jesus: why would a good and loving God require the death of a child (Isaac) or his own child (Jesus)? A structural analysis of the issues provides an answer to this question which is that it is through this offering of life that the ambivalent relationship of God with humanity as a God who tests and a God who blesses can be resolved.

Evaluation of structural criticism

One of the greatest values of structural criticism is that it avoids the complex detail of the New Testament text, in which many interpretations become involved, and looks instead for the network of relationships, or patterns of connection that exist between texts. The belief of structural critics that beneath the words and story-line of an individual unit lies a structure or mythic pattern that is shared by many, often very different, narratives, identifies deep connections between texts that would otherwise go unnoticed and unappreciated. Structuralism also allows for attempted resolutions of seemingly irreconcilable oppositions within the biblical narrative. Another value of structural criticism is that it makes the readers aware that there are many aspects of biblical texts (and of life) that one views as self-evident or coincidental which are in fact part of a shared mythic pattern that powerfully frames one's perception of life.

A problem for structural analysis/criticism is its obvious reliance upon and acceptance of the linguistic theory of Saussure and others, which is deliberately post-Enlightenment and thus postmodern (and mostly post-structural in that it rejects the anthropological philosophy of Lévi-Strauss even as it uses his theory). Unless one adopts their outlook and terminology, structural criticism can seem alien and bemusing. Indeed, for the non-specialist, structuralism involves the use of such specific terminology that it can be hard (not to say extremely confusing) to engage with the analysis; though the results of such technical analysis have also been presented without technical language. Nevertheless, it is the ability of structural criticism to see beyond the particular into the collective intelligence of language and human behaviour that has so much to offer the world of New Testament interpretation.

12

Poststructural criticism

What is poststructural criticism?

Poststructural criticism (also called poststructuralism) is a postmodern variety of structuralism in which the physical stuff of the text (the signifier) is seen as interfering with the understanding of the text's meaning or thought (the signified), with the result that no text ever presents a single, clear truth.

How did the theory develop and what are its main features?
George Aichele

A key question to ask of poststructuralism is at what point did structuralism become poststructuralism? An important point of transition is arguably the publication of Roland Barthes's *S/Z*, published in 1970, even though his *Mythologies*, with its ideological sophistication (here ideology refers to the organization of the conceptual world of some person or persons; the relation of consciousness to reality), had already appeared in 1957. One could even argue that poststructuralist **semiotics** had appeared much earlier in concepts developed by C. S. Peirce, one of the founders of modern structuralist thought (Peirce, 1998). Friedrich Nietzsche's understanding of truth as perspective and interpretation has also influenced a large number of poststructuralist thinkers, including Jacques Derrida, Michel Foucault, and Gilles Deleuze. In other words, poststructuralism is already there in the roots of structuralism. As a result, it is not surprising that poststructural criticism appeared almost as soon as structural criticism did in New Testament (and Hebrew Bible) studies, perhaps most notably in books by John Dominic Crossan (Crossan, 1976) and in many articles in the journal *Semeia*, which played an active role from 1974 until 2002 in promoting both structuralist and poststructuralist analyses of biblical texts. Even earlier than this Barthes himself had developed poststructural readings of Genesis 32 and Acts 10—11 (reprinted in Barthes, 1988).

Structuralism is concerned with the structure of texts – that is, with the various linguistic mechanisms through which a signified (meaning as concept or referent) is connected to a signifier (formed matter, such as spoken or written words). A 'text' may be any meaningful thing or event, either artificially constructed or naturally occurring. Poststructuralism is also concerned with the structure of texts, but it focuses on the breakdown or failure of meaning, as well as the impact of ideology on understanding. The breakdown of meaning occurs when meaningful structures within a text are fractured or subverted by the text itself. The channel that connects signifier to signified is interrupted by physical features within the text, and meaning is shaped and directed by extra-textual factors that repair or correct that interruption. Thus structuralism pays more attention to the signified meaning, and poststructuralism pays more attention to the signifier as that which both supports and resists meaning. Poststructural criticism is a deconstructive form of structural criticism. What deconstruction means here is that poststructuralism disassembles some signifying structure and identifies the incompleteness or meaninglessness that requires the reader to do something to make meaning possible. As a result, there can be no clear distinction between these two approaches that will not itself inevitably break down.

Poststructural criticism has developed around two important concepts: 'intertextuality' and 'unlimited semiosis'. These concepts are closely related to one another. Although both concepts are already implicit in structuralism, when either or both of them become explicit in the analysis of a text, that analysis becomes poststructuralist.

Intertextuality

Poststructuralists maintain that texts do not mean by themselves, but always in relation to other texts. The text is part of an intertextual machine through which readers make meaning. For structuralism, the meaning of a text derives not only from the arrangement or sequence of signs that make up the text (the syntagm) but also from the coded relations between those signs and other similar or different signs in the reader's linguistic repertoire (the paradigm). This second dimension of meaning arises because every reader inevitably brings to each text other similar or different texts that she has read. Various codes govern the reading of the text, limiting the paradigm and thus channelling the flow of semiosis. The usual invisibility of these codes makes them all the more effective. This is one way to describe the reader's ideology. Every reader is in effect a living repository of texts, a network of potential connections, and thus each reader is herself both product and producer of what Julia Kristeva calls 'intertextuality'.

Unlimited semiosis

In other words, the reader is a point at which an intertextual network comes to bear upon a text. This intertextual network controls or limits the text's possibilities for meaning. The reader wants the text to convey a message – that is, to have a single coherent meaning. However, the meaningful connection between signifier and signified is neither tight nor exclusive, and it is entirely artificial. Different intertextualities will attach different signifieds to the same signifier. Furthermore, this connection itself must be explained (that is, the message must be decoded), which inevitably requires yet other signs which themselves must also be explained, and so on. The signifying channel is deconstructed, and instead of a channel there is a flood: every signifier may also be signified, and every signified is itself the signifier of yet another signified. This opens up unlimited semiosis or flows of signification, in both the direction of the signifier and that of the signified.

Thus intertextuality and unlimited semiosis stand in a peculiar relationship to one another. Unlimited semiosis produces and disperses texts, and therefore it makes intertextuality possible. However, intertextuality brings semiosis to a halt, 'breaking' the potentially endless signifying flows. Intertextuality provokes and directs semiosis, elaborating but also confining the significance of each text through its interplay with other texts. Reading inevitably and arbitrarily limits semiotic unfolding by drawing upon intertextuality to break the flow of signification. Thus both unlimited semiosis and intertextuality imply that meaning is not *in* the text, to be dredged out by careful exegesis, but rather it only appears *between* texts, as they are brought together in the various understandings of readers. Meaning must be attached to the text through some exterior process, an ideological stopping of the flow of semiosis in the act of reading. Ideology defines a proper intertext, establishing a field in which acceptable ('natural') readings can occur. Ideology also appears in fundamental linguistic structures that are usually invisible but which control the possibility or impossibility of saying any particular thing at some particular time. These structures inevitably involve an exclusion or omission which they cannot justify; thus there is always an irrational element in the production of meaning.

Unlimited semiosis occurs in relation to every text, and it is particularly apparent both within the Bible (for example, in the appropriation and transformation of texts from the Jewish scriptures by New Testament texts) and in the 'afterlives' of biblical texts in extra-canonical cultural products such as popular art, novels and movies. At the same time, the Bible is itself a very powerful intertext, bringing together numerous diverse texts so that they illuminate one another and speak to the faithful reader. When biblical texts are juxtaposed with nonbiblical texts, a change of inter-textuality results, leading sometimes to remarkably different meanings for the texts involved.

G. A.

What are the landmark publications on poststructural criticism?

Roland Barthes (1970) *S/Z*. Paris: Éditions du Seuil.

Translated into English as (1974) *S/Z*. New York: Hill & Wang. Roland Barthes bridges structural and poststructural criticism and *S/Z* remains arguably the finest example of poststructuralist analysis of a text; rich with theoretical detail. The application of this theory to Acts 10—11, a significant moment in the application of poststructuralism, appears in 'The Structural Analysis of Narrative: Apropos of Acts 10—11', now published in English in Roland Barthes (1988) *The Semiotic Challenge*. New York: Hill & Wang, 217–45 and also available in (2001) D. Jobling, T. Pippin and R. Schleifer, eds, *The Postmodern Bible Reader*. Oxford: Blackwell, 58–77.

Julia Kristeva (1974) *La Révolution Du Langage Poétique: L'Avant-Garde À La Fin Du XIXe Siècle, Lautréamont Et Mallarmé*. Paris: Éditions du Seuil.

Translated into English as (1984) *Revolution in Poetic Language*. New York: Columbia University Press. In this, and other works, Kristeva explored the concept of intertextuality.

John Dominic Crossan (1976) *Raid on the Articulate: Comic Eschatology in Jesus and Borges*. New York: Harper & Row.

Crossan's early adoption of poststructuralism in this book marks a significant moment in the adoption of some features of poststructural criticism for New Testament interpretation.

The Bible and Culture Collective (1995) *The Postmodern Bible*. New Haven: Yale University Press.

Although it covers much more than poststructuralism, this important volume includes an exploration of poststructural interpretation of the Bible which was a significant marker in the development of general perception of the criticism.

Poststructural criticism in practice

One of the complexities of presenting a practical example of poststructural criticism is that poststructuralism argues that the reader brings with her a network of texts and referents through which she views the New Testament. By definition, then, one practical example cannot encapsulate the almost infinite possibilities of poststructural criticism. For this reason, then, it seems most profitable to choose not just any poststructural analysis of the New Testament but one which has been influential, and few have been as influential as Roland Barthes's seminal essay 'The Structural Analysis of Narrative: Apropos of Acts 10—11'.

Peter and Cornelius in Acts 10—11: through the eyes of Roland Barthes

It may seem odd to use an essay entitled 'The Structural Analysis of Narrative' as an example of poststructural analysis and yet its use here illustrates something important about poststructuralism: poststructuralism is really simply a mode of response to structuralism. Very few scholars would designate themselves poststructuralist; instead it is a label used of them by others. Barthes bridges structuralism and poststructuralism in that he employs some of the techniques of scholars such as Saussure while still holding to the view that there is no one possible meaning but instead 'a plurality of meaning or meaning as plurality' (Barthes, 1988, 228). Thus he maintains that what he is doing 'cannot be a method of interpretation' because it does not seek to interpret the text. It differs from other criticisms because 'it does not seek the secret of the text: for it all the text's roots are in the air; it does not have to unearth these roots in order to find *the main one*' (Barthes, 1988, 228).

The codes in the text

Barthes begins by exploring 'codes' within the passage. By codes he means the words and phrases that refer outside of the text to a network of references brought to the text by the reader. He notes initially that, in contrast to a nouvelle (that is, a short novel) by Balzac that he has been working on, the codes are both scarce and poor in this text (Barthes, 1988, 231). This, of course, communicates a lot about Barthes as a reader, since Acts is rich with 'codes' for someone steeped in Hebrew Bible and extra-biblical literature, though it has many fewer codes for someone, like Barthes, steeped in European literature.

Some of the codes that he identifies in this passage are:

- *The inaugurations of narratives*: 'there was' (Acts 10.1), Barthes maintains, refers to all 'inaugurations of narrative'. Within literature, particularly that influenced by rhetoric, there are strict protocols which govern the beginning of a story because humanity is prone to aphasia (the inability to write or speak) and so needs a set means of beginning; since it is perilous to emerge for the first time from silence and begin a discourse (Barthes, 1988, 232–3).

- *Topographic code*:
  - Barthes identifies 'in Caesarea' (Acts 10.1) as a *topographic code* which relates to the system of locations referred to in the text. In Acts 10—11, Barthes identifies that an opposition is established between two places (Caesarea and Jaffa) and notes that it implies knowledge on behalf of the reader as to the cultural code employed here. What he does not say is that Caesarea was a Roman city (as its name suggests) and was strongly associated with the Roman occupying forces, whereas Jaffa was an ancient Jewish city and was one of the cities apportioned to the tribe of Dan during the settlement of the land in Joshua (Josh. 19.40–46). Thus the opposition between the two cities and the two key characters – Cornelius who lives in Caesarea and Peter who is in Jaffa – is established.
  - A second topographical feature identified by Barthes is the reference to Peter being on the housetop (Acts 10.9) so that he does not hear the arrival of the men sent by Cornelius and has to be informed by an angel. Barthes notes of this code that it has cultural reference (to a setting in which roof terraces were common), a literary function and symbolic resonance. Barthes identifies the literary function as the *actional code*, or code of actions; in this instance it requires the intervention of an angel. Alongside this he places the symbolic resonance of Peter being in a high place which 'implies an ascensional symbolism' (Barthes, 1988, 233–4).

- *A citation from the symbolic field*: another example of a citation from the *symbolic field* is the sheet let down to earth full of animals, reptiles and birds (Acts 10.11–12). This is one of two transgressions described in the text: one is concerned with eating and the other with circumcision. Barthes is interested that both transgressions in this text are corporeal – and so become symbolic in a psychoanalytical sense – and are united in the text. This he understands to mean that 'alimentary transgression' (that is, transgression related to digestion) serves as 'an *exemplum* for the transgression of the law of exclusion by circumcision' (Barthes, 1988, 236–7).

- *Semic code*: Acts 10.2 ('He was a devout man who feared God with all his household; he gave alms generously to the people and prayed constantly to God') contains *semic code*. For Barthes a *semic code* was something that provided a second layer of meaning with emotive associations. An example often given is that of the word 'spring', which has associations of new birth, renewal and hope. For Barthes being a 'God-fearer' had such emotional associations, and thus contained a *semic code*.
- *Phatic code*: drawing on Jakobson's classification of the six functions of language, Barthes draws attention to the angel's address to Cornelius in Acts 10.3 when the angel says simply 'Cornelius', and Barthes describes it as *phatic code*. *Phatic code* is the means by which a word such as 'hello' (here 'Cornelius') both opens and maintains contact with someone.
- *Anagogic code*: the *anagogic code* is the hidden, deep meaning of the text, which Barthes here identifies as the problem of the integration of the uncircumcised into the Church and possibly also the problem of hospitality in general.
- *Actional code*: one of the most important codes that Barthes identifies is the code of actions to which he dedicates a whole section. This is where Barthes' indebtedness to structuralism becomes apparent, although the *actional code* relates not only to classical structuralism but to the whole history of literary theory, going back to Aristotle's discussion of plot. The *actional code* consists of looking in detail at the sequences of actions (such as Cornelius sending messengers to Peter, Peter's visit by the angel and so on) and at how the 'interlacing of sequences form the *braid* of a narrative' (Barthes, 1988, 239). Somewhat importantly Barthes recognizes the problems inherent in this approach and notes that such an analysis can seem obvious and trivial, but he argues that the importance of the task is the concern to ask 'What makes the text *readable*?' and thus produces the 'grammar of the *readable*'.
- *Metalinguistic code*: Barthes describes metalinguistics as speaking a language about another language. The example he gives is writing a French grammar, which is the speaking of a language (that is, his own grammar) about another language (French). Thus a summary within a text is a metalinguistic episode because it speaks a language (the summary) about another language (the narrative). These are important in this narrative because we have numerous summaries within the text, such as the messengers' summary of the order given to Cornelius (10.22) and Cornelius's summary of his vision to Peter (10.30–32).

The significance of these summaries here is that they refer to something that is already a narrative, and hence not reality. Barthes's interest then becomes focused on any continuity gap, or hiatus, that might exist between the summary and the narrative it summarizes. The presence of a hiatus raises the question of which account is correct and often then points onwards to the possibility of a pre-narrative: in this case, that of Peter or of Cornelius whose account of what happened that might have existed before the text was written might be deemed to be the 'absolute referent' and hence to have links to 'reality'. Jacques Derrida has argued that in the world there is no such thing as the absolute referent or the final signified of a piece of writing. All writing, Derrida maintains, simply points onwards to another piece of writing. As Barthes notes, when dealing with Scripture this argument becomes even more relevant than elsewhere because theology is ultimately concerned with the final signified, that is, God. Yet the very name 'Scripture' suggests to Barthes that there is a greater ambiguity involved here as though 'the base, the *princeps*, were still a Writing and always a Writing' (Barthes, 1988, 242).

The hiatus that Barthes identifies in this text is that despite the numerous summaries that exist within the narrative, what Cornelius must say to Peter is never articulated. What Cornelius must ask Peter is not the message itself but the act of communication; this is what Barthes calls 'the structural meaning of the absence'. In Barthes's words the 'content of the message is therefore the message itself, the destination of the message, i.e. the Uncircumcised – that is the very content of the message' (Barthes, 1988, 245).

Conclusions

One thing that becomes clear from Barthes's article on Acts 10—11 is that his method of approaching the text is not an interpretation but an interrogation. His purpose is not to uncover one or more meanings of the text but to establish how the text communicates, what its major features include and where the gaps lie between the different versions of what is said. His approach is almost the diametric opposite of the historical critical methods, whose concerns are to uncover the reality behind the text; whereas Barthes's concern lies solely within the written word.

Evaluation of poststructural criticism

Like structural criticism the value of poststructural criticism lies in a careful, almost intricate, reading of the text. The emphasis placed upon the way in which meaning is evoked by the interplay between texts is valuable because it reminds the reader of the processes of cross-referencing that take place often subconsciously as we read, and which affect the way in which we read a text. One of the other great values of poststructural criticism is the emphasis it places on absence, or gaps in the text. Thus it is as interested in what is not there as in what is there. Often the gaps are significant for understanding the way in which the text functions as a text. The other major contribution that poststructuralism offers to New Testament interpretation is its critique of modern concerns to discover what a text means. Poststructuralism questions whether meaning is ever in a text and able to be discovered through careful interpretation.

In many ways it is difficult to evaluate poststructural criticism because it takes many forms. Those forms more influenced by Julia Kristeva may demonstrate an interest in intertextuality, whereas those reliant on Jacques Derrida may make more use of deconstruction, and adherents of Michel Foucault would explore the interplay of power within the text. What holds these approaches together is greater interest in interrogating the text than in interpreting it, and a certain playfulness, which explores ideas and tries new thoughts.

Poststructuralism, like structuralism, has an internal language of words like semic, signified, phatic and so on that often feels exclusive and confusing to non-specialists. This, coupled with the different motivation in approaching the text (interrogation not interpretation) can mean, for some, that poststructuralism feels alien and off-putting. Nevertheless, it is the use of philosophy with playful intent that continues to produce many stimulating explorations of the New Testament.

Part 3

FROM TEXT TO READER

Introduction

This final part of the book incorporates all those criticisms which, in some way or another, focus on the role of the reader in interpretation. As noted in the general introduction to this volume, it is here that the classification of criticisms into three parts breaks down, since many of the criticisms included here are not methods in the way that the criticisms in the first two parts have been: they are **standpoints** which utilize many of the methods already explored in this book. Another problem for this third part is that although the primary focus of the criticisms explored in Part 1 is historical and in Part 2 textual, a number of them also focus on the role of the reader. For example, both rhetorical and narrative criticism are concerned with how a reader, implied or actual, engages with and interprets the text. As such they would have a proper place in this part, just as a historical critical black criticism would have a proper place in Part 1.

It is in full awareness of all these problems that we turn to the role of the reader in interpretation in Part 3. The first two criticisms focus on the meaning of the text:

- Reception history (Chapter 13) traces the way in which New Testament texts have been received, as well as the way in which they have influenced societies, throughout Christian histories.
- Theological interpretation (Chapter 14) focuses on the meaning of the New Testament, with an emphasis either on what it meant or on what it continues to mean.

Theological interpretation is one of those criticisms which could fit into more than one part of the book. The emphasis of the form of the criticism in this volume is on what the text means now, which places it in this part, but if the emphasis had been on what the text meant it might have fitted better in Part 1 among the historical critical methods.

- Chapter 15 focuses on reader-response criticism and the overt focus on the role of the reader. This is a broad criticism with many different emphases, though all focus around the idea that it is the reader that completes the meaning of a text.

Chapters 13–15 all hover on the edge of providing 'tools of interpretation'. Although there are many different ways of doing reception history, theological interpretation or reader-response criticism, each criticism is held together by methodological approaches, rather than a particular standpoint, such as postcolonialism, from which the text is viewed. The distinction, however, should not be pressed too far. There is a difference between the criticisms in Chapters 1–15 and those in 16–23, but it would be wrong to make too much of it; not least because, as well as being a criticism in its own right, reader-response criticism could be used as an umbrella term for the chapters that follow it, which each employ 'readers' responses' to the text.

- Chapters 16–23 contain criticisms which are derived from certain 'standpoints'. Here, again, we need to be alert to certain issues that arise. The problem with the use of the term standpoint, which I have already employed in this volume, is that it implies:
  - that the standpoint adopted is in some way optional or voluntary, that is, one could either choose to read the text 'normally' or adopt a standpoint. Standpoint criticisms are not optional, they are often the only possible way of reading the text for those who read from that perspective;
  - that 'mainstream' New Testament interpretations do not adopt a standpoint from which they read the text. All criticisms are in effect standpoint criticisms, it is just that the perspectives of the dominant white, male, heterosexual, Western, industrialized countries' criticisms are assumed to be normal, and all others 'abnormal';
  - that there is a 'normal' way of reading the text from which standpoint criticisms deviate. While standpoint criticisms do seek to disrupt the dominant, traditional readings of texts, they should not be viewed as 'abnormal' but as establishing a wider range of 'normal'.

The use of the phrase 'standpoint criticisms' is not intended to suppose any of these assumptions.

It has also been very difficult to decide how to order the criticisms among Chapters 16–23. A chronological order is impossible since it is difficult to work out which, if any, of these criticisms predate the other; but any kind of order could imply some form of hierarchy which is not my intention here. The current order attempts to group the criticisms roughly but in such a way that, where mutual interdependence between criticisms exists, it makes sense. For example, some of the practical examples used are influenced by feminist criticism, so that needed to come earlier in order that the later examples would make sense.

These eight final criticisms are, perhaps, the hardest to include well. As a rule they are so broad that one practical example of how the criticism works cannot even begin to communicate the breadth of issues involved; nevertheless, they are so important that to omit them would be to present an incorrect portrayal of New Testament interpretation. The chapters must be read in full knowledge that a similar volume to this could be written on each one of the chapters. So to take feminist criticism as an example, one could have a volume with chapters on feminist historical critical approaches, on feminist reception history and on feminist post-colonial criticism, to name but a few. The only way to engage with these chapters properly is to use them as a springboard into more reading.

13

Reception history

What is reception history?

Reception history is the study of the way in which a text's interpreters have read that text in their various social and religious contexts.

How did the theory develop and what are its main features?
Christopher Rowland

Reception history and *Wirkungsgeschichte* are terms which have been used interchangeably in discussion of the history of the interpretation of the Bible. There is a difference of theoretical explanation, but it is becoming increasingly difficult to make a precise distinction between them. It is a convenient distinction to make that the concern of reception history is on how a text has been read through history, while *Wirkungsgeschichte* places more emphasis on the text as an effective agent, which influences cultures as well as being received by them and whose peculiar character and details may explain why that particular text has had the effects it has.

Hans-Georg Gadamer (1900–2002) pioneered the use of the word *Wirkungsgeschichte* in his influential book *Truth and Method* (first published in 1960), where he reminded readers that they are creatures of culture and of a history of interpreting texts in particular ways. For Gadamer, our prejudices indicate the fact that we are part of a particular human history formed by a complex of traditions. Acknowledgement of this is the key to all understanding. This he termed '*wirkungsgeschichtliches Bewusstsein*', that is, knowing that is affected by tradition and history and the awareness of the character of this influence. If we accept this, then we acknowledge that no reading is unbiased or unaffected by context.

Reception history has been a growing interest in modern biblical studies and is part of a wider movement in the humanities, in which there has been a greater readiness to understand the history of the reception of literary texts at different points in history (a parallel example is the revival of interest in Greek and Latin literature and the effects of this literature during the Renaissance).

In biblical studies this interest led to the production of the Evangelisch-Katholische Kommentar zum Neuen Testament (EKK – the Evangelical/Catholic Commentary on the New Testament) series, which has done much to pioneer *Wirkungsgeschichte* in biblical studies. This series of commentaries emerged after the Second World War, during the growth of ecumenism, and in response to the need for religious and national reconciliation. The interpretation of the text through history offered a point of meeting between Catholic interest in tradition and Protestant emphasis on the original meaning of the biblical text. So it included theological, and reception history, interests, which were given a greater emphasis than in many historical–exegetical commentaries. As biblical scholarship has become more and more preoccupied with the emergence, and meaning, of the texts in antiquity, there has been a consequent recognition that the biblical texts are remote from modern people and their theological interests. Various attempts have been made to bridge the gap between ancient and modern, and the history of interpretation has been a significant part of that process.

Throughout the history of interpretation many different ways have been explored to search for meaning in texts, whether they be the Homeric legends or the Bible. The techniques are broadly similar. When this has happened, commentators have found that often the typical moves made by modern interpreters have been anticipated by their pre-modern predecessors. For example, there are contrasting ways of interpreting the book of Revelation: either as a map of the end of the world or as a heuristic lens for understanding church and world better. Both of these have their antecedents in patristic and medieval exegesis of the book. Another example is the dialectic between concern with the literal meaning of the text and the allegorical meaning (an interpretation that understands everything that happens as being a sign or symbol of something else), which is as old as the Bible itself and can be found illustrated in the parable of the Sower (Matt. 13.1–9) and its interpretation (Matt. 13.18–23), or in Paul's allegorical reading of Genesis 16, 17 and 21 in Galatians 4.24.

One of the most important changes in biblical interpretation took place with the **Enlightenment**, when there was both an increased interest in history and a suspicion of the authority of institutions – books and people included – so that what a church taught no longer determined how we understood a text so much as what 'I' as a rational and intelligent interpreter thought that it meant. As a result the Bible gradually ceased to be read as a part of a history of interpretation, in which the great (usually male) theologians of the Church were the context of reading, and instead texts, presumed to be written at the same time as the Bible, were the context of reading. Consequently the rabbinic texts (on the Jewish side) and Augustine, Aquinas, Luther and Calvin (on the Christian side) have become less important as ways of interpreting the Bible than texts like the Dead Sea Scrolls.

One of the greatest significances of a return of interest in the way in which the Bible has been interpreted through the centuries is that it is an acknowledgement that biblical interpretation is *affected* by what has gone before it and has *effects* on what comes after it. It places biblical interpretation in a strand of tradition that stretches for many years both forwards and backwards.

C. R.

What are the landmark publications on reception history and *Wirkungsgeschichte*?

Hans-Georg Gadamer (1960) *Wahrheit und Methode: Grundzüge einer philosophischen Hermeneutik*. Tübingen: Mohr.

Translated into English as (1975) *Truth and Method*. London and New York: Sheed & Ward. In his work Gadamer developed the idea that all knowing is affected by tradition and history and that awareness of this will affect the way in which we interpret texts.

Evangelisch-Katholischer Kommentar zum Neuen Testament (EKK) series.

Although unfortunately most of this series is not translated into English, it remains a significant example of *Wirkungsgeschichte* on the New Testament. From this series one of the commentaries that has been translated into English is

Ulrich Luz (1985–97) *Das Evangelium nach Matthäus*. Zurich: Neukirchener Verlag.

This magisterial commentary on Matthew has been translated into English as (2001–7) *Matthew: A Commentary*, 3 vols, Hermeneia Series. Minneapolis: Fortress.

Also important is and will be the Blackwell Bible Commentaries *Through the Centuries* titles, which, when complete, will contain a reception history commentary on each book of the Bible.

Reception history in practice

The remit of reception history is huge, as, potentially, its focus is every single piece of commentary, literary writing, artwork, drama and music that in any way appears to be influenced by the book. One of the most complex tasks for the reception critic, after finding the uses and allusions, is to sift them, order them and lay them out in such a way that communicates something, rather than in just the jumble in which they may have been retrieved. As a result reception history is interpretation on two levels: first, it interprets the Bible itself; and second, it interprets the interpretations of the Bible. For all attempts to organize information are, in their way, an interpretation.

One of the best of the Blackwell Bible Commentaries so far produced is the volume written by Judith Kovacs and Christopher Rowland on the book of Revelation (Kovacs, Rowland and Callow, 2004) and it is their treatment of Revelation 4 that underpins the practical exploration of reception history below.

The throne of God: Revelation 4

At the heart of the book of Revelation lies the vision of John of Patmos, of the throne of God. After the initial three chapters in which an angel gives to John the letters to the angels of the seven churches, John has a vision in which heaven's door is opened and he is summoned into heaven, where he sees the throne of God surrounded by the thrones of the elders and the four living creatures. Although for twenty-first-century readers this vision is odd and hard to comprehend, it, along with the rest of Revelation, has been hugely influential throughout Christian history.

Revelation 4 and Ezekiel 1

Before we can explore the ways in which Revelation 4 has been interpreted in Christian tradition, we need to acknowledge the fact that this chapter is itself an interpretation of Ezekiel 1. Ezekiel's fantastical vision of the divine chariot which is described in chapter 1 gave rise to extensive speculation. This took the form not only of exegesis and exposition but also an entering into the vision with the aim of seeing it again (Rowland, 1979; Kovacs, Rowland and Callow, 2004, 60). Revelation 4 is one of the earliest examples of this form of visionary appropriation, which enters so fully into Ezekiel 1 that another similar vision can be engendered by it.

Seeing the vision again

Just as Revelation 4 appears to be drawn from a tradition which believed in the importance of 'seeing again' the vision of Ezekiel 1, so also, in its turn, it gave rise to a tradition about visionary experiences. Numerous mystics found themselves so inspired by John's vision that they had visions of their own.

Visions inspired by Revelation 4. One particular characteristic of these visions is that the recipients believed themselves to have a greater and clearer understanding of Scripture as a result of meditating on Revelation 4.
  Two examples of this are:

- Hildegard of Bingen (1098–1179), who recorded a visionary experience in which fiery light permeated her brain so that she could understand Scripture in ways impossible before.
- Joachim of Fiore (*c.* 1135–1202), who struggled with reading the book of Revelation until, while meditating upon it, he had a vision after which he could grasp the fullness not only of that book but of the whole of Scripture (Kovacs, Rowland and Callow, 2004, 61–2).

There are of course many other instances of people whose reading of and meditation upon Revelation has caused them to have either similar visions or a conviction about the meaning of the text (this kind of visionary tradition in Judaism is the subject matter of Patrick White's novel *Riders in the Chariot*) but these two examples illustrate the fact that texts about visionary experiences can be interpreted through an appropriation of the vision itself, experienced anew in the reader's own context.

Artwork inspired by Revelation 4. Fascination with the vision of John of Patmos in Revelation 4 is not only found among mystics; it has also inspired works of art, and there are numerous depictions of God seated upon a throne surrounded by the 24 elders. It is worth noting that in nearly all the depictions of John's vision chapters 4 and 5 are conflated so that the Lamb and the scroll are often featured as well. For example, Hans Memling's depiction of John on Patmos (St John's Hospital Bruges, late fifteenth century) is an altarpiece which depicts scenes from the opening chapters of Revelation all happening at once, but what attracts John's attention is the vision of God in heaven with the Lamb adjacent to the Almighty. It appears as if seen through a giant eye, and dominates the whole picture. This scene of heavenly worship links the viewer with the worship, which would have been taking place in front of the altar-piece, and links the heavenly worship described in Revelation 4—5 with that enacted on earth in human worship. The *Très Riches Heures du Duc de Berry* (Musée Condé, Chantilly), a book of Hours commissioned by the Duke of Berry in 1410, portrays the scene from the perspective of a John of Patmos still on earth. Above John is God seated on his throne, again with the Lamb on his lap, with God holding a book, and with the 24 elders seated on medieval-looking pews, in two rows of 12 on each side. In this depiction the four holy creatures are depicted as cherubim, each a face surrounded by four wings. This iconography of heaven played an important role in shaping popular perceptions of what heaven was like.

The artist who was, perhaps, more affected by the imagery of apoca-lyptic literature than any other was William Blake (1757–1827). As Kovacs and Rowland note, the links between Blake's picture *Ezekiel's Wheels* (Museum of Fine Arts, Boston) and *The Four and Twenty Elders* (Tate Britain, London) indicate that Blake clearly associates Ezekiel 1 with Revelation 4—5 (Kovacs, Rowland and Callow, 2004, 64).

Verbal interpretations of Revelation 4

Revelation 4 (and 5) is described as being what John of Patmos *saw*. It is natural therefore that some interpretations attempt to 'see again' what he saw, either through a vision or through artwork. Another strand of trad-ition, however, focuses not on seeing the vision but on understanding the words used.

Victorinus and Revelation 4. Kovacs and Rowland note that Victorinus, bishop of the city of Pettau in the third century, interprets the chapters as a parable on Christian preaching (Kovacs, Rowland and Callow, 2004, 62). Victorinus adopts a classically allegorical interpretation of the pas-sage (an interpretation that understands everything that happens as being a sign or symbol of something else), such as was common in the writings of the early fathers. So for Victorinus John's ascent into heaven was more concerned with clarity of insight than with visionary experiences. He under-stands the opening of the door into heaven as an inference that previously it had been shut, and that Jesus' death and resurrection are the means by which the door is opened (Roberts and Donaldson, 1886, 347).

Victorinus then goes on to interpret the throne of God as the seat of judgement and the features of the throne as a means of the judgement. Thus, since jasper looks like water and carnelian like fire, Victorinus declares that the judgement by water has already taken place but that the judgement by fire is still to come (Roberts and Donaldson, 1886, 348). The rainbow and the sea of glass, in their turn, are associated with the promise to Noah as a promise that judgement will no longer come by water but by fire and with baptism through which one can repent before the Day of Judgement arrives.

Victorinus' interpretation continues in a similar vein throughout the rest of Revelation 4, interpreting the vision as a confirmation that Christians will be saved on the Day of Judgement due to their repentance and acceptance of the gospel. The importance of preaching is that it is the means by which the message of salvation can be proclaimed to the world.

Shelley and Revelation 4. Kovacs and Rowland note that the poet Percy Bysshe Shelley (1792–1822) introduces a similar theme of judgement into the throne vision in variations on Revelation 4, 6 and 20, in which he combines later parts of the book of Revelation with the throne scene in chapter 4 so that the later judgements become linked with John's vision:

> The Father and the Son
> Knew that strife was now begun,
> They ken that Satan had broken his chain,
> And, with millions of demons in his train,
> Was ranging over the world again.
> Before the Angel had told his tale,
> A Sweet and creeping sound,
> Like the rushing of wings was heard around;
> And suddenly the lamps grew pale –
> The lamps, before the archangel seven,
> That burn continually in heaven.
>   (Shelley, 1960, 2:299, cited in Kovacs,
>   Rowland and Callow, 2004, 65–6)

Conclusions

Revelation 4 has had a great and continuing influence on Christian history both visually and verbally, not least in connection with the liturgy. For some, the visual nature of the passage has caused them to enter into the vision to such an extent that a similar visionary experience is evoked; others focus more on what the heavenly scene would have looked like and attempt to depict the arrangement of the four holy creatures and the 24 elders around the throne. Interpretations governed more by words have attempted to discern what the vision meant, and by far the most common understanding of the throne vision is that of the coming judgement. This emphasis on judgement has been influential at different points in history in shaping an understanding of the end of the world and what it will mean.

Evaluation of reception history

The concern of reception history is not so much with what a passage means, or meant to its first author and readers, but what it has meant through-out history. Reception critics seek to remind readers that New Testament interpretation is around 2,000 years old and that, as a result, some 'new' interpretations are not as new as some may think. The great value of this is that it can revive an interest in the many profound Christian thinkers that have engaged with and interpreted the biblical text. A treasure trove of biblical interpretation exists, accumulated through the centuries; recep-tion history helps the reader to dip into this treasure trove and to discover some of the insights of our forebears. *Wirkungsgeschichte* also reminds us of the ways in which Christian culture has itself been shaped by the New Testament. The New Testament is not just received; it is an active agent in changing and shaping the world in which we live.

Reception history, however, is complex. The illustrative piece above demonstrates how selective one must be in compiling a reception history. Even a multiple-volume work on the interpretations of Revelation 4 would not exhaust the material that could be used. The selective nature of the technique reveals its subjectivity; one person's choice of inter-pretations of Revelation 4 differs widely from another person's choice. Not only this, but once the selection has been made, the reception critic must decide how to organize the material. All of this affects and shapes the narrative that is told about interpretations of the passage. This is not a problem, but it is important to recognize it as an issue.

Critics of reception history raise another issue. One of the aims of the historical critical method has been to achieve a 'better quality' interpret-ation of the text. Pre-Enlightenment interpretation was often characterized by harmonization, lack of attention to the original language and fanciful, figurative or allegorical interpretation which seemed to depart from the literal sense of the text. In some people's eyes, the danger of reception his-tory is that it places too much attention on pre-Enlightenment interpret-ations which seem to be unscholarly and lack that sense of detachment which is so typical of most modern academic exegetes. A reception critic's riposte to such a critique might be that reception history and historical criticism might seem to be attempting to do two different things, but in fact they are more similar than appears at first sight, as both are interested in the historical, one in what the text meant *at one point* in its history, the other in how the text has been interpreted *through* history. Such an attempt does not imply any acceptance of the interpretation; the task is descriptive, not necessarily evaluative.

14

Theological interpretation

What is theological interpretation?

Theological interpretation is concerned with exploring the relationship of
the New Testament to subsequent Christian theology and to understanding how it functions in worshipping communities.

How did the theory develop and what are its main features?
A. K. M. Adam

Although contemporary readers evidently feel the need for a method for
theological interpretation of the New Testament, ancient readers managed
comfortably without any such theoretical superstructure. Interpreters
in the first centuries – and many since that time – perceived no great
discontinuity between biblical narrative and exhortation and their
own situations in life. That discontinuity emerged at the convergence of
several cultural and ecclesiastical forces: the conflicts that splintered the
Western Church, and the ideological power of **modernity**, to name two
prominent such influences. In the first instance, political and theological
disagreements set Roman Catholic Christians against Protestant Christians,
and set various divergent sorts of Protestants against one another. In the
second instance, modern cultural premises such as the importance of
scientific objectivity, the value of distinct specialized fields of knowledge,
and the continuous progress of humanity from ignorance towards enlightenment all undermined the conventional grounds for theological
interpretation of the Bible. The specifically modern model for theological
interpretation dominated theological hermeneutics of the nineteenth and
twentieth centuries; though many interpreters remain convinced that
modern premises should continue to determine legitimate interpretation
of the Bible, an increasing constituency of scholars has imagined an
approach to theology and Scripture that does not stand or fall with
strictly modern premises.

The earliest Christian interpreters were, of course, reading and theolo-
gizing on a Bible that comprised the books of the Hebrew Bible, gradually supplemented (and in some circumstances 'supplanted') by Gospels,

apostolic letters, and apocalypses. They brought to their interpretations of the nascent New Testament the same imaginative vision of patterns and characters in the Hebrew Bible that enabled them to recognize these figures as narrative precedents for Jesus' ministry and the apostles' vision of an expansive communion of Gentiles and Jews. As they clarified the doctrinal exposition of Jesus' identity, or the Trinity, of the Spirit and the Church, they deployed a richly allusive, typological (interpreting events and persons as prefigurations of events and figures in the New Testament), figurative understanding of God's ways and God's communication to humanity in Scripture (both Old and New).

The Church's conflicts over doctrine gradually elicited a body of theory concerning interpretation. In response to questions about what makes some interpretations sounder than others, theologians began to articulate a critical practice of theological interpretation; the best-known of these early hermeneutical works is Augustine's *On Christian Doctrine*. Subsequent theologians developed a variety of approaches to exegetical theology. The well-known *quadriga* that differentiated literal, allegorical (doctrinal), tropological (ethical), and anagogical (eschatological) senses of Scripture, did not so much mandate four different meanings for each passage as it described four sets of criteria within which one might develop interpretations. From late antiquity through medieval interpretation, readers dwelt comfortably with a bounded variety of interpretations. They saw this diversity as a sign of God's abundant grace operating through the imaginations of authors and interpreters, as long as the interpretations upheld the Church's teaching.

The Protestant Reformation and the culture of modernity disrupted this situation in several ways. The divisions that set European Christians against one another heightened the urgency that biblical interpretations did not just fit soundly within the limits of a bounded plurality of acceptable readings, but that they were correct in a way that excluded alternative readings. The Reformers' antipathy to interpretive variety strengthened their insistence that the Bible yielded a single, clear, simple sense (although this rarely helped resolve any interpretive conundrums). With the Reformation, an insistence on the singularity and plainness of meaning did not diminish the proliferation of interpretive alternatives but intensified the stakes of disagreements among interpreters.

Modernity made the temporal quality of 'progress' a self-evident element in the ways that European cultures imagined their relation to the past, making plausible the assumption that a historical gap separates us from our biblical forebears. A modern interpreter needs to ascertain what a text meant, and subsequently to devise an application of the archaic meaning to contemporary life, or to insist that some meanings escape cultural specificity (while others remain captive to their contexts of origin). Likewise, modern premises warrant interpreters' confidence that interpretations from the past fatally lack the legitimation of up-to-date scholarship. Especially where modernity and the Reformation converge, biblical interpreters face the daunting challenge of determining the single historical sense of a passage that in some way informs radically different (modern) cultural circumstances.

While many scholars continue to refine and enhance modern approaches to theological interpretation, others propose promising alternative paths. The scholars who sponsor these alternatives typically allow greater latitude for diversity in interpretation (comparable to the bounded plurality of pre-Reformation interpretive practice). They expand the scope of their hermeneutical imagination beyond modernity's strict historicism, pursuing the theological interpretation of Scripture as a properly (and unabashedly) theological endeavour. Their interpretations embrace doctrinal and ethical concerns alongside questions of dates and historical background. Such scholars see the discourses of drama, the visual arts, literature and music (among others) as models of fields where critical evaluation and imaginative expression inform one another. Theological interpreters can take up a comparable practice of representing the faith of biblical antecedents afresh, accountable to criticism on historical and theological, aesthetic or ethical grounds. Thus imagined, the theological interpretation of Scripture finds strands of continuity with generations of previous interpreters from the earliest to the most modern.

A. K. M. A.

What are the landmark publications on theological interpretation?

Augustine (397–426) *De Doctrina Christiana.*

Translated into English as *On Christian Doctrine*, and available in a range of editions. In this four-volume work Augustine set out to identify and to teach the truth that, in his view, is contained in the Scriptures, and to teach others to defend this truth.

Johann Philip Gabler (1787) *Oratio: De iusto discrimine theologiae Biblicae et dogmaticae regundisque recte utriusque finibus.* Altdorf.

Translated into English as J. Sandy-Wunsch and L. Eldredge (1980) 'J.-P. Gabler and the Distinction between Biblical and Dogmatic Theology: Translation, Commentary and Discussion of his Originality',

Scottish Journal of Theology 33, 133–58. Widely recognized as the lecture which gave birth to modern understandings of biblical theology.

Wilhelm Wrede (1897) *Über Aufgabe und Methode der sogenannten neutestamentlichen Theologie*. Göttingen: Vandenhoeck & Ruprecht.

Translated into English as (1973) *The Task and Methods of New Testament Theology*. London: SCM. Although Wrede believed himself to be producing a faithful outworking of Gabler's argument, this important book argued biblical theology to be a historical report of the beliefs of the first Christians.

Theological interpretation in practice

Although the works given above are indeed landmark books in the exploration of theological interpretations of the Bible, which includes biblical theology, it is important to recognize the difference between theological interpretation and biblical theology. Stephen Fowl distinguishes between the two on the grounds that biblical theology is a 'child of modernity and subject to the limits modernity attempted to set on intellectual activity' (Fowl, 1996, xvi), whereas the scope of theological interpretation is much wider. He identifies four key ways in which theological interpretation differs from biblical theology:

- It is interested in pre-modern interpretation as well as modern.
- It is shaped by Christian communities rather than academic communities.
- It resists the fragmentation of theology into discrete disciplines.
- It is pluralistic in its methods.

When explored like this, it becomes clear that theological interpretation comes close to numerous other techniques explored in this volume; it has overlaps both with the reception criticism of the previous chapter (p. 111) and with criticisms which overtly interpret the Bible from their own experience, such as feminist (p. 135), or black (p. 167) criticisms. The feature that differentiates this criticism from those is its central concern with the theology of a passage, whereas in the other techniques often the central concern lies in context or experience.

The New Testament text which has, perhaps, been the subject of most theological interpretation is the epistle to the Romans, where Paul explores some of the theology that is crucial to his kerygma (proclamation of the gospel). The problem of exploring Romans here is that using Romans as an example of theological criticism appears to do precisely what theological interpretation of Scripture strives not to do, which is to compartmentalize; it is all too easy for Gospels to become the site for historical critical and narrative concerns, 1 Corinthians for social-scientific concerns and Romans for theology. This is not the intention in including this interpretation here. There are many New Testament passages that could be used to illustrate theological interpretations of the text, but Romans has most often been used in theological interpretations, and so provides a helpful example here.

The message of Romans 9—11

One of the key issues for understanding Romans 9—11 is working out what Paul is trying to say in this section of the epistle. A brief exploration of scholarship indicates that views on this differ. Opinions of this subject are so numerous and wide-ranging it is impossible to be exhaustive. Instead we shall explore four contrasting views on these chapters and reflect on their significance as examples of theological interpretations.

For some chapters 9—11 function as a sort of appendix to the epistle (see Sanday and Headlam, 1895), where for others it is the epistle's climax (see Stendahl, 1976, 40). In fact Stendahl sees these chapters as the key to understanding the whole epistle. Thus Stendahl argues that Romans 9—11 allow us to see how the mission to the Gentiles is essential to God's overall mission to the world (see Stendahl, 1976, 4; 1995, ix). This he maintains is the purpose of Paul's writing of Romans in the first place: so that the Roman Christians can gain an insight into Paul's mission and purpose.

J. A. T. Robinson on the other hand agrees with Sanday and Headlam that Romans 9—11 should be read as an excursus to the rest of Romans. Indeed he goes so far as to say that it could be detached from its context without affecting its argument and structure. In order to support this he cites from Dodd, who argues that this would have been the kind of sermon that Paul would have preached regularly on the Jewish question and may in fact have been drawn from a manuscript of a sermon like this that he kept to hand for when need arose (Robinson, 1979, 108). He regarded these chapters as running in parallel to 3.1–21 and answering the question posed in Romans 3.9 about whether Jews are any better or worse off than the Gentiles.

In contrast, scholars such as Ziesler see this part of Romans as Paul's struggle with theodicy: 'Paul cannot accept that "the word of God has failed" (v. 6), so he must now begin to find a solution to the problem that does not leave him with a God who changes his mind' (Ziesler, 1989, 234). Ziesler contends that Paul solves the conundrum by, in chapter 9, redefining Israel as a faithful group within Israel, rather than historic, racial Israel. The reason for this is that being Israel is a matter of calling not of racial descent. The fact that parts of Israel are now outside the people of God is due to Israel's disobedience (chapter 10) but Paul believes that ultimately Israel's present rejection will lead to a full reinstatement of the people of Israel (chapter 11; Ziesler, 1989, 234–5).

E. Elizabeth Johnson suggests that the development of Paul's argument between Romans 3.9 and 8.39 has highlighted the twin themes of God's impartiality and faithfulness which then underpin the argument in Romans 9—11. For Johnson, Paul's ability to hold these two together means that the one balances out the other, so that 'divine faithfulness never becomes blind loyalty nor does divine impartiality obliterate God's eternal promises' (Johnson, 1996, 367). The crucial factor in the balance is human response and the taking of responsibility for decisions made. God acts but also waits for humans to respond. God's integrity remains intact in that he remains faithful to Israel and impartial, to the extent of welcoming Gentiles into the covenant; the key factor in both of these is how human beings – whether Jew or Gentile – respond to the divine initiative of redemption.

Conclusions

All four of these readings of Romans 9—11 are theological but the latter two (Ziesler and Johnson) fit more comfortably into the criteria of theological interpretation as 'what a text means', rather than what it meant, than do the former two (Stendahl and Robinson). Both Stendahl and Robinson are concerned to expound what Paul was trying to do in his epistle to the Romans and have provided an answer which falls, more or less clearly, into the category of what the text meant: for Stendahl this involved the historical issue of Paul's mission and its communication to Roman Christians, and for Robinson it was 'the Jewish question' which he envisaged Paul preaching on numerous occasions to his audiences. Both of these address theological issues that were particularly pertinent in the first century.

Ziesler and Johnson, however, raise issues that are as much pertinent to the question of what a text means now as to what it meant then. Whether Ziesler intended to or not, his interest in how this passage engages with the issue of theodicy, and in particular with whether God can be deemed to have failed or not, is of great modern relevance. In a similar way Johnson's concern for the balancing of divine faithfulness with impartiality has modern relevance for our understandings of God. This is highlighted in her work by a reference to a contemporary confession of faith which demonstrates that she is aware of the way in which her discussion impacts and has influence in faith communities (Johnson, 1996, 367).

Evaluation of theological interpretation

In many ways theological interpretation offers a response to the criticism that has often been levelled against New Testament interpretations on the grounds that they make the text solely an ancient document or a dry academic text and forget the fact that it is used in communities of faith who are interested in what the text means to them today. Theological interpretations seek to discover more about what the New Testament means to contemporary Christians and are, therefore, for many, a welcome exercise.

The emphasis on the plurality of theological meaning is likewise a valuable contribution to the understanding of the New Testament, recognizing as it does the fact that the New Testament has made valuable contributions to the faith of Christian communities for many centuries though in different ways at different times. We begin to understand that theological meaning is fluid but none the less valuable for that fluidity.

Nevertheless, theological interpretations of the New Testament have experienced serious criticism from other New Testament scholars. The concern of biblical theology, and indeed of many historical critical New Testament interpretations, is to discover 'the' meaning of the text, by which is meant the author's original intention in writing. Adherents to this method of reading the New Testament are clear that the only true meaning possible is what the text meant in its original context. For them the purpose of professional biblical studies is to provide reliable, careful scholarship that aims to uncover as far as possible the original meaning of the text. Theological interpretations prefer to uncover a plurality of meanings which speak into the current context of the reader; between these two approaches to the New Testament lies a gulf that is hard to bridge.

15

Reader-response criticism

What is reader-response criticism?

Reader-response criticism encompasses a range of criticisms which emphasize the role of readers as active agents in completing the meaning of a text by the way that they read it. It is a method that originates in the critical study of literature and has been adapted by biblical scholars for interpreting the Bible.

How did the theory develop and what are its main features?
Robert M. Fowler

The emergence of reader-response criticism in literature in the 1970s and 1980s is often narrated as a rebellion within literary studies against **new criticism**, which emphasizes close examination of the form of a text with minimum regard for the biographical or historical circumstances in which it was produced. Reader-response criticism shifts attention away from the text and its formal features, to the reader of the text and the reading experience. Most reader-response critics would argue that meaning is not an inherent property of texts, rather meaning is made by a reader, in the act of reading. Within biblical studies, the embrace of reader-response criticism was also part of a rebellion against the hegemony, or dominance, of historical criticism of the Bible. Rather than seeking an ancient author's intention in writing, or insight into the ancient historical context in which the text was written, biblical reader-response critics have sought to shift attention to the omnipresent and yet often neglected central actor in biblical exegesis – the reader.

Although reader-response criticism has by now achieved the status of a standard critical approach to the reading of texts, there has never been anything resembling agreement on what reader-response criticism is. Rather than a clearly defined methodology, it is a diverse assortment of critical approaches that focus upon readers and reading. In spite of their diversity, however, it is possible to arrange most versions of reader-response criticism along a continuum from individual to community readings.

- At one end would be psychological or subjective approaches. Such approaches often seek out, validate and assess the personal and, indeed, idiosyncratic reading experiences of ordinary readers (Bleich, 1978; Holland, 1975), whether students in a college classroom, or members of a church congregation.
- In the middle of the continuum would be interactive or phenomenological approaches. Here a balance is often struck between the role of the text and the role of the reader in shaping or controlling the reading experience (Iser, 1972; 1976). Thus the reader has a role in interpreting the text but the text itself shapes the way in which the reader reads it.
- At the other end of the continuum would be social or structural approaches to readers and reading. Here the emphasis is placed upon the social location of the reader and the 'interpretive community' of which one is a part (Fish, 1980).

So who is 'the reader' of reader-response criticism? The answer varies widely, depending upon where the critic stands along the continuum. Some approaches focus on particular, individual readers, while other approaches focus upon the reader as a member of a community. The individual reader might well be an average reader, the reader in the classroom or the pew, so to speak; while the socially constructed reader is often understood to be a hypothetical expert reader, a critical reader deeply imbued with the history and values of a given community.

In biblical reader-response criticism, 'the reader' has usually meant the '**implied reader**', a term popularized by Wolfgang Iser (Iser, 1972) and inspired by Wayne Booth's concept of the '**implied author**' (Booth, 1983). Both concepts, however, are already present in the work of Booth: 'the author creates, in short, an image of himself and another image of his reader; he makes his reader, as he makes his second self, and the most successful reading is one in which the created selves, author and reader, can find complete agreement' (Booth, 1983, 138). To be accurate, Iser's understanding of the implied reader envisions a larger role for the reader than does Booth's, but both versions of the concept attribute a great deal of authority to the text to shape and control the reader's experience. Biblical versions of reader-response criticism that have been guided by Booth or Iser have thereby often stayed in the comparatively safe and comfortable middle position of the critical continuum, where the reader is acknowledged to have a major role in making meaning, but the text still remains dominant. More adventuresome critical approaches (such as feminist reader-response criticism) may choose to challenge the traditional authority of the text and read against its grain (Fetterley, 1978), by shifting the critical focus away from the text, either to a politicized individual reader or to a reader in a community seeking liberation or justice.

What is the 'experience of reading' that is addressed in reader-response criticism? Again, the answer is, it depends upon one's understanding of who the reader is, and where one stands along the critical continuum. However, one aspect that is often emphasized is painstaking attention to the temporal flow of the reading experience. Here again the insights of Wolfgang Iser into the phenomenology of reading have been influential. Iser claims that every text is characterized by 'gaps' and 'spots of indeterminacy', and so reading is inevitably a challenge to fill the gaps and to clarify the indeterminacies, as best one can. Even more broadly, to read is to experience a 'wandering viewpoint' that travels along, within and with the text, as one looks ahead, in anticipation of moments to come in the reading experience, and as one looks behind, in review of and reflection upon what has already transpired: 'We look forward, we look back, we decide, we change our decisions, we form expectations, we are shocked by their nonfulfillment, we question, we muse, we accept, we reject; this is the dynamic process of recreation' (Iser, 1978, 288).

Today reader-response criticism is no more unified than it ever has been, but at the same time attention to the reader and the reading experience is almost ubiquitous in theory and criticism. The central concerns of reader-response criticism are sharply visible within criticisms like feminist, post-structural, liberationist and postcolonial, as well as a host of other critical approaches. It is little wonder that some have suggested that we live in 'the era of the reader' (Leitch, 1988, 211) or 'the Age of Reading' (Abrams, 1979, 566).

R. M. F.

What are the landmark publications on reader-response criticism?

Wayne C. Booth (1961) *The Rhetoric of Fiction*. Chicago: University of Chicago Press.

Booth's original work was republished in a 2nd edition in 1983; his theory was that all narrative was a piece of rhetoric in which an author sought to persuade the reader of moral commitments. The author presents himself or herself to the reader in the guise of a second-self, or implied author, whose character is created through the choices made by the author.

Wolfgang Iser (1972) *Der implizite Leser. Kommunikationsformen des Romans von Bunyan bis Beckett.* Munich: Fink.

Translated into English as (1974) *The Implied Reader: Patterns of Communication in Prose Fiction from Bunyan to Beckett.* Baltimore: Johns Hopkins University Press.

Wolfgang Iser (1976) *Der Akt des Lesens: Theorie ästhetischer Wirkung.* Munich: Fink.

Translated into English as (1978) *The Act of Reading: A Theory of Aesthetic Response.* Baltimore: Johns Hopkins University Press.

In these two books Iser sets out his theory that each text has an 'implied reader' but that it is the 'actual reader' who engages not only with the role of implied reader but also with the gaps in the text itself to complete the 'meaning' of a text.

David Bleich (1978) *Subjective Criticism.* Baltimore: Johns Hopkins University Press.

In this book David Bleich explored the way in which intensely personal responses to a text affect the way in which it is read. His focus is thus on the response of an individual.

Stanley E. Fish (1980) *Is There a Text in This Class? The Authority of Interpretive Communities.* Cambridge, MA: Harvard University Press.

Stanley Fish's concern is not so much the individual as the community that shapes that individual. In his view communities form the way in which individuals think and this, in its turn, forms the way in which a text is interpreted.

Reader-response criticism in practice

As Robert Fowler has made clear above, reader-response criticism is the umbrella term for many different sorts of criticisms that pay particular attention to the role of the reader in interpretation, either individually, informed by the text or as shaped by community. Consequently there are methods of interpretation which fulfil the criteria of reader-response criticism but which are treated in dedicated chapters within this book. Thus those which are drawn from the ideological adherence of the reader fall under this umbrella (feminist, liberation, sociopolitical, black, Asian, ecological), as does reception history, which explores how the New Testament has been received in history, and indeed, to a certain extent, also structuralism and poststructuralism. One area not explored elsewhere, however, but which is important within reader-response criticisms, is the way in which the *process* of reading informs interpretation.

Reader-response theory includes so many different approaches that it is almost impossible to incorporate them into a single, short example. For this reason, the practical example will focus on one particular reader-response interpretation as proposed by Mark Allan Powell.

Magi from the East: Matthew 2.1–9

In his book *Chasing the Eastern Star: Adventures in Biblical Reader-Response Criticism* Mark Allan Powell pays great attention to the process of reading in interpretations of the magi in Matthew's birth narratives (Powell, 2001). Part of the significance of his argument here is that he is not interested in whether an interpretation is 'right' or 'wrong' but on whether it is 'expected' (that is, an implied audience might be expected to have understood it in that way) or 'unexpected' (an implied audience might not be expected to have understood it in that way). The importance of this is that this gap between what an implied reader might have expected in an interpretation and what interpretations have been produced can tell us a lot about ourselves in the act of reading. In order to illustrate this, Powell explores the interpretation of the magi as kings and then as wise people and thus reveals what is, in his view, the expected understanding of them in the text as well as the unexpected.

The magi as kings

The magi of Matthew's Gospel were widely regarded as being kings, from the sixth century to the time of the Reformation. As Powell notes, however, from the Reformation to the present day it has been accepted that, historically, the magi were not kings and had no connection to royalty (Powell, 2001, 136–7). This is now so much the case that many modern commentaries do not even discuss whether or not they were kings. Nevertheless, allusions within the text open up the possibility of interpreting the magi as kings.

Lying behind the Matthean story are Isaiah 60.3 and Psalm 72.10–11. Isaiah 60.3 refers to kings coming 'to the brightness of your dawn' and Psalm 72.10–11 to the kings of Tarshish and Sheba bringing gifts and bowing down in worship. This causes Powell to conclude that, although the magi were not kings historically, there was room in the text through intertextual allusion to make a connection between the magi and kings.

This does not mean, however, that the implied readers of Matthew's Gospel would have made such a connection. Powell argues that the implied readers of Matthew's Gospel would be 'expected' to know that magi were in fact the servants of kings and not kings themselves. He brings forward evidence of this material from Graeco-Roman texts, from Jewish **midrash** and also from Daniel 2.2 and 10 as clear indications that magi were widely considered to be royal servants. He also adds to this the fact that Matthew makes it very clear throughout the Gospel that the reign of God is in conflict with the reign of worldly powers and so an implied reader, who might know at least some of the references Powell cites, would assume that the magi were in fact just servants of kings; if they were actual kings they would be in conflict with God's reign, not paying homage to it. Powell pushes his argument one stage further. He maintains that the intertextual allusions with Isaiah and Psalms serve to undermine the tradition about kings bringing gifts to worship, rather than support it. The prophetic and psalmic tradition looked forward to a time when kings would come to worship; in the event of the fulfilment of the prophecy it was servants and not the kings themselves who brought gifts in homage of 'the king'.

The magi as wise people

While the majority of New Testament scholars would reject the identification of the magi as kings, many would accept their identification as 'wise people'. Powell expresses his own surprise that, after exploring the evidence, he feels that the interpretation of magi as wise people was also undermined by Matthew and that the implied reader was expected to take them as fools (Powell, 2001, 148–9). He begins by distinguishing between wisdom as learning and wisdom as astuteness (one is acquired through study, the other is natural) and he observes that most would accept that the magi were wise due to their learning in astronomy. Powell notes a gap in the text, however, which is the way in which Matthew describes the magi's report of seeing the star in the East (Matt. 2.2). Modern interpretation assumes that their sight of the star in the East implies a learned knowledge of astronomy. It is possible that this knowledge was no more than common knowledge and that the appearance of a star in the sky would have been widely understood to mean the birth of a new king.

Powell goes on to explore what the implied readers might be expected to know about magi. Drawing in particular from Daniel 2, though also from Graeco-Roman literature and Jewish midrash, he argues that the implied readers of Matthew would be expected to make the link that magi were only learned in matters that were known to be nonsense. Thus a distinction would be made between learned and wise; they may have been learned but certainly were not wise (Powell, 2001, 150–2). Powell supports this by exploring the concept of wisdom elsewhere in Matthew and notes that in passages such as 11.25, wisdom appears to be undermined as a virtue since it is accompanied by power. He concludes that wisdom is rejected by God in Matthew in the same way that royalty is.

This reading of the magi as 'fools' seems to be supported in the story of their search for Jesus, which is marked by ignorance and misinterpretation. They do not in fact know where Jesus was born and go to the wrong place before they arrive in Bethlehem (Matt. 2.1–8) and appear to be fooled by Herod into thinking that his concern for Jesus was genuine (Matt. 2.8–9). Thus Powell concludes that the implied readers are expected to respond: 'God revealed the truth about the Christ to a bunch of pagan fools while those who were clever enough to figure it out for themselves missed it' (Powell, 2001, 156).

Neither kings nor wise

Powell's conclusion, therefore, is that the implied readers of the narrative would have known that the magi were neither kings nor wise. As time went on, however, attitudes to royalty and wisdom changed so that after Constantine kings became highly regarded and, in the Renaissance, wisdom became prized so that the magi became associated first with kingship and then with wisdom. At this point, then, the expected reading (that which the implied reader might have adopted) was overturned in favour of the unexpected reading (that which the implied reader would not have adopted): the magi became characters endued either with royalty or with wisdom and thus worthy to receive a revelation of Christ. Powell interprets this as a resistance by the actual readers to the message of the gospel, which prefers the lowly and the outcast to the rich and powerful (Powell, 2001, 175).

Conclusions

Powell's reader-response criticism falls into the category that Fowler identified as a mid-point on the spectrum and includes influence as much by the text as by the reader. His interpretation here is an amalgam of quasi-historical criticism (the search for the expectations of the implied reader) with reception history (how the text has actually been interpreted by the Church). His reflection on the process of reading is to explore why and how the 'unexpected' reading of the actual reader became preferred over the 'expected' reading of the implied reader. He acknowledges later on in the book that, as a rule, he prefers the expected reading to the unexpected but that he recognizes that the unexpected reading (such as interpreting the manna in the desert, Exodus 16.31–36, through the lens of the Eucharist) can provide insights into the text that the expected reading cannot.

Evaluation of reader-response criticism

The breadth of reader-response criticism makes it very complicated to evaluate critically. Those, like Mark Allan Powell, whose preference lies in the 'expected' reading of the text have concerns very similar to those of historical critics. They work on the principle that there is a better reading of the text (in this case that which the implied reader would have adopted) and that, although it may be difficult to discern what it is this should be, this is the goal of the critic, who might then compare other interpretations to see how far they agree and how far they differ. Others may acknowledge the presence of the 'expected' reading and deliberately read the text in a different way. Such an 'against the grain' reading deliberately pits the reader against the obvious meaning of the text and attempts to read 'differently'. Other reader-response criticisms would dispute whether there is an 'expected' meaning and would argue for a plurality of meanings.

The crucial factor that holds all these approaches together is the emphasis that is placed on the reader and their role in interpreting the text. Some prefer to place more emphasis on the text than on the reader; others would put more on the reader than on the text but all are concerned to note the significance of the reader's role in interpretation either to correct that balance in favour of the meaning of the text or to emphasize it as the location for the discovery of meaning.

16

Feminist criticism

What is feminist criticism?

Feminist criticism interprets the Bible from a position which pays particular attention to gender issues as they affect women, both in the New Testament and in its interpretation.

How did the theory develop and what are its main features?
Kathy Ehrensperger

Awareness of gender issues in the New Testament and New Testament interpretation emerged as early as the middle of the nineteenth century. One of the most influential volumes that arose from this was published in 1895 and 1898. Influenced by the anti-slavery campaigns in the USA and the UK, a group of activists around Elizabeth Cady Stanton (1815–1902) edited *The Woman's Bible* in the USA. The passages of the Bible compiled in this volume were selected according to criteria which read the text with an awareness of the particular (male) gendered perspective of biblical texts, and thus, also, of the issue of presupposition in interpretation.

This early example of a gender-conscious interpretation of the Bible did not exercise a lasting or widespread influence at the time, and the issue of interpreting the New Testament from a specifically feminist perspective only resurfaced in the late 1960s and early 1970s. Prior to the emergence of feminist approaches, scholars had focused on what the New Testament says about the role of women and particular texts on women rather than addressing the issue of hermeneutical presuppositions in interpretation.

Research into the history and role of women in the New Testament and its first-century context continues to constitute a significant aspect of feminist research today; however, a critical feminist perspective developed in the aftermath of what Elisabeth Schüssler Fiorenza in her ground-breaking book *Bread not Stone* (1984) identified and labelled as the 'hermeneutics of suspicion' in which, unlike in earlier approaches, the discourse of biblical interpretation, and the Bible itself, were perceived as entirely entrenched within male-oriented and male-dominated perspectives. This not only decisively shaped the role of men and women in church and society but also the paradigms of thinking and acting in society: women's voices, experiences and perspectives are thus represented neither in New Testament texts nor in their interpretation. Feminist interpretation informed by a hermeneutics of suspicion searches for the silenced voices and hidden history of women in the text. The main focus lies in uncovering these submerged voices and at the same time revealing dominating and oppressing traditions in texts and their interpretation.

One of the implicit presuppositions of the earlier feminist approaches (1970s to 1980s) was the notion of a universal female experience of being silenced and oppressed. Women from non-white, non-Western traditions challenged some feminist interpretations as implicitly racist and/or anti-Jewish. A new wave of feminist interpretation emerged in the 1980s and 1990s making it obvious that feminist interpretation is characterized by diversity rather than universalism. **Womanist** interpretation drew attention to the perspective of Afro-American and Afro-Caribbean women; and *mujerista* to Hispano women; whereas the voices of Jewish feminists alerted Christian feminists to traps of anti-Judaism in New Testament interpretation which they often had taken over from male interpretive traditions. Another development focuses more on gender issues in general and has given rise both to gender criticism of the Bible in general (Sawyer, 2007) and to 'masculinist' criticisms (Moore and Anderson, 2003).

The necessity of self-critical assessment of hermeneutical presuppositions within feminist and gender-sensitive approaches also became obvious. Thus feminist interpretation cannot be described as one single approach to, or method of, interpretation but has rather developed into 'a set of interrelated perspectives' (Day and Pressler, 2006, xi), which include a wide range of disciplines and methods. Literary criticism ranges alongside historical criticism, social science, sociology, critical theory, political science and other approaches in the variety of feminist criticisms available. Some aspects however can with confidence be described as being shared by most feminist approaches:

- *The subjectivity of all interpretation*
  Feminist criticism, along with numerous other approaches such as postcolonial interpretation, does not perceive itself as an additional method for analysing a text but as a paradigm shift which assumes that all interpretations are *contextual*, that is, shaped by their *social location* (gender,

race, class, sexual orientation, age, etc.). This emphasizes their need to pay attention to the *hermeneutical presuppositions* which are influenced by the context of the interpreter and which guide any interpretation. As a result the notion of objectivity or of a text speaking for itself is perceived as a stance which cannot be upheld whatever perspective of interpretation is advocated. Particularity and diversity are thus inherent aspects of the process of interpretation, which itself is perceived as an ongoing conversation over the meaning of a text.

• *The importance of contemporary issues in church and society*
Another dimension shared by most feminist approaches is their aware-ness of, and relation to, contemporary issues in church and society. New Testament interpretation is seen and practised not as an innocent or detached 'purely academic' discipline but in both its potential and actual impact on the lives of men and women in church and society. Interpretations and the ethical responsibility for the impact/effects they may produce cannot be separated from each other. Feminist inter-pretations are concerned interpretations, concerned especially but not exclusively about the fate of women.

K. E.

What are the landmark publications on feminist criticism?

Elizabeth Cady Stanton and the National American Woman Suffrage Association Collection (1895) *The Woman's Bible*. New York: European Publishing.

The Woman's Bible contains a selection of passages considered to be particularly relevant to the concerns of women. It is the first book to have a particular interest in evaluating the way in which the Bible had influenced how women were treated; it concluded that it degrades women from beginning to end.

Elisabeth Schüssler Fiorenza (1983) *In Memory of Her: A Feminist Theological Reconstruction of Christian Origins*. New York: Crossroad.

Elisabeth Schüssler Fiorenza (1984) *Bread not Stone: The Challenge of Feminist Biblical Interpretation*. Boston: Beacon Press.

These two books are widely accepted to have begun to shape the field of feminist biblical interpretation by crafting a method for reading the Bible informed by a 'hermeneutic of suspicion'.

The series edited by Amy-Jill Levine, Feminist Companion to the New Testament and Early Christian Writings (published in the UK by

Continuum and in the USA by Pilgrim Press) aimed to provide collections of feminist interpretations of all the books of the New Testament. It has been influential in making feminist interpretation known to a wider audience.

Carol A. Newsom and Sharon H. Ringe (1992) *The Women's Bible Commentary*. London and Louisville: SPCK and Westminster John Knox.

In a conscious tribute to Cady Stanton's *The Woman's Bible*, Newsom and Ringe recognized the plurality of women's voices involved in feminist biblical interpretation and the importance of interpretation in reading the Bible (and so changed the name from *The Woman's Bible* to *The Women's Bible Commentary*). In the volume they gathered together a wide spectrum of feminist views on the Bible with the aim of producing commentary on each book of the Bible.

Feminist criticism in practice

One of the issues that affects feminist criticism is the question of what makes an interpretation 'feminist'. It is obvious that not all interpretations by women are necessarily feminist; furthermore many people, but not everyone, would accept that men can write feminist criticism. Therefore it is not necessarily the gender of the author of a piece of criticism that dictates whether it is feminist or not. Instead it is ideological intent that affects the feminist nature of a piece of criticism; the methods used will differ widely from scholar to scholar:

- Some feminist scholars choose to interpret passages in which women feature and so they look at passages which appear to undermine the equality of women (such as Paul's discussion of the role of women in 1 Cor. 11.1–16 or the portrayal of the whore of Babylon in Rev. 17.1–18) or those which appear to support their equality (such as Gal. 3.28 or passages which mention women in the early Church like Phoebe in Rom. 16.1 or Junia in Rom. 16.7).
- Other feminist scholars concentrate on how interpretation of the New Testament in general has affected the role or place of women.
- Still others explore issues such as power, either in the New Testament text itself or in interpretations of the text, which, while not overtly about women, have affected women and their place in society.

Consequently feminist criticism rarely, if ever, occurs on its own; instead it becomes a particular **standpoint** from which one does another form of criticism, so we can find feminist historical critics, feminist poststructuralists, feminist rhetorical critics and so on. All are feminist but they are very different from each other. A book the length of this one could be written to introduce feminist criticisms alone and could have very similar chapters to this volume.

Probably one of the most familiar forms of feminist criticism is the attempt to reconstruct the role of women in the earliest Christian communities. Within this attempt, Romans 16, with its double mention of Phoebe – a deacon – and Junia – an apostle – as well as numerous other women, has played an important role in the discussion and serves as a good illustration of the attempt to understand more about women and the early Christian communities.

Using the New Testament as a source for reconstructing the role of women

Among the very many contributions that Schüssler Fiorenza has made to this field is her constant reminder that extant canonical New Testament texts do not necessarily present a complete picture of the situation in the early church communities. In her view, the presence of women in the canonical material that we possess is indicative of 'submerged' information: '(t)hose passages that directly mention women cannot be taken as providing all the information *about women* in early Christianity' (Schüssler Fiorenza, 1986, 423). Layers and layers separate us from the women of these early communities: the selection of accounts recorded, the way in which scribal activity passed on these records, the selection of New Testament texts for the canon and centuries of Christian interpretation have all acted to obscure the role that women had in the first century (Schüssler Fiorenza, 1983, 41–95).

Beneath all these layers, various women remain visible in the Pauline epistles, and in the final chapter of Romans the presence of two women in particular has raised great discussion about their role in the Pauline communities.

Phoebe, a deacon of the church: Romans 16.1

At the start of Paul's greetings in Romans 16, he commends Phoebe, who is a *diakonos* of the church in Cenchreae and a *prostatis*. Both of these words have significance and are worth exploring further.

- The word *diakonos* has been extensively explored by those interested in the development of diaconate in early Christian communities, and it is possible to observe a growing consensus – illustrated in the definition

139

offered in the 3rd edition of Bauer, Danker, Arndt and Gingrich's Greek Lexicon (Danker, 2000, 229–31) – that a *diakonos* was to be regarded as an agent or go-between as much as a humble servant. Thus here Phoebe should probably be understood to be an agent of the church in Cenchreae. This seems to be enforced by the fact that Phoebe, a woman, is described using a masculine noun, *diakonos*. Ever since the time of Origen it has been assumed that Phoebe was an assistant and servant of Paul despite the fact that Paul uses the masculine *diakonos* of her which elsewhere is used of Paul himself, Apollos, Timothy or Tychios without the assumption of their being an assistant (see examples cited in Schüssler Fiorenza, 1983, 47 and 1986, 423–4).

• Of even greater interest is the word *prostatis*. This word most obviously means a patron in a gathering who bestows benefaction; such a person would be immensely wealthy and powerful as they had the means to support people and communities, or not, as they chose (Osiek, MacDonald and Tulloch, 2006). Again, as Schüssler Fiorenza points out, scholars have generally assumed that because Phoebe is a woman this must mean personal care and help received by Paul and his friends rather than the more usual 'patron' since women are deemed not to be able to adopt this role at the time of Paul (Schüssler Fiorenza, 1986, 425).

Feminist interpretations of this word posit an entirely different role for Phoebe. For example Robert Jewett argues that Phoebe is a leading light in the setting up of Paul's Spanish mission, and that because Paul does not know anyone in Rome, the wealthy and influential Phoebe is given the task to inspire the Roman Christians to support the mission.

The natural interpretations of both these words, as agent and patron, have often been discarded on the grounds that women could not adopt such positions. This leads to a somewhat circular argument about the position of women in the Church: women could not be in positions of influence, therefore, when texts appear to indicate that they were, they must be retranslated and interpreted on the grounds that they cannot be right.

Junia, prominent among the apostles: Romans 16.7

Another verse in Romans that has caused controversy is Romans 16.7, which appears to refer to Junia as a relative of Paul and prominent among the apostles. The discussion around Junia concentrates on two particular areas: whether she was a woman or a man and whether Paul's description of her says that she was prominent among the apostles or simply well known to them.

140

Man or woman? Although the early fathers understood Junia to be a woman, it seems to be only in the medieval period that Aegidius of Rome (thirteenth century) proposed that a change to the masculine would be more logical. Luther subsequently understood the name as masculine but the King James Version of the Bible did not. It was only in 1881, with the Revised Version, that Junia became Junias, and male in English translations (Thorley, 1996, 18). This position was exacerbated by the critical manuscripts of the Greek New Testament published by the United Bible Societies and Nestle-Aland between 1927 and 1993 which ranked the male Junias as a 'certain' reading (Epp, 2005, 49–52).

As Epp points out there is very little evidence at all for taking the Greek *Junian* as masculine, since the question of whether it was a masculine or feminine noun depends entirely upon the accents given to the word and there were few manuscripts before the seventh century which contained any accents at all and those that did have accents show the form of the word that can be either feminine or masculine. Add this to the fact that:

- Junia is a very common woman's name in the Roman empire,
- no examples of the masculine Junias have been found anywhere,
- Paul addresses other male/female couples in Romans 16

and the evidence for Junia being a woman seems rather compelling.

Prominent among the apostles? The other focus of discussion is whether *episēmoi en tois apostolois* means 'prominent among the apostles' or 'well known to the apostles'. The evidence here is harder to evaluate. The discussion focuses around other examples of the same phrase in Greek literature outside of the New Testament and what the phrase can be seen to mean in those contexts. Burer and Wallace argue that if the phrase had meant 'prominent among' a different Greek construction would have been used (Burer and Wallace, 2001) though their case has been heavily rebutted in subsequent work by various scholars including Belleville and Epp (Belleville, 2005; Epp, 2005), who argue that this phrase clearly means 'prominent among'.

If they are right, then the reference to Junia as an apostle is significant. The word apostle in this early period could refer to a broad range of activities, but the most common was a missionary agent, so if Junia were indeed prominent among these early agents of mission, she must have held an influential role within the community. To borrow words from John Chrysostom, 'how great the wisdom of this woman must have been that she was even deemed worthy of the title apostle' (*Epistle to the Romans* 21.2, cited in Epp, 2005, 32).

The leading women in the Roman community

We cannot leave Romans 16 without noting the other women to whom Paul sends greetings in Romans 16. Paul mentions 26 people by name and of these approximately a third are women (Schüssler Fiorenza, 1986, 427). Since many of those that he greets by name are known to be influential, this, again, seems to undermine the claim that women were unimportant and lacked leadership roles in the Pauline communities.

Conclusions

The feminist interpretations of Romans 16 explored above have sought to overturn the widespread belief that women did not have places of particular prominence in the Pauline communities. These interpretations use evidence about Phoebe, about Junia and about the other women greeted by Paul in this chapter to argue that there were numerous women within these early communities who held honoured, prominent positions as leaders and that it is subsequent male interpretation that has presented a very different position. If these interpretations are correct then Romans 16 does seem to present a very different picture from that commonly presented of the Pauline church in which women were not only present and respected by Paul but instigators of mission.

Evaluation of feminist criticism

Feminist criticism is not so much a 'method' in its own right, as an ideological standpoint from which to engage in other methods, such as rhetorical, historical or narrative criticism. The practical example given in this chapter is heavily influenced by historical criticism, in that although it employs the hermeneutic of suspicion to the apparent lack of women in the early Christian communities and to interpretations that further enforce this view, it seeks to rediscover a women's history (or 'her-story' as Schüssler Fiorenza calls it) which acknowledges and honours women's place within history and narrative. The values of this are that it shines a light onto the way that assumptions are so easily made in scholarship that, for example, a woman could not be prominent as an apostle and so must be a man, and celebrates a reconstruction in which women's places are visible. The problem of this particular approach is that it is easy to reach an impasse in scholarship. Again an example from Romans 16 is that Burer and Wallace argue strongly for one interpretation of a phrase and

Belleville and Epp for another; both evince large amounts of evidence to support their case but as a rule fail to persuade the other of the value of their position.

This highlights the issues at the heart of this approach. The advantage of feminist criticism is that it acknowledges, even celebrates, the subjectivity of an author. The fact that someone is writing from a feminist perspective will inevitably affect the way in which the New Testament is read and received. This in its turn highlights the fact that interpretations have an impact in communities which receive and use them.

One complexity is that it is harder to engage in debate with those who do not adopt a similar ideological standpoint. Those who reject or are ambivalent about feminism find it hard to engage with the interpretations it produces. This is noticeable in feminist historical critical studies which, though **postmodern** in attitude, are still driven by the **modern** concern to reconstruct the history that lies behind the text. Those who do not share the feminist standpoint often also do not share the historical reconstruction achieved by feminist historical critics.

17

Queer criticism

What is queer criticism?

Queer criticism uses sexual identity as a **standpoint** from which to interpret the New Testament.

How did the theory develop and what are its main features?
Teresa J. Hornsby

Queer, or gay, lesbian, bisexual and transsexual/transgendered (GLBT) New Testament interpretation is descended from historical critical methods, language studies, feminist hermeneutics and liberation theology and has evolved into multilayered, multidisciplinary and complex approaches to the New Testament texts. Once solely within the realm of historical studies, modern GLBT interpretations of the New Testament involve literary critical methods (including reader-response and **postmodernism**), the social sciences, **semiotics**, ethics and, I suspect, any method mentioned in this book. What makes GLBT criticism unique is its subject matter: people whose sexuality may differ from what a dominant culture may deem as 'normal', which tends overwhelmingly to be one man and one woman having intercourse within a religiously sanctioned marriage.

The New Testament has been used by many Christians to support a modern model of 'normal' sexuality. Romans 1.18–36, 1 Corinthians 6.9 and 1 Timothy 1.10 have been given a particularly heavy amount of attention because each verse has been traditionally interpreted as prohibiting homosexuality. Queer interpretations, for the most part, do not argue that the New Testament says that homosexuality, bisexuality, and so on is acceptable; rather, GLBT critics have tended to argue that homosexuality (defining a whole person by his or her sexuality) is a modern construction; for example, words, such as *malakos* (1 Cor. 6.9) or *arsenokoites* (1 Cor. 6.9; 1 Tim. 1.10), which have been translated as 'sodomites', 'homosexuals' or 'effeminate men', come from Greek words with no clear modern meaning. Dale Martin makes an especially strong argument on this matter (D. B. Martin, 1996). Others have also argued that the vilification of homoeroticism is a cultural rather than a theological phenomenon (for example, Nissinen, 1998).

Two significant studies in the area of New Testament GLBT interpretation were published in the early 1980s – John Boswell's *Christianity, Social Tolerance and Homosexuality* (1980) and Robin Scroggs's *The New Testament and Homosexuality* (1983). It would not be a gross overstatement to say that much of the GLBT New Testament work after 1983 has been in response to these two seminal works. Though Boswell is more a historian of the Middle Ages than a New Testament scholar, the influence of Boswell's book on GLBT New Testament scholarship is enormous. Matthew Kuefler published a book of essays in 2006, *The Boswell Thesis*, in which scholars from a wide range of disciplines consider the impact that Boswell's book had, the fundamental arguments the book engendered – the most notable being the 'essentialism vs. social constructionist' debate – and the new ideas that have emerged from Boswell's work. Scroggs's thesis that Paul's references were to the ancient practice of pederasty (an erotic relationship with an adolescent boy who was often a slave) and not homosexuality in general, is as controversial as influential, thus spawning decades of reactive scholarship.

Another example of innovative and rigorous historical-critical work in Queer New Testament interpretation is Bernadette Brooten's book, *Love Between Women* (1996). Brooten first published a precursor to this book in her 1985 article 'Paul's Views on the Nature of Women and Female Homoeroticism'. Her work stands alone as the landmark for lesbian historical-critical New Testament scholarship. Brooten argues that yes, the apostle Paul does not approve of homoeroticism between women, but that disapproval is based firmly in culture. Paul, like his contemporaries, assumes gender normatives are 'natural'. If a woman steps outside her God-given, passive nature, by for example being the sexual actor (a male role), she is being unnatural and against God, regardless of whether her sexual partner is a woman or a man.

Another genre of GLBT New Testament scholarship emerged in the late 1970s with Letha Scanzoni and Virginia Ramey Mollenkott's *Is the Homosexual My Neighbor?* and continued to the present with works such as *Our Tribe*, by Nancy Wilson (1995) and *Jesus, the Bible, and Homosexuality*, by Jack Rogers (2006). These books are written primarily for the non-academic Christian, but are founded on linguistic studies and historical criticism. They tend to move from the study of the usual texts (such as Rom. 1.18–36; 1 Cor. 6.9) in order to synthesize a broader theological reading that insists on love and acceptance of all people.

The most recent and dynamic work in the area of GLBT interpretation of the New Testament is from literary-critical scholars, particularly the postmodernists. Though the earliest work in postmodern biblical criticism comes from Hebrew Bible scholars (for example, Roland Boer, Ken Stone, Tamar Kamionkowski), GLBT New Testament postmodernists (such as Deborah Krause, Teresa J. Hornsby, Tina Pippin and Thomas Bohache) now read the Christian texts through the lenses of influential postmodern/ poststructuralist writers (Michel Foucault, Judith Butler, Jacques Derrida, Julia Kristeva and others). A **postmodern** literary critical approach to GLBT New Testament texts analyses the intersections of the production of meaning, power and the formations of modern Christianity. 'Queer' becomes the antithesis of the normative, and reveals that those in power determine the normative. Postmodernism suggests that not only is meaning located in the interaction of the reader with the text, but the reader herself or himself is produced by a dynamic community. By deconstructing, or exposing, the different ways in which the New Testament conveys meaning, the GLBT New Testament scholars also expose a constructed sexual normative, one that produces and maintains power; 'queer', then, is also revealed to be a construction that changes from time to time and from place to place. Thus, in this work, sexuality is stripped of its 'essentialness' or 'naturalness'. Postmodern GLBT New Testament scholars argue that there is no 'normal' human sexuality; the New Testament has been used to produce and preserve a monogamous heterosexuality (as sanctioned in marriage) as something ordained by God.

Though Queer New Testament interpretation is as diverse, multidisciplinary and as complex as all of the various biblical methods of interpretation, the hermeneutic seeks, for the most part, to reverse the damage that other New Testament interpretations have done to GLBT people.

T. J. H.

What are the landmark publications on queer criticism?

Letha Scanzoni and Virginia Ramey Mollenkott (1978) *Is the Homosexual My Neighbor? Another Christian View*. San Francisco: Harper & Row.

This is the first of a number of more popular books that attempt to look at broader issues about sexuality and homosexuality than simply the 'key' New Testament texts.

John Boswell (1980) *Christianity, Social Tolerance and Homosexuality*. Chicago: University of Chicago Press.

Boswell's book has become a classic in this field. In it he explores the history of attitudes to homosexuality from the Christian era to the fourteenth century. He also raises the crucial question of whether sexual identity was 'essential' (that is, inherent to a person) or socially constructed (affected by the society in which a person grew up).

Robin Scroggs (1983) *The New Testament and Homosexuality.* Philadelphia: Fortress.

Scroggs's argument, still hotly debated today, is that the references in the New Testament that are commonly understood to be about homosexuality are really about pederasty and have been regularly misunderstood.

Bernadette J. Brooten (1985) 'Paul's Views on the Nature of Women and Female Homoeroticism', in C. Atkinson, C. Buchanan and M. Miles, eds, *Immaculate and Powerful.* Boston: Beacon, 61–87.

Bernadette J. Brooten (1996) *Love Between Women: Early Christian Responses to Female Homoeroticism.* Chicago: University of Chicago Press.

Brooten's works are the most important in the area of lesbian criticism. She argues that Paul's comment on lesbian relations is located firmly within Paul's own culture and must be understood as such.

Queer criticism in practice

Like most of the 'standpoint' criticisms in this part of the book, GLBT interpretations of the Bible are not so much a method as a way of viewing the text using a variety of different methods. As Teresa Hornsby makes clear above, GLBT interpretations use a wide range of 'methods' of biblical interpretation; what holds them together is that they all read from a GLBT standpoint, which of course differs from reader to reader.

In some ways queer criticism has similarities with feminist criticisms in that GLBT interpreters must decide whether they will focus their attention on just those passages that have been used in the debate about attitudes to homosexuality in the Bible or whether a 'queer' perspective can be brought to other texts not so overtly focused on the issue. In the same way, feminist criticism can deal with just those passages that talk about women or can bring a 'feminist' perspective to other more disparate passages. In the feminist criticism chapter I used, as a practical example, a passage that talks about women and thereby demonstrated the aspect of feminist criticism that explores texts about women; in this chapter, I will use a passage not overtly concerned with the debate about homosexuality in the Bible and thus demonstrate how a GLBT approach can provide an insight into texts not overtly concerned with homosexuality.

No male and female: Galatians 3.28

In a recent collection of essays, *Sex and the Single Savior*, Dale Martin has published an article on 'The Queer History of Galatians 3:28: "No Male and Female"' (D. B. Martin, 2006, 77–102). In this article he has demonstrated how a heterosexual bias has affected interpretations of this important verse. He adopts two main methods: reception history as a means of noting how the verse has been interpreted through Christian history, followed by a postmodern approach. As this volume does not have a chapter dedicated to postmodern criticism, it is worth defining what this means here.

Postmodernism is notoriously difficult to define. It gained popularity as a term in the 1940s and 1950s as a means of critiquing 'modern' architectural designs but from there has grown to describe a wide variety of phenomena from interior design to adverts on television; from a novel to methods of interpreting literature. In short postmodernism arises from but critiques modernism and its concern for objectivity, rationalism and certainty. Many of the criticisms in this book can properly be called postmodern in that their stance is consciously subjective (for example, liberation criticism), prefers plurality to a single meaning (as with theological interpretation) and believes that meaning can be found as much outside of the text as in it (for example, poststructuralism), though some of the practical examples are more postmodern than others. When Martin describes his method as postmodern he means that it is playful, that it seeks to undermine traditional modern interpretations and opens up a space in which to see the text differently.

Galatians 3.28 and equality

Martin begins by demonstrating the difference that exists between interpretations of this passage. He notes that in academic circles the dominant view, influenced by scholars such as Stendahl and Schüssler Fiorenza, is that this verse argues for equality 'in Christ' (Stendahl, 1966; Schüssler Fiorenza, 1983, 205–36). This interpretation has become so influential that it is the lens through which other Pauline passages, such as 1 Corinthians 14.34–35, have been read. In the nineteenth century and for much of the twentieth century, however, Galatians 3.28 was viewed as saying that there was no distinction between men and women in relation *to* Christ but that sexual distinction elsewhere, in society, in the church and at home, continued. It is also interesting to note that language about equality – rather than lack of distinction – came into interpretations of this passage well into the twentieth century. The discussion continues and focuses around whether the verse argues for equality between the sexes or a lack of gender distinction and also whether what is the case 'in Christ' is also true in wider society (D. B. Martin, 2006, 81–2).

Androgyny and Galatians 3.28

An important development in the discussion of this verse arose from the publication of Meeks's article in 1974 in which he argued that what Paul was talking about here was androgyny like that of Adam. Adam, Meeks argued, was androgynous and only became male after the female Eve was lifted from him. Christian baptism, he argues, returns us to an original androgynous state. This view has spawned a wide variety of discussions about the nature of androgyny in the ancient world, and a consensus has developed that, within the ancient context, androgyny does not mean united male and female – as it does for us – but 'completed male'. As scholars such as Fatum have argued, Galatians 3.28 is not affirmative of women but 'fixes them in a state of asexuality dependent upon the androcentric concept of human normality' (Fatum, 1995, 79, cited in Martin, 2006, 84). Martin notes that this is the way in which this verse was understood by ancient Christian writers, for which there is widespread evidence, the most striking of which is the Gospel of Thomas (logion 114), which declares that Mary must become male in order to enter the kingdom.

This leads Martin to maintain that the current egalitarian reading of Galatians 3.28 (that man and woman are equal in Christ) is not in fact historical. He does not see Paul as arguing for sexual equality but for the abolition of the dichotomy between male and female, so that all human beings would be 'subsumed into the superior, perfected, and therefore (as it seems to us) male body' (Martin, 2006, 87). For Martin the modern, liberal tendency to view sexuality as a dichotomy between 'male and female' represents a dominant heterosexual reading of sexuality and of this passage. It is important to recognize that Martin is clear that what he calls the 'historical' reading of this passage (that is, that Paul's language here is to be understood as arguing that women should be subsumed in baptism into the 'completed male') is not the only possible one, but he puts forward this reading as a means of disrupting the current view on the text (that Paul is arguing for equality here). This chimes with his thesis throughout his book, *Sex and the Single Savior*, that the historical reading should not be allowed to control all other readings of the text.

A postmodern queer reading of Galatians 3.28

This causes Martin to begin to explore a more playful plurality of meanings of this text. He notes the importance of translating the Greek more accurately as 'no male *and* female' rather than the popular '*neither* male *nor* female' (such as is found in translations like the New International Version, the English Standard Version, or the New American Standard Bible). This may remind us of the ancients' view that there is not male and female, only male; equally he argues we may wish to resist the view of the ancient writers and understand this verse as saying that there is not male and female only female.

Another possibility is to focus on the 'and': we are not one or the other, male or female, but both male *and* female. He concludes that in 'ethical-prescriptive terms, this would be interpreted as meaning that all femmes must become as butch as possible, and all butches must work their hardest to become flaming queens' (Martin, 2006, 89). In Martin's view, even better would be to abandon the dichotomy of male or female altogether and recognize that gender is 'multiplex', which opens up new ways of being human in Christ beyond the duality of male and female.

Conclusions

Martin's argument in this chapter has been to challenge what he calls the dominant heterosexual reading of this verse (that is, the tendency to see male and female as a dichotomy and to argue that the verse seeks equality between the two), which, although he does not reject it, was probably not the 'historical' meaning of the verse. If it is not, but people still wish to hold the egalitarian view, then they have to accept a range of other interpretations of the verse that challenge the duality between male and female that is so dominant in most interpretations of the text. Thus a reading that argues for gender equality must be placed alongside one that argues for gender multiplicity in Christ, which allows for different ways of expressing gender such as GLBT interpretations call for.

Evaluation of queer criticism

The issues surrounding queer criticism are similar to those surrounding other standpoint interpretations, but are more sharply focused. Like other criticisms in the neighbouring chapters to this one, GLBT interpretations adopt a standpoint from which to view the text. This raises a number of connected issues. The standpoint approach assumes that the identity of the reader will affect the way in which the text is read. However, there is no such thing as a 'standard' gay, lesbian, bisexual, transsexual/transgender identity – any more than there is a 'standard' heterosexual identity – thus GLBT interpretations of the Bible will, by their very nature, be disparate and unlike each other.

Even more important than this are attitudes to the criticism; all standpoint interpretations are liable to critique from those who do not hold the same standpoint. Criticisms range from whether an interpretation is a 'good' one to whether it should be done at all. GLBT interpretations of the Bible are particularly susceptible to such arguments because of the fierce debate within Christian communities about the Bible's (and the churches') attitude to homosexuality. It is important to recognize here, and elsewhere in this book, that, although biblical interpretation inevitably overlaps with the concerns of confessional communities, this book presents the interpretations that can be found in academia. GLBT interpretations of the Bible exist and thrive in numerous academic institutions and so rightfully have a place in this volume.

The value of queer criticism is that it challenges our preconceptions about sexuality and gender, and reminds us that there are ways of understanding passages which talk about gender and sexuality other than the dominant heterosexual ones.

18

Liberation criticism

What is liberation criticism?

Liberation criticism is not so much a method of criticism as an ideological orientation which seeks to make common cause with the poor and the marginalized and to liberate them from oppression.

How did the theory develop and what are its main features?
Gerald O. West

Liberation criticism arose out of liberation theology, which emerged in the 1960s and 1970s, largely based in Latin America though now spread throughout the world with particularly important contributions from Africa and India. It has at its core five interrelated emphases, which can be found across a range of liberation theologies. These five areas of emphasis include, according to Per Frostin, 'the choice of "interlocutors", the perception of God, social analysis, the choice of theological tools, and the relationship between theory and practice' (Frostin, 1988, 6). I use Frostin's analysis of liberation criticism because it draws on a wide range of liberation theologies in dialogue with each other. The data Frostin uses are drawn substantially from the internal dialogue of Third World theologians working together in forums such as the Ecumenical Association of Third World Theologians (EATWOT).

With respect to the first and fundamental emphasis – the choice of interlocutors or conversation partners – the emphasis in liberation criticism has been on social relations, not ideas or techniques, as has been the tendency in post-Enlightenment Western theology and biblical studies. This emphasis leads to the central question in liberation criticism, namely, 'Who are the interlocutors of biblical interpretation?' Or (in the language used by Musa Dube and I (West and Dube, 1996)), 'Who are biblical scholars reading "with", when they read the Bible?' To these questions liberation criticism gives a decisive answer: liberation criticism grants a preferential option for the poor (Frostin, 1988, 6). This choice of interlocutors is more than an ethical commitment; it is also an epistemological commitment, requiring an interpretive starting point within the social analysis of the poor themselves. The other four emphases of liberation criticism each flow from this first, which is why liberation criticism must always be more than an interpretive technique. The actual presence and participation of the poor in any interpretive act is pivotal. And while the notion of 'the poor' is often extended to include the working-class and the marginalized more generally, the designation 'the poor' remains central to liberation criticism.

The choice of interlocutors, of course, 'has important consequences not only for the interpretation of social reality but also for the understanding of God' (Frostin, 1988, 7), which brings us to the second emphasis. As EATWOT so aptly expressed it, 'The question about God in the world of the oppressed is not knowing whether God exists or not, but knowing on which side God is' (cited in Frostin, 1988, 7). Liberation criticism accepts that oppressors claim to share the same faith as the oppressed, which is why it is so important for liberation criticism to name the faith of the oppressor as idolatry, for it deifies the ideologies of domination, sacralizing the structures of exploitation so as to make them appear to reflect the will of God (Frostin, 1988, 7).

The third emphasis, that of social analysis, also derives from the first, since the option for the poor, as the chief interlocutors of liberation criticism, is based on a conflictual perception of social reality which affirms that there is a difference between the perspectives of the privileged 'from above' and of the poor 'from below' (Frostin, 1988, 7–8). EATWOT reports characterize the world as 'a divided world', where theology and biblical interpretation can only be done 'within the framework of an analysis of these conflicts' (cited in Frostin, 1988). The poles of conflict or 'struggle' (to use the term common in South African liberation theologies (Mosala, 1989; Nolan, 1988) include: rich–poor (economic), capitalists–proletariat (classist), North–South (geographic), male–female (sexist), white–black (racist), dominant–dominated cultures (ethnic) (Frostin, 1988, 8). While EATWOT consistently stresses the interrelatedness of these struggles, particular contexts of struggle, of course, give priority to different aspects of oppression.

The fourth emphasis in Frostin's analysis of the methodology of liberation criticism has to do with the choice of interpretive tools: '(w)ith a different interlocutor and a different perception of God, liberation theologians need different tools for their theological reflection' (Frostin, 1988, 9). The starting point is the perspective of the poor, what Itumeleng Mosala refers to as 'eyes that are hermeneutically trained in the struggle for liberation today', which are then used 'to observe the kin struggles of the oppressed and exploited of the biblical communities' (Mosala, 1986,

196). From within this starting point, socio-historical tools are used to interrogate past and present power structures (Schüssler Fiorenza, 1983; Gottwald, 1979). While socio-historical modes of interpretation have been the preferred choice in liberation criticism, literary and semiotic modes of reading have also found a place (Croatto, 1987; Trible, 1984; G. O. West, 1995).

Given that power relations are central to liberation criticism, Marxist modes of analysis have been particularly significant, though 'the actual use of Marxist analysis differs from group to group', depending on the form of oppression which is the focus of a particular liberation struggle (Frostin, 1988, 9). So, for example, even though the relationship between capital and labour is clearly one dimension of the African struggle, African liberation criticism adopts a multi-dimensional analysis of the relationship between oppressor and oppressed, which includes race, gender and culture (Frostin, 1988, 182). Furthermore, while classical Marxism maintains that material production conditions human thought, African liberation criticism emphasizes the creativity and capacity of the oppressed in a way that differs fundamentally from classical Marxism (Frostin, 1988, 182–3; C. West, 1984, 17; G. O. West, 2003).

Frostin's fifth and final emphasis is the dialectic between praxis and biblical interpretation. In liberation criticism, biblical interpretation is 'a second act' (Frostin, 1988, 10). The first act is the praxis of action and reflection. The action is actual action in a particular struggle; integrally related to this action is reflection on the action; and integrally related to this action-induced reflection is further action, refined or reconstituted by the reflection on and reconsideration of theory (and so on goes the cyclical process). Out of this first act of praxis second-order liberation biblical interpretation is constructed. How liberation interpretations are constructed and by whom is the subject of ongoing debate. Frostin favours a strong role for socially engaged middle-class theologians and organic intellectuals in assisting the poor to break their silence 'and create their own language' (Frostin, 1988, 10), but others, including myself, argue for a much more prominent place for the poor themselves (G. O. West, 1995; 2003).

G. O. W.

What are the landmark publications in liberation criticism?

Gustavo Gutiérrez (1971) *Teología de la Liberación. Perspectivas.* Salamanca: Ediciones Sígueme.

Translated into English as (1988) *A Theology of Liberation: History, Politics and Salvation*. London: SCM.

This book arose out of a series of meetings between Roman Catholic, Latin American theologians in which the relationship between faith and poverty was explored. This gave rise to an articulation of theology as a critical reflection on praxis, a statement which became very important in the discussion of liberation theology.

Leonardo Boff (1972) *Jesus Cristo Libertador. Ensaio de Cristologia crítica para o nosso tempo*. Petrópolis: Vozes.

Translated into English as (1978) *Jesus Christ Liberator: A Critical Christology for our Time*. London and Maryknoll: SPCK and Orbis.

Boff was a member of the same group as Gutiérrez and this book represents another significant voice which was articulating some of the theological and ideological presuppositions behind liberation theology. Fourteen years after publishing *Jesus Cristo Libertador* he published with his brother Clodovis Boff (1986) *Como Fazer Teologia da Libertacao*. Petrópolis: Vozes. This rapidly became one of the most influential books on liberation theology. It was translated into English as (1986) *Introducing Liberation Theology*. London and Maryknoll: SPCK and Orbis.

(1985) *The Kairos Document: A Theological Comment on the Political Crisis in South Africa*. London: Catholic Institute for International Relations.

A significant moment in African liberation theology was 1985 when a group of black South African theologians, based in Soweto, South Africa, produced the Kairos Document, in which the churches' attitudes to apartheid were challenged.

Liberation criticism in practice

Producing a practical example of liberation criticism is extremely difficult because by its very nature it arises out of communities of faith based among the poor and marginalized who read the text from their own experience and, out of this, find inspiration and hope for their everyday lives. This in its turn transforms their everyday living so that when they return to the text they see it anew (this is known as the hermeneutical spiral). It is community based, politically active, transformative reading of the Bible. The paradox for liberation criticism is that in order to report it, it is necessary to squash this multi-dimensional, ongoing and active means of reading the Bible into a one-dimensional snapshot. Almost by definition the transforming element that lies at the heart of liberation critical readings of the Bible is lost when it is presented to an outside audience; thus its most valuable element cannot be communicated easily. Most liberation criticism is in fact the work of biblical scholars who have read the Bible with their local community and have then gone away to reflect further on the passage using the tools of biblical scholarship.

The example I have chosen to discuss below is an example of this. Monika Ottermann in her article ' "How could he ever do that to her?" Or, How the Woman who Anointed Jesus became a Victim of Luke's Redactional and Theological Principles' (Ottermann, 2007, 103–16) does precisely this. She began her study of the woman who anointed Jesus in Luke 7.36–50 with her local community but then went on to explore the text in more detail using redaction critical scholarship.

The woman who anointed Jesus' feet: Luke 7.36–50

Ottermann's initial engagement with this story began in a study day on the story of the woman who anointed Jesus, which she was asked to facilitate during Lent for the women's association in the Northern Brazilian region of Bico da Papagaio. Because it was Lent, Ottermann set up their discussion focusing on John's account of the anointing of Jesus by Mary of Bethany (John 12.1–18), which she understood to be both an act of comfort for Jesus before his death and a revelation of the murder plot against him. In small group discussion, one of the groups discussed whether the Mary who anointed Jesus was in fact Mary Magdalene and they turned to Luke's Gospel, where they found the woman unnamed and called a sinner. When the small groups came back together they did not share their own life stories inspired by this story as was the custom; rather they wanted to explore Luke's telling of this story (Luke 7.36–50).

Ottermann records that she attempted to explain that the difference between the accounts was due to Luke adapting the core story into a different situation for his own audience but also that the women with whom she spoke were horrified. These women generally believed that Luke was a supporter of women and were distressed to discover his attitude to this woman; from Luke's use of the word 'sinner' they understood him to be describing her as a prostitute. Ottermann records the reaction of one woman in particular, saying that she 'grew pale and with a voice nearly fainting, she said to me "But Monika – how can you defend that! You know what one is suffering when one is judged a prostitute! You know what people say and what they do to us!" ' (Ottermann, 2007, 105); this was then followed by many, many stories from the rest of the women present who recounted their experiences in which their participation in political action had drawn forth accusations about their morals and private lives.

This in its turn led on to a discussion about the way in which men can react when patriarchal values are challenged by women. Many of the women shared stories of the ways in which the men close to them had reacted when they, the women present, had attempted to liberate themselves from the expectations on women. The question which they explored for the rest of the day was why someone like Luke, who they still saw as a friend of Jesus and kind to women, might have told the story in such a way that the woman was both unnamed and designated a 'sinner'. They sent Ottermann away to ask the question of 'Why would he do that to her?' (Ottermann, 2007, 105).

So did Luke 'do it to her'?

The rest of Ottermann's article records her research into this question of what Luke did to the tradition about the woman who anointed Jesus. As is often the case in liberation criticism, Ottermann's scholarly investigations were grounded in historical critical concerns like Synoptic relationships and historical background.

She concludes that there is a relationship between the four accounts of this story (Luke 7.36–50; Mark 14.3–9; Matt. 26.6–13; John 12.1–8) and that there are significant similarities as well as differences between the Markan account and the Lukan one; and that although John shows knowledge of the Markan account some features can only be explained by a knowledge of a second account such as Luke. A detailed exploration of the differences between Mark and Luke leads Ottermann to conclude that Luke did, indeed, 'do it to her' and that his version of the story is an adapted version of Mark which was at times somewhat forced (Ottermann, 2007, 110).

Why did he do that?

One feature of the Lukan technique is indeed to present more pictures of women than any other of the Gospels. But as D'Angelo has pointed out, although there are more pictures of women in Luke, their roles are also more prescribed by the conventions of the Roman empire. D'Angelo goes on to argue that Luke's own motivation of presenting Jesus as the best of all prophets prevents him from acknowledging that the woman's action here is a prophetic one, pointing forward to Jesus' suffering and death (D'Angelo, 1990; cited in Ottermann, 2007, 112–13). From this

Ottermann concludes that Luke deliberately changed the tradition about this prominent early woman leader in order to 'control and to cut down women's leadership of his time' (Ottermann, 2007, 113).

The nature of Luke's writing

This causes Ottermann to conclude that Luke's literary style was 'androcentric, macho and Christocentric', so Christocentric in fact that he denied the dignity of the human beings that Jesus encountered during his ministry (Ottermann, 2007, 115). She believes that he 'dirtied' the reputations of characters within the text in an attempt to preserve his community in the face of Roman imperialism. Thus in her view Luke's theology does not correspond to Jesus' interest.

Conclusions

Ottermann's engagement with the story of the woman who anointed Jesus is an excellent example of liberation critical analysis. It arose out of the concerns and passionate reactions to the story of poor women in Brazil whose own life experiences led them to be much more sympathetic to the woman who was a sinner than many other interpreters are. Indeed perhaps it would be better to describe their reaction not as sympathetic but as outraged. Liberation criticism often begins in emotionally engaged reactions to the text and to life's experience, which then become the lens through which the text is read.

There is much in Ottermann's interpretation of Luke's account that might be disputed, but to do so would be to detract from the process of reading that has taken place. Ottermann's engagement with the story is based upon the **standpoint** of liberation theology which, as we have noticed already, is passionately and politically engaged with the experiences of the poor. Her reading of the text as well as her use of redaction criticism reflects this, and it is this ideological stance that informs and shapes this interpretation of the text as well as liberation criticism in general.

Evaluation of liberation criticism

Like many of the criticisms in this third part of the book, liberation criticism is a form of reader-response criticism in that it pays attention to the circumstances, experiences and motivations of the reader with an eye to informing the way in which the reader engages with the world. Liberation criticism is clearly and comfortably subjective and rejects the assumption that anyone can be objective in reading the New Testament. In fact liberation criticism deliberately brings to the fore the subjectivity of the context in which readers function so that their life experiences can be a primary factor in the interpretation of the text.

One of the difficulties of evaluating liberation criticism is that the contexts of community readings in South America, Africa or India are very different from Western academic readings. It is neither possible nor desirable to declare that, for example, Ottermann's women's group should not have reacted to the text in the way that they did. Such reactions are genuine, and based in life experience even if they do not sit comfortably in the academic context in which other biblical scholars function.

A slightly more complex issue is the use of historical critical tools by liberation critics. Here is the apparently uncomfortable meeting of objective scholarship (historical criticism) with subjective scholarship (liberation criticism and other similar criticisms). The crucial factor to bear in mind here is that although liberation critics use the tools of **Enlightenment** scholarship, they do not subscribe to the philosophy that underpins them; a philosophy which supports objectivity, a single meaning of the text and a reliance on what the text 'meant'. Liberation critics are driven by an ideology that supports plurality of meaning, the vital subjectivity of the reader and, of course, solidarity with the poor. Also important is the fact that historical critical tools are used together with sociological tools; the historical critical tools delimit the text being interpreted but the sociological tools then analyse the context of struggle in which the text was produced. Liberation criticism uses historical critical tools with a different ideological framework; as such it remains a powerful critique not only of contexts (both those in which the text was originally written and the context in which it is now read) but also of New Testament scholarship and the way in which New Testament interpretation has reinforced oppression and the imbalance of power.

19

Sociopolitical criticism

What is sociopolitical criticism?

Sociopolitical criticism (also know as socioeconomic criticism or political readings) draws on the insights of liberation criticism to explore oppression and the uses of power. Unlike liberation criticism, it is often based in Europe and the USA.

What are the key features of sociopolitical criticism?
Ched Myers

During the 1970s Christian liberation theologies percolated throughout Latin America, Africa and Asia, as well as among poor communities struggling within industrialized countries. These theologies were

- grounded in practices of popular education among the poor pioneered by Paulo Freire;
- generated out of contexts of violence, poverty and oppression;
- often (though not always) aligned with social movements of revolutionary dissent (see Hennelly, 1990; Abraham, 1990; and McGovern, 1989).

During this same period a variety of 'political theologies' and Christian–Marxist dialogues emerged in Europe and the USA (Downey, 1999).

Liberation theologies animated 'political readings' of both Testaments that focused upon God's attentiveness to the poor; the prophetic insistence upon social justice; and the vocation of the Church to stand in solidarity with the marginalized (for example, Nolan, 1978). Such perspectives elicited denunciations from political and ecclesial leaders, including the Reagan White House and Pope John Paul II. But some First World Catholic and Protestant theologians paid close attention to them – usually because they too had experienced conditions of oppression at home or abroad.

Academic biblical scholars were much slower to respond to liberation theologies. A notable exception, however, was Norman Gottwald, whose sociopolitical interpretation of Israel's origins (*Tribes of Yahweh*, 1979) was groundbreaking in its use of sociological method and political hermeneutics. Though initially controversial, this work eventually transformed the discipline of biblical studies and laid down principles that can be seen in the work of New Testament scholars such as Richard Horsley.

In 1993 Gottwald and Horsley gathered a collection of essays by exegetes impacted by liberation theologies entitled *The Bible and Liberation: Political and Social Hermeneutics*, which identified four key 'chasms' in biblical studies.

- The perceived chasm *between religion and the rest of life*: although this chasm is experienced by many in 'structurally differentiated' modern societies, sociopolitical readings of the Bible would not recognize it in biblical history and literature, where religion is integral to the rest of life.
- A related chasm is perceived *between the past as 'dead history' and the present as 'real life'*. Sociopolitical criticism would see the Bible as being about political-economic life which is inseparable from a religious perspective and inspiration and is full of political-economic-religious conflict and struggle.
- Likewise thought *and practice* are no more separated in the Bible than are religion and political economy.
- The fourth chasm, the chasm *between biblical academics and popular lay Bible study* remains; but as biblical scholars recognize that their own enterprise and points of view are historically determined and parochial, and further recognize that certain popular readings display an affinity or analogy with certain views or struggles represented in biblical literature, even this chasm begins to seem bridgeable (see Gottwald and Horsley, 1993, xiv).

These four chasms represent an enduring statement of the problems addressed, and approaches embraced, by sociopolitical readings of the Bible (see also Rowland and Corner, 1990).

The conservative turn of culture and politics through the Reagan/Thatcher and Bush/Blair eras has seen liberation theology increasingly relegated to the activist margins of First World seminaries and churches. Ironically, however, a slow but steady stream of political and sociological readings of the Bible has emerged among a new generation of exegetes (compare Jobling, Day and Sheppard, 1991). Even excluding the categories that are treated separately in the present volume (such as feminist, black, and postcolonial), the field is broad enough to divide into four interrelated trajectories.

- There are a large number of *thematic studies*, driven by contemporary social concerns. These works survey biblical perspectives on specific issues such as economics (Miranda, 1974; Oakman, 1986; Schottroff and Stegemann, 1986; Ringe 1985), violence/nonviolence (Edwards, 1972; Weaver, 2001; C. Marshall, 2001; Swartley, 2006) and politics (Brandon, 1967; Yoder, 1972; Wink, 1984).
- A second trajectory of sociopolitical criticism can be seen in the way in which liberation theologies continue to fertilize engaged biblical study, despite less interest among First World publishers, whether this influence takes the form of methodology (Segovia and Tolbert, 1998; Clevenot, 1985; De La Torre, 2002; Ekblad, 2005) or of the reading of a specific text (Cassidy, 1987; N. Elliott, 1994; Tamez, 2007).
- A third trajectory overlaps with other techniques in this volume such as social-scientific criticism and explores social history (Horsley and Hanson, 1985; Horsley, 1989; Stegemann and Stegemann, 1999), socio-logical context (Stegemann, Malina and Theissen, 2002) and again the reading of specific texts from a sociological perspective (J. H. Elliott, 1990; Malina and Rohrbaugh, 1992; Herzog, 1994).
- The fourth, and final, trajectory is more interested in the narrative as a historically situated ideological production (Myers, 1988; Carter, 2000; Walsh and Keesmaat, 2004; Howard-Brook and Gwyther, 1999), or concentrates on 'reading against the grain' and exercising suspicion about how power functions within and around the text (Collins, 2005; Pippin, 1999).

Liberation hermeneutics and political readings disrupted whatever aca-demic consensus may have existed in biblical studies prior to 1975. As a result the field now is quite fragmented; it is hard to state with any certainty what approach to the text may be adopted in any one work of sociopolitical criticism. Nevertheless a significant watershed exists between those who engage texts from within and on behalf of ongoing social movements for change, and those who are content with academic 'deconstructionism'.

C. M.

What are the landmark publications in sociopolitical criticism?

Norman Gottwald (1979) *The Tribes of Yahweh: A Sociology of the Religion of Liberated Israel, 1250–1050 B.C.* Maryknoll: Orbis.

Gottwald was the first biblical scholar to apply political hermeneutics to the biblical narrative.

Norman Gottwald and Richard Horsley, eds (1993) *The Bible and Liberation: Political and Social Hermeneutics*. Maryknoll: Orbis.

Horsley applied a similar political approach to New Testament texts and in this volume collected together a range of 'liberative' interpretations of the Bible.

Neil Elliott (1994) *Liberating Paul: The Justice of God and the Politics of the Apostle*. Maryknoll: Orbis.

In this book Elliott explores the various different passages in Paul that have been used to support oppression and argues that they have been misunderstood and that Paul's message has been distorted.

Wolfgang Stegemann, Bruce Malina and Gerd Theissen, eds (2002) *The Social Setting of Jesus and the Gospels*. Minneapolis: Fortress.

This collected work explores the ways in which a clearer understanding of the social setting of both Jesus and the Gospels helps us to see how ancient economics and politics functioned within the teaching of Jesus.

Sociopolitical criticism in practice

The crucial difference between sociopolitical criticism and liberation criticism (explored in the previous chapter) is not so much the emphasis or aim of the criticism as the context out of which it emerges. Although there is a lot of overlap between these two, and in fact a blurring of terminology so that liberation criticism is also called socioeconomic or sociopolitical criticism, the difference is that the readings described in the previous section arise out of a community context which faces poverty and oppression; whereas the readings described in this section arise primarily in industrialized countries which are more isolated from communities which experience extreme poverty. Both have the same concern for transformation but arrive at their reading via a different route.

Wealth and power in 1 Timothy

Elsa Tamez's recent book on 1 Timothy, *Struggles for Power in Early Christianity* (Tamez, 2007) is an interesting example of a sociopolitical reading, both because she grounds her reading in a thoroughly academic context and also because she envisages her study being used among communities of the poor. Thus illustrating that any distinction that may exist between liberation criticism and sociopolitical criticism cannot be drawn too clearly; there are divergences but also convergences between the two.

As Tamez notes in her introduction, 1 Timothy is not an obvious choice to illustrate sociopolitical criticism in practice. Its emphases on a certain type of leadership, on women and on slaves do not make it a natural text for those seeking a reading from the perspective of the poor. Nevertheless, the epistle has certain sharp criticisms to make of the wealthy and it is these, as well as the passages on women and slaves which form the focus for Tamez's book. She follows a method derived from Schüssler Fiorenza (Schüssler Fiorenza, 1983; 1984) in which a historical reconstruction of the community is offered as a means for understanding why the text is saying what it does. The overall argument of the book is that it is written into a context in which the wealthy are seeking power on the grounds of their wealth.

Rich women in 1 Timothy 2.8—3.1a

Against a backdrop which appears to support hierarchy, the social systems of the day, and which appears to pay no attention to the needs of the oppressed, such as women and slaves, a few passages in 1 Timothy stand out. The first concerns one of the most discussed passages in the whole of 1 Timothy: 2.8—3.1a which attends to women's dress and whether they should teach within the community. This stands in stark contrast to the instruction to men and how they should behave within the Christian community, which is brief and instructs them only on posture (to pray with their hands raised 2.8) and on emotion (without anger or argument 2.8). Tamez's question, then, is why the disparity of instruction in this instance?

One of the key features of this passage, which Tamez notes, is that the description of the women's apparel indicates that they were wealthy: only those who were rich could afford to braid their hair, wear gold pearls or expensive clothes (2.9–10). Such a command in a context in which there were many poor women, she suggests, draws the attention to the fact that the criticism is about ostentation more than about indecency.

In order to understand this context more clearly Tamez points to the patronage system that existed in Graeco-Roman society. The patronage system established a relationship, albeit unequal, between the wealthy and the poor of a community: the patron gave protection and often money to someone in need, and in return that person would praise them for all their virtues and remain loyal to them. As Tamez notes, '(b)ecause honor was one of the fundamental values at that time, patrons needed praise in order to conserve their status and power in society' (Tamez, 2007, 9). Women as well as men could be a part of this system. Thus she reads the criticism in 1 Timothy 2 as directed not against women per se (though she recognizes that the epistle is negative about women as well) but against the rich women who had developed power and influence within the community, and supposes that the epistle might have been written in response to a complaint by the male leaders of the community whose authority these rich, powerful women were challenging.

Should the wealthy be rewarded for their favours? 1 Timothy 6.17–19

Tamez observes a similar principle taking place later on in 1 Timothy when the rich are exhorted not to be haughty, not to set their hopes on riches, to do good works, be generous and ready to share. As is often the case, exhortations such as these are only necessary when they are not generally being kept. Here the author directly addresses the rich, and the Greek word, here, can refer to rich men or the rich women featured in 2.8. When this command is set against the patronage system, outlined above, it makes even more sense. The rich are not to look to the patronage system for praise, honour and recompense. They should share their wealth as a matter of course and expect to receive reward from God and not from human praise.

Money is the root of all evil: 1 Timothy 6.3–10

Tamez finds a clue to what might have been going on within the community in 1 Timothy 6.3–10. She notes that

- verse 3 refers to those who teach 'otherwise' and whose teaching 'does not agree with the sound words of our Lord Jesus Christ and the teaching that is in accordance with godliness';
- verse 5b refers to those who believe that 'godliness is a means of gain';
- and verse 10 asserts that the root of all evil is love of money and that those who desire money will cause people to wander from faith and cause themselves pain.

Therefore, those who were advocating other teachings were those who believed that it was right to gain from godliness and who wandered from the faith in order to achieve this. In other words, those whose love of money drove them were preaching among the community a message that was contrary to Jesus' message in the gospel that they should give everything they owned to the poor. This seems to indicate that there was a group of people within the community – who either were already wealthy or sought to become so – who used what money they had to exert power within the community and to wrest leadership from others.

Conclusions

In her book Tamez uses the principles of historical criticism to reconstruct the community that lies behind the writing of 1 Timothy. What she sees is a community riven by issues of power, torn between the 'true' leaders of the community and those with wealth who sought extra power and indeed gain by seizing leadership. This, she believes, explains not only the attitudes to wealth in the epistle but also the extensive criteria for leadership set out in chapter 3 and the attitude to women in chapter 2, which she believes is really a critique against wealthy women who sought to abuse their power within the community.

Tamez's study is a classic example of sociopolitical criticism because it reads carefully the social, political and economic implications of the text to understand how power functioned within Timothy's community and challenges us to reflect further on how similar issues of power are raised within our own communities today.

An evaluation of sociopolitical criticism

In many ways the evaluation of sociopolitical criticism is the same as that for liberation criticism: both operate out of a belief in the need for the liberation of the poor and oppressed, and out of a desire to critique and overturn attitudes, including methods of biblical interpretation, which reinforce that oppression. In many, though not all cases, both combine the principles of reader-response criticism with historical critical methods, and the aim of both is to be transformative in as much as they affect what people do.

As mentioned above the main difference between the two is between the settings out of which they arise. Liberation criticism arises from local communities in which the poor and oppressed meet to read Scripture together; sociopolitical criticisms arise more within industrialized countries which, as a rule, have less experience of the extreme poverty we see in developing countries. Thus sociopolitical criticism seeks to transform the interpretation of those with power and wealth and to encourage them to take action in the world. A good example of this is Ched Myers's excellent commentary on Mark, *Binding the Strong Man* (Myers, 1988), which has been widely used within industrialized countries (as well as in the developing world) as a means of understanding how biblical interpretation can be a call to action.

20

Black criticism

What is black criticism?

Black criticism explores the New Testament from the experience and perspective of black readers, pointing to the ways in which black people have been treated both in the text and in subsequent New Testament interpretation.

How did the theory develop and what are its main features?
Emerson B. Powery

Most scholars (Mosala, 1989; Brown, 2004) recognize that black New Testament criticism developed out of the black theology movement which was formed out of black consciousness struggles (in the USA and in South Africa) in the 1960s and 1970s. This is true if 'criticism' is defined as the application of standard forms of *higher biblical* criticism among academically trained minorities. On the other hand, 'critical' approaches to biblical texts have a much longer and more complicated history within black reading practices (Wimbush, 2003).

In academic circles, the turning point for black engagement with the Bible came with the publication of two books: Itumeleng Mosala, *Biblical Hermeneutics and Black Theology in South Africa* (1989), and a collective effort, *Stony the Road We Trod: African American Biblical Interpretation*, edited by Cain Hope Felder (1991). These volumes have become 'standards' in theological seminaries and divinity schools throughout several continents. Both volumes take seriously the experience of black communities from which they derive and not only the scholarly assumptions and methodological practices of white, European tradition(s) on biblical interpretation.

Itumeleng Mosala's project appropriates a historical-materialist reading of Micah and the Gospel of Luke for the purpose of providing a hermeneutically liberating interpretation 'tested on the grid of black history and culture' (Mosala, 1989, 5). One of the primary assumptions behind his interpretative decisions was the ideological bias of the Bible itself. As he concludes, '(I)t is liberating to recognize that not every God of every biblical text is on the side of the poor'; sometimes the text depicts God's favour for those who are privileged (Mosala, 1989, 8).

The *Stony* project is a collection of essays written by a group of US scholars who gathered together regularly, over a five-year period, to discuss their experiences within the Academy. This effort generated working papers, which eventually led to this publication. Their goal was to establish, in the words of Felder, 'precedent that would begin a tradition of African American collaboration in biblical scholarship' (Felder, 1991, xi). Aware of a common goal, their exegetical methods were nonetheless diverse and the group also included the two 'mothers' of **womanist** biblical scholarship (Clarice Martin in New Testament and Renita Weems in Hebrew Bible).

More recent developments within black New Testament criticism have come in larger cultural-ethnographic and cultural-literary projects, such as Musa Dube's work *Postcolonial Feminist Interpretation of the Bible* (2000), the collective effort organized by Vincent Wimbush (2000) *African Americans and the Bible*; Gay Byron's (2002) *Symbolic Blackness and Ethnic Difference in Early Christian Literature*; Allen Callahan's (2006) *The Talking Book: African Americans and the Bible*; and the most recent engagement in a collective commentary project by African American New Testament scholars and edited by Brian Blount and others (2007) *True to Our Native Land*.

Fundamental to any 'black' approach to any biblical text are the notions of 'liberation' and 'survival' (D. Williams, 1993), both of which are derived from the history of black experience worldwide. Randall Bailey has helpfully divided black scholarship on the Bible into four categories (see Bailey, 2000, 696–711):

1 interpretations on the African presence in the Bible;
2 responses to racist interpretations of the text;
3 cultural interpretation from the perspective of black readers;
4 ideological assumptions of the biblical text itself.

None of these areas of scholarship are limited to persons of black descent only. Yet, in each area of investigation, there is a particular stance an interpreter assumes. In categories (1) and (2), the 'black' reader frequently must 'read against the grain' of much scholarship which (un)intentionally overlooks the role and presence of 'Africans' in biblical accounts or deliberately offers an interpretation to foster the myth of white supremacy. In categories (3) and (4), the 'black' reader must occasionally 'read against the grain' of the biblical text itself when its own ideological tendencies hinder the full humanity of all peoples, as in cases in which texts support enslavement and violence directed by 'God'.

To place race, gender, class and ideology on the forefront of engagement with a biblical text establishes readers' assumptions (and the texts' assumptions, for that matter) *and* assists interpreters to make evident both the politics of their own social locations and biases and that of the ancient stories. Teresa Okure has offered a Nigerian proverb as an appropriate guide to interpretation, '*Inuen afruroke ke enyong ukot asiwot isong*' ('the legs of the bird that flies in the air always point to the ground'). In like manner, 'black' biblical interpretation will consider the implications of its conclusions for the liberation and survival of *all* peoples.

E. B. P.

What are the landmark publications in black criticism?

James H. Cone (1969) *Black Theology and Black Power*. Maryknoll: Orbis.

James Cone is widely regarded as being one of the founders of the black theology movement, from which black New Testament criticism emerged.

Itumeleng Mosala (1989) *Biblical Hermeneutics and Black Theology in South Africa*. Grand Rapids: Eerdmans.

In his influential book, Mosala seeks to develop a hermeneutic with which he could rescue the liberative themes that exist in the Bible, from other strands in the Bible which work against liberation.

Cain Hope Felder, ed. (1991) *Stony the Road We Trod: African American Biblical Interpretation*. Minneapolis: Fortress.

This volume contains a diverse range of methods of biblical interpretation from an African-American perspective and was influential in raising the profile of black criticism within biblical studies.

Brian Blount, Cain Hope Felder, Clarice Martin and Emerson B. Powery, eds (2007) *True to Our Native Land: An African American New Testament Commentary*. Minneapolis: Fortress.

This significant collection of essays focuses attention on the broad range of methods employed within black criticism and also on issues that black interpretations highlight within the text.

Black criticism in practice

In common with most of the chapters in this part of the book, it is impossible either to present an interpretation which is 'representative' of black criticism, or even to draw together a number of examples on a single text to illustrate what black criticism is like. Black criticism is as varied and diverse as the readers who interpret the text. The example below explores Clarice Martin's seminal article on the 'household codes' (the sections of the epistles that deal with how people, particularly women and slaves, should behave within the household, Colossians 3.18—4.1; Ephesians 5.21—6.9; 1 Peter 2.18—3.7) and the impact that these passages have had on the lives of African-Americans (see C. Martin, 1991, 208). Martin's article also represents a womanist critique of her own African-American background. Womanist criticism is particularly critical of the patriarchy within African-American churches but also of the ways in which white feminists have colluded in the oppression of their African-American sisters. Since womanism does not have a dedicated chapter in this volume Martin's article provides a helpful way of seeing some of the concerns of womanism as well.

Subordinate relationships within the household codes

One of the first features to notice about the household codes is that they establish three separate groups of people (women, slaves and children) who are each subordinate to a single male/master/father, although not all the codes have all three: Ephesians 5.21—6.9 and Colossians 3.18—4.1 have the three pairs but 1 Peter has only husbands and wives, and slaves (but not masters) (see C. Martin, 1991, 208). These household codes reflect Graeco-Roman norms. Households within the Graeco-Roman world were strongly hierarchical, based around a *paterfamilias*, or head of the household, upon whom the rest of the household depended for its livelihood. This role as *paterfamilias* was regarded by many ancient writers as the fundamental structure for the whole of society. For example, Martin gives the illustration of Philo, who argued that the household was the training ground for all future statesmen: once they learned to govern the households sufficiently they would be in a position for high office within the state (Philo, *On Joseph* 38–9, cited in C. Martin, 1991, 209).

One of the major areas of dispute among scholars is how the household codes functioned within Christian communities. There are many possible positions to take on this subject, but Martin identifies three major ones (see C. Martin, 1991, 210–12):

- One view, proposed by Herzog, is that the codes were taken by the Church from the world outside and given a new motive within Christian communities not based so much on Graeco-Roman society as on acting 'as is fitting in the Lord'.

- The second view, held by scholars such as Balch, regards following these codes as a form of *apologia* or witness to the world outside. Conforming to societal norms would have increased outsiders' respect for the community and thus, potentially, prevented their suffering from persecution.
- The third view, as maintained by Schüssler Fiorenza, argues that the household codes were in fact a retreat from the principle of the 'discipleship of equals' (Schüssler Fiorenza, 1983, 140–54) found in earlier forms of New Testament discipleship, a retreat that was thought to be necessary in order to resolve the tensions that had arisen within the patriarchal households of the early Christian communities, where people no longer observed the loyalties to the *paterfamilias*.

Whatever view is taken of the reason that the Christian communities had for enforcing the submission of slaves, women and children to the *paterfamilias*, or head of the household, the effect has been the same on those who have been deemed to be subordinate to the *paterfamilias*-type character in that they have been treated as inferior both socially and intellectually.

Slaves and African-American interpretation

The household codes formed the centre of the debate about slavery in the eighteenth and nineteenth centuries. These passages were interpreted by the pro-slavery lobby as a divine mandate for slavery and the way in which slaves were treated. Martin cites a particularly famous case from North Carolina in 1829, when the court argued that a slave 'was to labor "upon a principle of natural duty" without regard to his or her own personal happiness', a judgement which is thought to have been influenced by a certain interpretation of the household codes (see C. Martin, 1991, 214).

As Martin notes, African-American and white abolitionist sympathizers' responses to interpretations such as these were fundamental in the fight against slavery and she cites the example of H. D. Ganse, who argued that this passage was designed to *limit* the power of the slavemasters not to *confer* it. Thus they were to treat the slaves with respect and dignity (see C. Martin, 1991, 216). African-American interpretations of passages such as these are a significant example of liberatory hermeneutics at work as early as the nineteenth century. African-Americans remained faithful both to the Bible and to their call for freedom, and interpreted the text accordingly. James Evans has argued that three major principles under-girded such interpretations:

171

- Slave regulation was regarded as not exemplifying the gospel, nor as being central to its main thrust.
- Slavery was not considered to be the main focus of the epistles in which the household codes are found.
- Probably most importantly, Paul was understood as 'not Christ', and although he strove to attain the fullness of the gospel he did not possess it (Evans, 1981, cited in C. Martin, 1991, 217).

This **hermeneutic** is important because it illustrates an attitude to humanity not shared in the pro-slavery readings of the texts. Such African-American interpretations function out of the understanding that all humanity shared an equal kinship with God which ruled out any form of human bondage; whereas pro-slavery readings of the text operate a more hierarchical perspective in which the equivalent of the *paterfamilias* can hold authority over his subordinates.

Free slaves and submissive women?

In her article, Martin then went on to explore similar questions about the relationship between husbands and wives, though as she notes this has widely become used 'to reinforce patterns of male domination of women in church and society' (C. Martin, 1991, 221). Thus the husband and wife relationship has become interpreted as the relationship between men and women in general. Women are widely regarded as 'complementary' to men, thus as Carter Hayward and Suzanne Hiat notably commented, '(the) Masculine model is the rational, orderly head and leader; the feminine model the emotional, chaotic, submissive heart, which follows and supports' (Hayward and Hiat, 1978, 160 cited in C. Martin, 1991, 222).

This dynamic, however, is different in African-American contexts from in white contexts, since, although there are strictures against women's leadership in certain African-American churches, women have always exercised power and influence; whereas in white contexts this has not been the case.

Reflections on hermeneutical paradoxes

One of the intriguing features of black criticism of the New Testament, however, is that, although a clear and well articulated method of interpretation has been brought to bear on the household codes as regards their attitude to slavery, a very different approach is used as regards attitudes towards women: 'New Testament narratives that prescribe hierarchical patterns of dominance–subordination between men and women have *not* been perceived to be as troublesome and offensive as those that prescribe hierarchical patterns of dominance–subordination between slavemasters and slaves' (C. Martin, 1991, 225). It is hard to understand why a fully worked-out hermeneutic that addressed one aspect of the household codes (slavemasters and slaves) was not then equally applied to another element of it (men and women).

Martin raises this question starkly by asking why it is that those people who use liberating hermeneutics when discussing the relationship between slaves and slavemasters use a literalist one when talking about women and men (see C. Martin, 1991, 226). Martin proposes two major factors that might explain this apparent paradox.

- She notes that the liberation of the Hebrews from slavery in Exodus 14 has played a vital role in the shaping of African-American attitudes to slavery. This has caused them to challenge the presuppositions behind literalist interpretations of slavery in the household codes; but since nothing similar to Exodus 14 exists that might have shaped an attitude to women, a similar challenge towards interpretations of the texts about women has not been forthcoming.
- Also important, she believes, is that many African Americans accept patriarchy as the norm and have not challenged this attitude.

Conclusions

Martin's article is a helpful illustration of black criticism on many levels, since it demonstrates some of the major issues that have (and others that have not) shaped black criticism of the New Testament. Martin's argument functions both as critical reception history, noting where and how passages like the household codes have been interpreted through Christian history in ways that have added to the oppression of black people and of women, and as sociological exploration of the factors that might have caused such a passage to be written in the first place. Her comments highlight how easy it is to develop a liberating hermeneutic about one area of human experience, while omitting to notice that a second area of oppression goes unnoticed and uncritiqued.

Evaluation of black criticism

Martin's article helpfully demonstrates the variety and breadth of writing that exists within black criticism: she writes from an African-American perspective as well as from a womanist **standpoint**. Some of the points she makes about African-American experience and interpretations of the New Testament are specific to her own context, and would be only partially reflected in a black British or African interpretation of the text. Of course, examples from other scholars would have presented a different range of issues and concerns.

Black criticism is an essential voice within New Testament scholarship, reminding readers of the ways in which the biblical writers have portrayed black characters within the Bible; of the ways in which New Testament interpretation through the centuries has ignored, overlooked and entrenched prejudice towards black people; and of the consequences of these attitudes in the lives of black people both throughout history and today. The way in which the Bible was used to support the slave trade is a particularly shameful example of the impact of New Testament interpretation on the lives of black people; black criticism reminds us, however, that such attitudes did not end with the demise of the slave trade and are as much in need of critique now as ever before.

21

Postcolonial criticism

What is postcolonial criticism?

Postcolonial criticism interprets the Bible from the perspective of those who seek to engage with the legacy of colonial rule.

How did the theory develop and what are its main features?
R. S. Sugirtharajah

Postcolonial studies emerged in the 1970s; first in departments of English literature and later making its way into other disciplines. It is associated with the study of sacred texts, historical documents, colonial records and fictional accounts of societies which had been invaded and disrupted by European colonialism and was initiated in Edward Said's book *Orientalism* (Said, 1978). The task of postcolonial studies is twofold:

- to analyse how European scholarship codified and studied colonial cultures;
- to recover how the resistant writings of the colonized tried to redeem their cultures and restore their identity and dignity.

Postcolonialism began its career as a resistant and creative literature, and only later was turned into a theoretical category. It is seen no longer as a natural evolutionary progression following on from the departure of imperial powers, but as a series of critical and political protests since the beginning of modern colonialism.

The central aim of postcolonial criticism is to situate empire and imperial concerns at the centre of the Bible and biblical studies. In doing so, it has enhanced biblical studies in a number of ways.

1 It has brought to attention the importance of empire – Assyrian, Egyptian, Persian, Greek and Roman – at the centre of many biblical narratives, providing the social, cultural and political framework. While mainstream scholarship restricts our understanding to theological, spiritual and historical aspects of these narratives, postcolonialism adds the often neglected dimension of politics, specifically the politics

of imperialism. In doing so, it interrogates the text in various ways, asking, for example:

- How does the author portray the empire – as benevolent or oppressive?
- Does the text support the imperial intentions of the empire, or oppose these?
- Where do the loyalties of the author lie – with the imperial power or with those subjugated by it?
- How does the author represent the occupied – as victims or as grateful beneficiaries?
- Does the author provide space for their resistance?

When reading a text like the Gospel of Mark, postcolonialism highlights both the imperial oppression of the Roman empire and the absence of ordinary people from the imperial loop. It also investigates ways in which the book has been interpreted, drawing attention to the marginalized and the outcast.

2 Postcolonialism has been vigilant about representation and has exposed how both biblical figures and the colonized and their cultures have been distorted and defamed in the colonial and theological literature. One such much maligned figure is Mary Magdalene. Utilizing the discarded Gospel of Mary, postcolonialism attempts to reconfigure the story of Mary Magdalene, showing how a once exemplary leader has been turned into a repentant sinner by later male ecclesiastical writers (e.g. King, 2006). It has also exposed stereotypical images of the 'other' as 'lazy' and 'unreliable' in the writings of so-called liberal scholarship.

3 The retrieval hermeneutics embarked on by postcolonial criticism has unearthed the imaginative ways in which the colonized have appropriated the Bible. Taking advantage of the biblical idea of salvation history, the victims of European colonialism were able to justify both their resistance to colonial rule and their defence of their disparaged culture. The presence of the Bible played an influential role in re-linking the newly converted Christians to their own scriptural traditions. This enabled them not only to draw attention to God's presence in their own religious traditions, which had been disparaged by missionaries, but also to claim, in certain cases, that the spiritual insights in their own scriptures were more illuminating than those in the Bible. The Indian convert K. M. Banerjea's claim that the Hindu Vedas contained superior notions of the sacrificial lamb is a notable case in point (Banerjea, 1875). These resistant discourses were a timely reminder that the colonized were capable of recovering and restoring the 'pure gospel' which had been distorted

by the vested interests of Western denominationalism and cultural imperialism.

4 Postcolonial criticism has been able to intervene in the area of biblical translation and repair the cultural and theological damage often done in that process. An illustration of this is that when the Bible was translated into Shona (the native language of the Shona people of Zimbabwe and southern Zambia) the translation made God a male, whereas the Supreme Being of the Shona people has no gender specificity.

5 Postcolonial criticism has been vigorous in addressing issues that have emerged in the wake of colonialism such as nationhood, migrancy, diaspora, multiculturalism and hybridity.

Although eclectic in its use of methodologies, postcolonialism can call contrapuntal reading its own. Unlike the earlier and questionable comparative method, which was binary and judgemental, contrapuntal reading sees connections and creates bonds between texts and treats them as equal partners. By juxtaposing texts – Christian and non-Christian, sacred and secular, Western and Eastern – postcolonialism not only avoids the rhetoric of blame and denunciation but also draws attention to discrepancies and complementarities in them.

Postcolonial reading has made Western interpretation more accountable and sensitive to the 'other'. Unlike other liberative movements, which try to replace, for instance, a sexist Bible with a feminist version, postcolonialism is not in the business of cleansing the Bible of its colonial impulses and substituting a counter-imperial version. Postcolonialism sees the Bible as a contested and ambiguous book. At a time when there are new forms of colonialism, the usefulness of postcolonial insights becomes even more evident and urgent.

R. S. S.

What are the landmark publications in postcolonial criticism?

Edward Said (1978) *Orientalism*. London and New York: Routledge and Pantheon.

In this book Said critiqued the assumptions made of the West by the East and laid the foundations for much subsequent postcolonial theory.

Musa W. Dube (2000) *Postcolonial Feminist Interpretation of the Bible*. St Louis: Chalice Press.

In her book Dube critiques Western biblical interpretation for the way in which it reinforces patriarchy and the oppression of those who live in other parts of the world; but she also proposes alternative reading strategies which pay particular attention to the needs of women from the two-thirds world.

Fernando F. Segovia (2000) *Decolonizing Biblical Studies: A View from the Margins*. Maryknoll: Orbis.

In this significant book, Segovia explores the principles that underpin a wide range of contextual readings of Scripture, and shows the ways in which they critique the dominant paradigm of biblical interpretation.

R. S. Sugirtharajah (2000) *Postcolonial Criticism and Biblical Interpretation*. Oxford: Oxford University Press.

Sugirtharajah is widely regarded as one of the most influential Sri Lankan voices writing in the area of postcolonial criticism of the Bible. This book explores the origins, principles and significance of postcolonial criticism.

Moore, S. D. and F. Segovia, eds. (2005) *Postcolonial Biblical Criticism: Interdisciplinary Intersections*. London and New York: T&T Clark.

The value of this book is that it not only explores the significance of postcolonial criticism, but also offers an internal critique of the way in which it functions.

Postcolonial criticism in practice

One of the most significant passages for many of the criticisms in this third part of the book is the story of the Syro-Phoenician woman in Mark 7.26–30, with its parallel in Matthew 15.22–28 where the woman is described as a Canaanite. This story has had great impact because it recounts the story of a woman who has no power or place within Jesus' society and who insists that Jesus help her and her daughter. One of the most thorough and specifically postcolonial interpretations of the story can be found in Musa Dube's book *Postcolonial Feminist Interpretation of the Bible*, which addresses issues of feminism as well as colonialism in her interpretation of the passage.

The Canaanite woman: Matthew 15.22–28

In the first half of her book Dube establishes a method of reading the Bible which she then employs on Matthew 15.22–28, the healing of the Canaanite woman's daughter. Dube calls her method of interpreting the Bible 'Rahab's prism', drawn from the story of Rahab in Joshua 2.1–21. The power of this story for Dube is that Rahab, as a harlot, is vulnerable both to her male compatriots in Jericho and to foreign men, who seek

178

to destroy her city and possess her land. Dube understands both of these (patriarchy and invasion by a foreign army) as colonizations which 'overlap and intertwine but are not identical or translatable to one another' (Dube, 2000, 121). 'Rahab's prism' is valuable insomuch as it reveals the layers of colonization and oppression that exist and invites those variously engaged in colonization or decolonization to recognize the layers of oppression that function in different communities.

Matthew's community as colonized but seeking favour with the Empire

Dube begins her exploration of this story by assessing the **implied author** of Matthew's attitude to the Roman empire. She notes that, throughout Matthew's Gospel, representatives of Rome are presented as having a capacity to perceive God, whereas the local Jewish leaders are portrayed as hypocritical and intransigent. For example, Pilate in the trial scene in Matthew 27.11–26 is presented as keen to let Jesus go; he is advised by his wife that he should not kill Jesus and is determined to maintain his innocence about Jesus' death. In contrast, the Jewish leaders are determined that Jesus should die and thwart Pilate's every attempt to proclaim Jesus innocent. Dube's conclusion is that Matthew is an example of a 'collaborative postcolonial narrative' which deflects the root cause of oppression from the empire and focuses on other oppressors, in this case the Jewish leaders. The implied author of Matthew, she concludes, is attempting to gain 'favor with the Empire for his/her community' and stands in conflict with a rival group of Jewish leaders (Dube, 2000, 135) and this affects the way in which he presents his narrative.

Matthew 15.21–28 and decolonization

Dube identifies this story as a 'land possession type-scene' (Dube, 2000, 144). What she means by this is that encounters with a woman in a story often symbolize the colonization of the land she represents. The story of Rahab is an excellent example of this; the spies' encounter with Rahab prefigures the subsequent conquering and colonization of her land. Matthew 15.21–28 is emphasized as such a scene by the author's changing her name from 'Syro-Phoenician' woman to 'Canaanite' woman; as Dube notes, Canaan is not just a place name but also an ideologically loaded geographical marker since it brings to mind Joshua's subjugation of the land and allies the woman with the victims of the settlement (Dube, 2000, 146).

This dynamic is highlighted by the characters in the story. Dube identifies two major types of character in a land possession-type scene: 'imperializing characters' and their 'foreign victims' (Dube, 2000, 146). It becomes clear, early in the story, that Jesus is superior as a result not only of his divine authority but also his privileged class and race that allow him to travel beyond his own land; the Canaanite woman, by contrast, is emphasized as racially inferior (as a 'dog' who 'can only eat crumbs from under the table', Matt. 15.27) and a foreigner who had no input into the writing of this story. In Dube's opinion this contrast is exacerbated by the way in which the implied author of Matthew has edited the Markan source by introducing the woman as a Canaanite (ripe for subjugation and conquest) and by increasing the condition of her daughter from having an unclean spirit (Mark 7.25) to being 'severely possessed' (Matt. 15.22).

The dialogue between Jesus and the woman further exacerbates the contrast between the characters. Jesus first ignores the woman, then informs her that his concern is only for the house of Israel and finally identifies her as a dog; the woman in contrast perseveres, driven by her great need of Jesus and accepts Jesus' insult towards her. In this first stage of reading, then, Dube explores the text for signs of imperialism and notes the ways in which location, description, character and dialogue enforce the ideology of empire within the story itself.

White Western readings of Matthew 15.21–28 and decolonization

Dube's next step is to turn to interpretations of the text. Dube believes that all interpretations are shaped either by communities that 'advance and collaborate with colonizing institutions of education' or by those that 'reject and decolonize the imperializing texts in their critical practices' (Dube, 2000, 157). She analyses various 'white western male' interpretations (Dube, 2000, 158–69) followed by a number of 'white western feminist' interpretations (Dube, 2000, 169–82). She reaches a range of conclusions (see Dube, 2000, 168–9 and 182–3), some of the most important of which are:

- that these interpreters do not take into consideration the context of the implied author of Matthew within an imperial occupation for understanding how issues of power, and relationships to the Romans as well as other 'rival groups', might affect the portrayal of the story;
- that male interpreters, in particular, read the Gospel as an antiquated text and not one that might inform relationships between nations and genders in the modern world;

- that although the feminist writers are more alert to issues of power in gender relationships, they seem unaware of the ways in which 'privileged races' have achieved this position by constructing themselves as superior to other races;

- that discussions of mission seem to 'continue to reassert that biblical religions are universally valid for all cultures, despite the disputation of non-Christian worlds'.

All of this reinforces for Dube the importance of depatriarchalizing as well as decolonizing texts before it becomes possible to reclaim them.

Liberating interdependence as a means of interpreting the text

Dube proposes a reading technique which she calls 'liberating interdependence'. What she means by this is the acknowledgement that most current interconnection is oppressive and exploitative; liberating interdependence seeks to build up the connection in such a way that honours, values and affirms the dignity of all people. Thus Dube asked women from the African Independent Churches (AIC) to answer questions about the passage based on a questionnaire and did not rely solely on her own interpretation of the text.

Dube called the reading grid that she developed the 'Semoya Reading Grid'; Semoya means 'of the spirit' and it was this that guided most of the interpretations proposed by the AIC women. Dube argues that it is Moya, the spirit, that enabled members of the AIC to resist the dominant colonial readings of the missionary-founded churches and to found their own independent churches. This spirit she sees in their refusal to see Israel or Canaan as exclusive terms. Within their readings of this passage Israel was reinterpreted to mean all those who believe and Canaan to be a 'rich land of faith, sought by all Israelites' (Dube, 2000, 188 and 192). She notes that the women insisted on reading the text in line with a belief in inclusiveness and in the significance of the healing of relationships between people.

Another important feature is that AIC women refuse to be limited to the written word. They hear and are affected by the word of the spirit and so refuse to reproduce stories told about them which reinforce their oppression; instead they 'retell and weave their own stories of healing and empowerment'. They see beyond the written text, therefore, to places where God is at work healing all kinds of social ills; the AIC women, like the Canaanite woman, 'join hands with God in a constant protest and struggle against institutional oppression' (Dube, 2000, 195).

Conclusions

Dube's reading of the text has three levels:

- The first level identifies the ways in which the implied author of Matthew has shaped the narrative from a perspective that seeks support from the Empire, that differentiates between those who are superior (Jesus) and those inferior (the Canaanite woman) and reinforces the oppression of the Canaanite woman by associating her with a land, Canaan, historically dominated by the Israelites.
- The second level critiques the way in which both male and female white Western critics overlooked aspects of oppression within the text.
- The third level presents a different way of reading – a method that celebrates the liberating potential of true interdependence and that relies on community reading as a means of resisting the oppressions enforced both in the text and in interpretations of it.

These three together seek to decolonize the text's interpretation and then to reclaim it for those most affected by such colonization and to find liberation from the oppression that flows from this colonization.

Evaluation of postcolonial criticism

Dube's form of postcolonial criticism has much in common with liberation, feminist and womanist criticisms.

- Like liberation critics, she seeks to identify and overturn the oppression of poor communities, and to read the text with people from within these communities.
- Like feminist critics, she seeks to identify the ways in which patriarchy functions both within the New Testament and in interpretations of it to reinforce the oppression of women.
- Like womanist critics, she critiques the attitude of white Western feminist criticism which ignores the differences of power that exist between white Western women and their sisters from around the world.

But while postcolonial criticism (in common with the other criticisms in this part of the book) is a varied discipline that draws on other criticisms, it also remains distinct from all of these criticisms insomuch as its major critique is of the ideology of colonialism and empire and the many effects of colonization. It highlights how the often unacknowledged acceptance of an empire's domination shapes texts and interpretations, as well as attitudes towards those who are victims of such domination. One of postcolonial criticism's biggest contributions is the way in which it draws attention both to the impact of empire and colonization on ancient and modern societies and to the widespread implicit acceptance of that impact by New Testament authors and interpreters alike. It is fair to say that those unaffected by oppression can often remain blind to its effects and postcolonialism battles against this.

22

Asian criticism

What is Asian criticism?

Asian criticism explores the Bible from the wide-ranging experiences and perspectives that readers have of Asia. It can sometimes overlap with postcolonial interpretation since some readers read both the Bible and Asia from postcolonial contexts.

How did the theory develop and what are its main features?
Tat-siong Benny Liew

It is important to realize that Asian criticism of the New Testament is both fluid and diverse. Besides the cartographic politics of continental and national demarcation (that is, the questions that surround where boundaries should lie between continents as well as countries), one needs to realize that methodological, theological and linguistic differences exist between and within nations in Asia. This is important since, with the continually growing population of mixed or multi-raced persons and the ever-expanding Asian diasporas, debates over what or who is 'Asian' become more complicated and cannot be limited to the geographical borders of nations within the Asian continent. Without denying that non-Asians may participate in Asian criticism of the New Testament (especially white missionary preachers and theological educators in Asia), I will, keeping in mind not only the power differential between Asians and whites but also the context of this volume, restrict my discussion to Asian scholars who have published in English as I proceed to discuss the history and sensibilities of Asian criticism.

When early Christian traditions from Palestine reached today's so-called Asia proper is debatable (although Indian traditions have suggested that it had happened as early as the mid-first century CE – that is, before most of the New Testament books were written, not to mention canonized). Because this volume deals with New Testament criticism since the beginning of modern, critical biblical scholarship in Europe, I will start with the colonial and missionary movement by whites around the modern era. These two overlapping movements (critical biblical scholarship and the colonial and missionary movement) have continued to influence Asian criticism, whether the methodological emphasis is on 'event', 'text' or 'reader', although criticisms that give explicit attention to readers and/ or ideologies are more likely to bring about readings that are also more explicitly 'Asian'. Put differently, the practice of Asian criticism is fluid and diverse enough to engage basically all of the criticisms represented in this volume (see for example, Kinukawa, 1994; Yamaguchi, 2002). The fact that Asian criticism has connections and similarities with other criticisms – and at times even uses them all in one big *bricolage* (something made by putting together a wide range of objects) – does not mean that it does not have its own distinctions.

Almost as soon as the New Testament became available in Asian lan-guages – thanks largely to Protestant missionaries in the eighteenth and nineteenth centuries, and their Reformation emphasis on the Bible – Asians have put the New Testament into conversation with their own native traditions and/or sociopolitical realities (see also Kwok, 1995, 8–19). These native traditions may be literary texts and/or religious beliefs that have long been honoured, recognized and/or practised, although one should remember that literary and religious traditions can be one and the same, since many Asian religions have their own collection of sacred texts. When attempts are made to put these religiocultural traditions alongside the New Testament, they tend to go in two distinguishable though not necessarily mutually exclusive directions.

- On the one hand, there are attempts that try to establish some kind of correspondence between the New Testament and Asian traditions to make the New Testament more culturally accessible or agreeable. Yeo Khiok-khng, a Chinese Malaysian who teaches on both sides of the Pacific, has compared the *yin–yang* worldview of the Chinese with the concept of 'rest' in the book of Hebrews, as well as the Chinese understandings of *li* and *jen* with Paul's emphasis on torah and spirit in Romans (1998, 65–105 and 129–61). Similarly, India's Vengal Chakkarai had, several decades earlier, compared Jesus' incarnation in the Gospel of John to the Hindu concept of *avatar*, the bodily manifestation of a divine being on earth (1930).
- On the other hand, there are attempts that take the more aggressive path of using parallels or similarities within their own traditions to diminish the New Testament's claim as a unique divine revelation, or highlight-ing differences to challenge the New Testament's adequacy. An example would be Stanley J. Samartha of India, who questions the exclusive claims

185

of and for Christ in the New Testament, and proposes that different faith traditions and sacred texts need to engage and enrich each other (1987; 1994).

Since these religiocultural traditions often have long and continuous influence, their separation from contemporary sociopolitical situations is also more heuristic (a tool used to facilitate or further investigation) than absolute. Raja Rammohan Roy, a Bengali Brahmin in India, for example, used the Synoptic Gospels even before the historical-critical methods had been fully developed, to urge for moral reform among his fellow Hindus *and* usurp simultaneously the white missionaries' interpretation of the New Testament (1820). This is a common feature of Asian criticism, which often employs similar dialogical moves (that is, moves akin to the give-and-take of a back-and-forth dialogue) between the New Testament and a particular sociopolitical situation, so that the New Testament informs the situation or the situation is used to critique the New Testament. Examples of this include:

- Yeo, mentioned above, who has also used Paul's writings to challenge Mao Zedong's understandings and policies (2002).
- Byung-mu Ahn of Korea, who has argued for identifying Mark's *ochlos* or 'crowd' as the oppressed minjung of Korea, and thus the latter as the audience and recipients of Jesus' message and mission of liberation (1981).
- Carlos H. Abesamis of the Philippines, who has referred to both Mark and Q to contend for the liberating nature of Jesus' mission (1987; see also Abesamis, 1990).
- Dhyanchand Carr of India, who has used Matthew to establish 'a biblical basis for Dalit theology' (1994).
- Jean K. Kim, a Korean American feminist, who reads John's Gospel and Korean nationalist movements of the twentieth century alongside each other to conclude that both are guilty of sacrificing women for masculinist causes (2004).

This dialogical emphasis of Asian criticisms has two more characteristics. First, with its emphasis on native traditions or sociopolitical situations, these readings tend to be rather explicitly theological. Employing theological resources from both within and beyond Asia, the line between theology and biblical studies in Asian criticism is much more blurred than has been traditional within New Testament studies.

Second, references to native traditions and/or sociopolitical situations also place Asian criticism into closer and greater connection with postcolonial criticism. R. S. Sugirtharajah, a Sri Lankan who teaches in England, has done much to develop Asian criticism in this direction (1998). While Sugirtharajah tends to use Asian traditions and situations to 'talk back' to the New Testament, postcolonial criticism also intersects with Asian criticisms that employ the New Testament as a resource or an ally for postcolonial resistance (see for example Joy, 2005; S. H. Kim, 2006), although, again, Asian criticism does not always engage the New Testament in such binary terms. Simon Samuel of India, for example, has read Mark as a 'colonial conundrum' with both pro-colonial and anti-colonial dynamics (2007).

T.-s. B. L.

What are the landmark publications in Asian criticism?

Asian criticism is so wide-ranging that it is not really possible to provide 'landmark' publications as it is with other criticisms: the volumes listed below have been influential but many, many others could – and probably should – have been included before any sense of 'landmark' publications can be achieved.

Rammohun Roy (1820), *An Appeal to the Christian Public, in Defence of the 'Precepts of Jesus'*, Calcutta.

This volume is significant because it demonstrates that as early as 1820 Roy was using the New Testament in dialogue with his own context, both urging reform and critiquing the New Testament interpretation of the missionaries.

Kwok Pui-lan (1995) *Discovering the Bible in the Non-Biblical World*. Maryknoll: Orbis.

Kwok Pui-Lan is known internationally for her pioneering work in Asian feminist theology. This book illustrates the many levels and methods at work within Asian criticism and argues for the Bible as a 'talking book', that is, one which engages in conversation with its readers.

Yamaguchi Satoko (2002) *Mary and Martha: Women in the World of Jesus*. Maryknoll: Orbis.

Yamaguchi explores the women in John's Gospel from a Japanese feminist perspective and argues for the importance of historical re-imagination.

Yeo Khiok-khng (2002) *Chairman Mao Meets the Apostle Paul: Christianity, Communism, and the Hope of China*. Grand Rapids: Brazos.

This book illustrates the significance of dialogue with the context of the author and shows, through conversation with the writings of Chairman Mao, the mutually transforming value of such a conversation.

Mary F. Foskett and Jeffrey Kah-Jin Kuan, eds (2006) *Ways of Being, Ways of Reading: Asian American Biblical Interpretation.* St Louis: Chalice.

This significant volume presents a range of articles which illustrate the variety of methods that exist even within Asian American criticism of the Bible.

Asian criticism in practice

As Liew has illustrated so well above, Asian criticism is broad and wide-ranging. Like many of the criticisms in this part of the book, any one practical example chosen cannot capture the entirety of the criticism. Asian criticisms range from Japanese feminist approaches to Indian postcolonial studies and Korean liberative interpretations, to mention only three of an ever expanding range. There are many practical illustrations that I could use to demonstrate Asian criticism in practice, and choosing only one will, of course, simply show one way in which one scholar has interpreted the New Testament from an Asian perspective. With this in mind, I have decided to use an article that has been influential in subaltern interpretation – that is, relating to people thought to be of lower status in a society (see for example Joy, 2005) – but which is somewhat different from the other texts used in, for example, the chapters on postcolonial criticism or black criticism in this volume.

Ahn Byung-mu produced an essay in 1981, reprinted in 1991 in *Voices from the Margin*, called 'Jesus and the Minjung in the Gospel of Mark', in which he explored the role of the crowd in Mark's Gospel from a subaltern perspective. 'Minjung theology' grew up in the 1970s in South Korea and is a people's theology which seeks to overturn the social injustice that affects all those who are marginalized, oppressed or exploited within society.

The crowd in Mark and minjung theology

One of the central groups of people within Mark's Gospel is the crowd, who follow Jesus' ministry and are amazed by what he does. Interestingly, one of the effects of form criticism and redaction criticism has been to downplay the significance of the crowd in Mark. Form criticism has focused on the sayings of Jesus to the exclusion of the framework, including the crowd, in which they are embedded; while redaction critics, more interested in the framework of the Gospel, focused more on the understanding of Jesus' identity and mission than on the role of the people in the story (see Ahn, 1991, 87–8).

The people play an important role in Mark's Gospel. Ahn notes that they initially appear unnamed and unidentified in the narrative, being referred to as *polloi* or 'many', until in Mark 2.4 they are designated with the Greek word *ochlos* or crowd, which then occurs 36 more times in the Gospel. Ahn also draws attention to the fact that Mark seems to choose not to use the word *laos* or people, which occurs about 2,000 times in the **Septuagint**. Both of these factors seem to indicate that this word was important for Mark, and that it was he who introduced it into the vocabulary of the New Testament, since it does not appear in any texts written before Mark, whereas it is common in the Gospels and Acts which post-date it (see Ahn, 1991, 88).

Characteristics of ochlos *in Mark*

Ahn notes that the people who make up the *ochlos* have five major characteristics in Mark (see Ahn, 1991, 89–90):

1 they follow Jesus around and form the backdrop to his ministry (for example, 'the whole crowd gathered around him, and he taught them', Mark 2.13);
2 they are often sinners: *ochlos* is the collective noun often used to describe the tax collectors and sinners (for example, 'many tax collectors and sinners were also sitting with Jesus and his disciples – for there were many who followed him', Mark 2.15);
3 they are differentiated from the disciples whom Jesus teaches on other occasions without the *ochlos* (for example, 'And leaving the crowd behind, they took him with them in the boat, just as he was', Mark 4.36);
4 they are opposed to the Jewish leaders, who attack Jesus as their enemy (for example, 'Now some of the scribes were sitting there, questioning in their hearts, "Why does this fellow speak in this way? It is blasphemy! Who can forgive sins but God alone?"', Mark 2.6–7, as opposed to, 'they were all amazed and glorified God, saying, "We have never seen anything like this!"', Mark 2.12);
5 the Jewish leaders were afraid of them and tried not to provoke them (for example, 'And when the chief priests and the scribes heard it, they kept looking for a way to kill him; for they were afraid of him, because the whole crowd was spellbound by his teaching', Mark 11.18).

He also notes that Jesus has compassion towards the crowd, calling its members his family, and that he taught them many things. The contrast with the Jewish ruling classes emphasizes that the *ochlos* was poor, marginalized and alienated from the centre of power and was also from Galilee and not Jerusalem, where the power was focused. The crowd consisted of sinners, tax collectors, the sick and others who were on the outskirts of society. Thus when Jesus states that he came to call sinners and not the righteous, this seems to imply a particular relationship with the *ochlos*.

The meaning of ochlos

Ahn then goes on to explore what the word *ochlos* might have meant for Mark, causing him to use it so prominently in his Gospel. Although there is extensive discussion about the precise nature of the '*am ha'aretz* in Jewish tradition, Ahn maintains that Mark's usage of *ochlos* is to be understood as the equivalent of this phrase, which literally means 'people of the land'. Although before the Exile the '*am ha'aretz* were the wealthy aristocrats, during the Exile, the land passed to those who remained in the land and so the phrase became used of the lower classes, who had not been taken away at the same time as the exiles. Later Rabbinic Jewish texts proscribe interaction with the '*am ha'aretz*, and there are numerous derogatory references to them in the Talmud, where the word seems almost synonymous with 'ignoramus'. Ahn argues that during the time of Jesus '*am ha'aretz* designates social status and so is the equivalent of Mark's *ochlos* (see Ahn, 1991, 99–100).

The ochlos *and the minjung*

Ahn concludes that *ochlos* and minjung are equivalent terms. Both words, he maintains, refer to all those who are marginalized by virtue of their unequal relationship to those in power: the word *ochlos* is not an abstract concept but a relational one. Tax collectors fit into the category, not because they are poor, but because they are despised by and marginal within the society in which they live. The term is fluid and includes all those who are on the outskirts of society, for whatever reason. He also maintains that the *ochlos*, or minjung, have great power because they are feared by the rich and powerful, even though they do not use this power for their own gain.

There is a strong relationship between Jesus and the *ochlos*: he accepts them as they are and never rebukes them; he does not try to organize them into anything that they are not:

> He does not forcibly demand anything from them. He does not ask to be their ruler or head. He 'passively' stands with them. A relationship between

190

Jesus and the minjung takes place and then is broken. They follow him without condition. They welcome him. They also betray him. (Ahn, 1991, 100)

Conclusions

In this article, Ahn demonstrates how context and the New Testament text can dialogue with each other: he considers a particular aspect of his own context – an understanding of the minjung as marginal to society – and reads this alongside the *ochlos* of Mark's Gospel. Thus Jesus' attitude to the *ochlos* is understood to demonstrate his attitude towards all minjung. The contribution that Ahn's article makes is that it identifies a group in Mark's portrayal of Jesus' ministry which are often overlooked or identified simply as a foil for Jesus or the attitudes of the disciples. Ahn argues that they are important in their own right and, in fact, are central to Jesus' calling: tax collectors and sinners are part of the *ochlos* and hence of the minjung, and it is to them that Jesus has come. Thus Ahn brings to the New Testament an acute understanding of marginal groups within society, from his own context, which he uses to comprehend more fully the marginal groups of Mark's Gospel so that, in turn, Jesus' attitude towards this group, the *ochlos*, might be applied to Ahn's own context, the minjung.

Evaluation of Asian criticism

Like many criticisms in this third part of the book, Asian criticism engages both with the text of the New Testament and with the context of the interpreter, and often brings the two into dialogue with each other using the insights gained from one to illuminate the other (Bible to context, context to Bible, or both). The nature of many Asian contexts means that there is overlap between Asian criticism and postcolonial criticism; although the example given in the previous chapter happened to be drawn from Musa Dube, a prominent African postcolonial interpreter, it could just as easily have been drawn from a number of different Asian postcolonial interpretations.

The many different Asian contexts inform a wide variety of possible Asian interpretations. It is impossible to propose any one 'contribution' that Asian criticism makes to New Testament scholarship and to do so would be to miss the point. Asian criticism consists of many different ways of reading the text that arise in Asian contexts and from Asian readers; they do not so much contribute to New Testament scholarship as open up new worlds of meaning centred around the many experiences, cultures and insights of the continent of Asia.

23

Ecological criticism

What is ecological criticism?

Ecological criticism refers to a recent but growing interest in reading biblical texts in the light of the environmental and ecological challenges that face us in the twenty-first century.

How did the theory develop and what are its main features?
David G. Horrell

Unlike some of the well-established forms of biblical criticism, eco-logical criticism does not represent a clearly defined or widely practised 'method' in biblical studies. Since a variety of perspectives and approaches are adopted, any definition (like the one above) must remain somewhat broad.

The general reason for the rise of this approach to biblical interpreta-tion is the growth of ecological concerns, and increasing awareness of the impact of human activity upon the planet. A more specific stimulus was the critique of the Christian tradition provided in a classic article by Lynn White, Jr, published in 1967. White argued that the Christian worldview, rooted in the creation stories and the notion of humanity made in God's image, had introduced a dualism between humanity and nature, and established the notion that it was God's will that humanity exploit nature to serve human interests. Thus Christianity, according to White, bears 'a huge burden of guilt' (White, 2000, 40) for introducing the Western worldview that has essentially permitted and fostered what White called 'our ecologic crisis'.

Many ecologically orientated readings of the Bible have thus been con-cerned to defend it against the charge that it necessarily promotes a human-centred ('anthropocentric') ideology which legitimates aggressive and damaging exploitation of the natural world. Such readings have sought to show how the biblical texts offer resources for a positive attitude towards non-human creation. For example, attention has been drawn to the emphasis on the goodness of all creation (Gen. 1.4, 10, 12, etc.), to God's covenant with the whole earth (Gen. 9.9–17), to the idea of creation's praise in the Psalms (Pss. 96; 148), to the decentring of humanity in the book of Job (38.1—42.6), and to the visions of a peaceable, non-violent new creation in the book of Isaiah (Isa. 11.6–9; 65.25).

In the New Testament, ecotheologians have found valuable material in Jesus' attitude to creation (Matt. 6.25–34; Luke 12.22–31), in the Pauline descriptions of creation's liberation and of the whole cosmos reconciled in Christ (Rom. 8.19–23; Col. 1.15–20), and in Revelation's visions of a renewed heaven and earth (Rev. 21—22). At the same time, passages apparently speaking of the future destruction of the earth (such as Joel 2; Mark 13; 2 Pet. 3.11–13) have been re-examined in an effort to rehabilitate them.

Particularly influential, and important in response to White's critique, is the emphasis on the notion of 'stewardship' as a biblical model for the relationship of humanity to the rest of creation. On this reading of the potentially negative concept of 'dominion' (Gen. 1.26–28; Ps. 8.6), humanity is not empowered to dominate creation for human benefit, but is, rather, given a responsibility for careful and compassionate management of the world's resources. Indeed, a focus on stewardship as a biblical image of humanity's role in the world is central to the recent realignment of major evangelical leaders and bodies behind a more environmentally conscious vision of Christian responsibility.

However, the most methodologically developed approach to ecological criticism is represented in the five volumes of the Earth Bible series, produced by the Earth Bible Team between 2000 and 2002. In contrast to the approach outlined above, the members of the Team are somewhat sceptical of attempts to portray the Bible as 'ecofriendly'. They do not by any means deny that there is ecologically valuable and instructive material in the Bible, but insist that an engagement must be critical, prepared also to expose and resist the material which is anthropocentric and damaging to Earth. Their approach to the biblical material is guided by a series of ecojustice principles (see Habel, 2000, 24):

1 *The principle of intrinsic worth.* The universe, Earth and all its components have intrinsic worth/value.
2 *The principle of interconnectedness.* Earth is a community of interconnected living things that are mutually dependent on each other for life and survival.
3 *The principle of voice.* Earth is a subject capable of raising its voice in celebration and against injustice.

4 *The principle of purpose.* The universe, Earth and all its components are part of a dynamic cosmic design within which each piece has a place in the overall goal of that design.

5 *The principle of mutual custodianship.* Earth is a balanced and diverse domain where responsible custodians can function as partners, rather than rulers, to sustain a balanced and diverse Earth community.

6 *The principle of resistance.* Earth and its components not only suffer from injustices at the hands of humans, but actively resist them in the struggle for justice.

The key task for an ecological reading of a biblical text, then, is to discern whether 'the text is consistent, or in conflict, with whichever of the six eco-justice principles may be considered relevant' (Earth Bible Team, in Habel and Balabanski, 2002, 2). This leads different authors to be critical of some texts, appreciative of others, and, as with feminist criticism, requires the operation of both suspicion and retrieval. In this way, the writers in the Earth Bible project practise a form of ecological criticism which engages biblical texts from a perspective committed to an explicit model of eco-justice. However, if such an approach is to contribute significantly to an ecological reconfiguration of Christian theology, through a new engagement with the biblical texts, it would seem necessary not only to read the texts in the light of 'ecojustice principles', but also to show what kind of ecojustice principles can emerge from, and remain congruent with, the biblical and Christian tradition.

D. G. H.

What are the landmark publications on ecological criticism?

The relative infancy of ecological criticism, in comparison to the other subjects of this book, means that there are fewer landmark publications in the field. Two, however, stand out:

Lynn White, Jr (1967) 'The Historical Roots of our Ecologic Crisis', *Science* 155, 1203–7, reprinted in R. J. Berry, ed. (2000) *The Care of Creation*. Leicester: IVP, 31–42.

This brief but influential article placed the blame for the current ecological crisis on the worldview introduced by Western Christianity, which gave humans a divine commission to exploit the earth for human ends.

Norman C. Habel, ed. (2000) *Readings from the Perspective of Earth*, Earth Bible 1. Sheffield: Sheffield Academic Press.

Norman C. Habel and V. Balabanski, eds (2002) *The Earth Story in the New Testament*, Earth Bible 5. Sheffield: Sheffield Academic Press.

The first and fifth volumes in a five-volume collection present a range of readings of biblical texts, including New Testament texts, which are informed by the ecojustice principles outlined above.

Ecological criticism in practice

Generally speaking, much more work has been done on the Hebrew Bible from an ecological perspective than on the New Testament. This is illustrated by the five-volume Earth Bible series, which has only one of those five volumes dedicated to the New Testament. Although the New Testament has attracted less attention from ecological criticism, one passage has been especially important, Romans 8.18–22, because of its emphasis on the groaning of creation in relation to salvation. A recent example of an ecological approach to this text is Brendan Byrne's article 'Creation Groaning: An Earth Bible Reading of Romans 8.18–22' (2000).

The groaning of creation: Romans 8.18–22

Byrne acknowledges that Paul may seem to be an unlikely conversation partner in the area of ecological criticism. For many years Pauline scholarship was so preoccupied with justification by faith and, as a result, with the relationship between God and humanity, that all else was squeezed out of discussion. Yet different trends in Pauline scholarship over the past thirty years or so have widened discussion of Paul's theology in such a way that other themes have become important once more. In Byrne's view one of the key features of Paul's argument is the conflict between human sinfulness and God's grace and, within this, Paul discusses the creation traditions of Genesis 1—3. These allusions form the backdrop to Romans 8.18–22 but also to Romans 5.12–21 (see Byrne, 2000, 194–5).

Interconnectedness, the 'sin story' and the 'grace story'

Byrne understands Paul's argument in Romans 5 to be about the interconnectedness of humanity and the ways in which the actions of one person impact upon others: 'There is an interconnectedness binding all together – for good or ill' (Byrne, 2000, 195). Adam represents the negative side of this interconnectedness and Christ the positive. Byrne argues that for Paul sin is not to be identified with 'concrete acts' but with the tendency to act 'selfishly and destructively' (195), but that this is set against 'grace'. Thus Romans 5 tells two parallel stories, the 'sin story' and the 'grace story', with the clear understanding that 'the grace story is the more powerful of the two' (196). It is against the foundations laid down in Romans 5 that Byrne believes that Romans 8.18–22 should be read, because here Paul picks up, once more, the 'grace story' that was so clear in chapter 5.

Romans 8.18–22 and Genesis 1—3

Although Romans 8 does not quote directly from the creation narratives of Genesis, they are woven deeply into its fabric. The whole of Paul's argument here is based on the principle that since humanity and the rest of creation were created by God alongside each other, they share a common fate: 'When the situation of human beings deteriorates, so does that of the rest of the creation and, vice versa, when it goes well, the creation shares in the same blessing' (Byrne, 2000, 197). Byrne points to the cursing of the earth as a result of Adam's sin, as the origin of this idea, but also identifies numerous other moments when the earth joins in with Israel's fate; most notable are Isaiah's prophecies of the mountains singing for joy (Isa. 44.23), trees clapping their hands (Isa. 55.12) and deserts becoming oases at the return from exile (Isa. 35.1).

Thus in Romans 8.21–22 the same principle is at work: creation yearns for the revealing of the children of God because its fate is linked to theirs; only once it comes to pass will creation also be set free from its bondage. It is in bondage against its will (8.20) and the groaning is a symbol of positive yearning for a time when, along with God's children, it will be free from 'the subduer' (8.20).

Creation and anthropocentrism

Byrne acknowledges that Paul presupposes a triangular pattern, derived from Genesis 1.26–28, of relationship between God, humanity and the created order in which humanity has supremacy over the created order. He argues, however, that although this anthropocentrism exists, Paul's argument here critiques such an attitude and proposes a new way of being which, though still anthropocentric, is less exploitative.

Byrne views the reference in verse 20 to the 'subduer' as referring, not to God as it has often been presumed to do, but to Adam and hence humankind. The significance of this for Byrne is that then this verse becomes a part of the 'sin story', in which humanity dominates and maltreats creation. As he established in Romans 5, however, the 'sin story' is only half of Paul's narrative here; the other half is the 'grace story'. Just as exploitation is a part of the 'sin story', so care and responsibility for the planet are a part of the 'grace story' when humanity acts in accordance with God's will. Humans remain in dominion over the planet but they act differently.

Byrne acknowledges that Paul does not go as far in his argument as one might wish him to. His discussion of the interconnectedness of all humanity does not stretch to the non-human created world: a marked contrast still exists between humanity and the rest of creation in that human beings still control the non-human created order. Nevertheless, Romans 8.18–22 expresses a connection between the fate of human beings and that of creation: a positive outcome for humanity will transform creation.

Resurrection and redemption of the body

One of the intriguing features of Romans 8.18–22 is that Paul does not, here, choose to talk about resurrection, an idea so central to his theology elsewhere, but of 'the redemption of our bodies' (8.23). Byrne suggests that this is because Paul did not, here, wish to suggest the discontinuity of death followed by resurrection and instead spoke of continuity and transformation. A mention of resurrection might have implied that the world whose fate was so tied to that of humanity was disposable and temporary, whereas Paul's emphasis here seems to be more on the continuity of the current world.

Conclusions

Byrne does not pretend that Paul's theology provides easy pickings for those who wish to provide ecological criticism, but what he does is to demonstrate that Paul is not as dualistic, nor as influenced by the idea of the dominance of the non-human created order by humanity, as some might suppose him to be. Romans 8.18–22 certainly does seem to point to an attitude that values the created order and its connection to the fate of humanity. As Byrne points out, if we add this to Paul's emphasis on the importance of the body, then his theology becomes much more affirmative of the created order than some have supposed. Although it has been traditional to view Paul as downplaying creation in favour of the realm of the spirit, passages like Romans 8.18–22 disrupt such assumptions and challenge us to look again at Paul's theology of the non-human created world.

Evaluation of ecological criticism

In comparison with the other criticisms presented in this volume, ecological criticism is new and still developing. Its standpoint on matters of ecology means it raises similar issues to other criticisms in the third part of this book. As White's influential article indicated, Western Christianity and its interpretation of the Bible have played an important part in shaping attitudes that have led to the practices that threaten the welfare of the planet. Ecological critics, therefore, may choose either to challenge traditional interpretations of the text and propose readings that are more ecologically friendly (as Byrne has done in the example above) or to read the text against the grain and to challenge its presuppositions (as for example Habel, 2000, 76–82). The work that is emerging so far indicates that both these approaches are being adopted.

It is unlikely that we will ever reach a stage in which the Bible can be demonstrated to be 'eco friendly'. Even if the layers of environmentally damaging interpretations can be stripped away, attitudes such as Byrne describes in Paul, which see humanity as given predominance over creation, are woven deeply into the text. Nevertheless, there are numerous passages which disrupt assumptions of human domination of creation to such an extent as to challenge our attitudes and relationships to the non-human created order. Only time can tell whether ecological criticism will become as great a force in New Testament interpretation as some of the other more established disciplines, but its current contributions which confront our assumptions about the planet and the New Testament's attitudes to creation are valuable in and of themselves.

Glossary

'am ha'aretz: literally the people of the land, in later Rabbinic literature the phrase was synonymous with people who are to be despised and avoided.

Enlightenment: a movement that believes in the importance of the application of human reason.

Hellenistic: the literature and culture of the Greek empire in all its forms.

Hermeneutics: the science of interpretation (particularly of Scripture) and hence a particular method by which it is done.

Implied author: a term used in literary criticism, as well as elsewhere, to refer to the notional person or people 'implied' by the text as the original author of the text, who may or may not be the same as the actual author. For example in English literature the actual author might be male but might create a fictional female – an 'implied author' – to tell his story.

Implied reader: a term used in literary criticism, as well as elsewhere, to refer to the notional person or people 'implied' by the text as its original recipient(s). The implied reader stands in contrast to the actual reader who is reading the text in the twenty-first century.

Midrash: a form of Jewish interpretation of Scripture, used particularly by the Rabbis, which often explored the link between two passages of Scripture.

Modern/modernity/modernism: a period of time (nineteenth–twentieth centuries), and hence attitudes adopted by those who live in that time, which emphasizes the importance of human reason. In New Testament studies, it gave rise to a concern to discover the original meaning of the text by the careful use of seemingly scientific techniques such as source criticism.

New criticism: a method of interpretation widely used in English and American literary criticism which believes that texts can have multiple meanings at any one time.

Postmodern/postmodernity/postmodernism: responses to or reactions against modernism's concerns for rationality, science and objectivity.

Q: thought by many scholars to be a common source shared by Matthew and Luke. An abbreviation of the German *Quelle* meaning source.

Semiotics: sometimes called semiology by French scholars, is the study of the connection between words and the concepts that they represent.

Septuagint: a Greek translation of the Hebrew Bible with some additional texts in Greek, probably translated between the third and first centuries BCE. The legend that it was translated by 72 different translators has given rise to its abbreviation **LXX** (70), the nearest round number to 72.

Standpoint/standpoint criticism: an approach to the New Testament which arises from a particular and conscious subjective standpoint, for example feminist or liberation criticism. For more on the difficulties with using this term, see p. 108.

Synoptic problem: the question of the literary relationship between Matthew, Mark and Luke.

Two-source hypothesis: the theory proposed by source critics which argues that Mark and Q form the two earliest written sources of Gospel material.

Womanism/womanist criticism: a movement or criticism which emerges from the experience of women of colour, often African Americans.

References

Abesamis, C. H. (1987) 'The Mission of Jesus and Good News to the Poor: Exegetico-Pastoral Considerations for a Church in the Third World', *Asia Journal of Theology* 1/2, 429–60.

Abesamis, C. H. (1990) 'Some Paradigms in Re-reading the Bible in a Third-World Setting', *Mission Studies* 7/1, 21–34.

Abraham, K. C., ed. (1990) *Third World Theologies: Commonalities and Divergences.* Maryknoll: Orbis.

Abrams, M. H. (1979) 'How to Do Things With Texts', *Partisan Review* 46, 566–88.

Adam, A. K. M. (2006) *Faithful Interpretation.* Minneapolis: Fortress.

Adam, A. K. M., S. Fowl, K. Vanhoozer and F. Watson (2006) *Reading Scripture With the Church.* Grand Rapids: Baker Academic.

Ahn, B.-m. (1981) 'Jesus and the *Minjung* in the Gospel of Mark', in Commission on Theological Concerns of the Christian Conference of Asia, ed., *Minjung Theology: People as the Subjects of History*, Maryknoll: Orbis, 138–52, reprinted in R. S. Sugirtharajah, ed. (1991) *Voices from the Margin: Interpreting the Bible in the Third World.* London and Maryknoll: SPCK and Orbis, 87–102.

Aichele, G. (1997) *Sign, Text, Scripture: Semiotics and the Bible.* Sheffield: Sheffield Academic.

Anderson, R. D. (1996) *Ancient Rhetorical Theory and Paul*, Contributions to Biblical Exegesis and Theology 18. Kampen: Kok Pharos.

'Asian Women Doing Theology' (2004), *In God's Image* 21/4 (special thematic issue).

Bailey, R. (2000) 'Academic Biblical Interpretation among African Americans in the United States', in V. Wimbush, ed., *African Americans and the Bible: Sacred Texts and Social Textures.* New York and London: Continuum, 696–711.

Banerjea, K. M. (1875) *The Arian Witness: Or the Testimony of Arian Scriptures in Corroboration of Biblical History and the Rudiments of Christian Doctrine, Including Dissertations on the Original and Early Adventures of Indo-Arians.* Calcutta: Spink & Co.

Barthes, R. (1970) *S/Z.* Paris: Éditions du Seuil (ET (1974) *S/Z.* New York: Hill & Wang).

Barthes, R. (1972) *Mythologies.* London and New York: J. Cape and Hill & Wang.

Barthes, R. (1985) *The Fashion System.* London and New York: J. Cape and Hill & Wang.

Barthes, R. (1988) *The Semiotic Challenge.* London and New York: J. Cape and Hill & Wang.

Barthes, R. and H. D. Balzac (1974) *S/Z.* London and New York: J. Cape and Hill & Wang.

Barton, J. (2002) *The Biblical World.* London and New York: Routledge.

Bauckham, R. (1998) *Gospels for All Christians: Rethinking the Gospel Audience*. Edinburgh and New York: T&T Clark.

Bauckham, R. (2006) *Jesus and the Eyewitnesses: The Gospels as Eyewitness Testimony*. Grand Rapids: Eerdmans.

Belleville, L. (2005) 'Ἰουνιαν . . . ἐπίσημοι ἐν τοῖς ἀποστόλοις: A Reexamination of Romans 16.7 in Light of Primary Source Materials', *New Testament Studies* 51, 231–49.

Berry, R. J., ed. (2000) *The Care of Creation*. Leicester: IVP.

Betz, H. D. (1979) *Galatians: A Commentary on Paul's Letter to the Churches in Galatia*, Hermeneia: A Critical and Historical Commentary on the Bible. Philadelphia: Fortress.

Beuken, W. and S. Freyne (1995) *The Bible as Cultural Heritage*. London and Maryknoll: SCM and Orbis.

Bible and Culture Collective (1995) *The Postmodern Bible: The Bible and Culture Collective*. New Haven: Yale University Press.

Blasi, A. J., J. Duhaime and P.-A. Turcotte (2002) *Handbook of Early Christianity: Social Science Approaches*. Walnut Creek, CA: Alta Mira.

Bleich, D. (1978) *Subjective Criticism*. Baltimore: Johns Hopkins University Press.

Blount, B. K. (1995) *Cultural Interpretation: Reorienting New Testament Criticism*. Minneapolis: Augsburg/Fortress.

Blount, B. K. (2001) *Then the Whisper Put on Flesh: New Testament Ethics in an African Context*. Nashville: Abingdon.

Blount, B. K., C. H. Felder, C. Martin and E. B. Powery, eds (2007) *True to Our Native Land: An African American New Testament Commentary*. Minneapolis: Fortress.

Bockmuehl, M. (2006) *Seeing the Word: Refocusing New Testament Study*. Grand Rapids: Baker Academic.

Boff, L. (1972) *Jesus Cristo Libertador. Ensaio de Cristologia crítica para o nosso tempo*. Petrópolis: Vozes (ET (1978) *Jesus Christ Liberator: A Critical Christology for our Time*. London and Maryknoll: SPCK and Orbis).

Boff, L. and C. Boff (1986) *Como Fazer Teologia da Libertacao*. Petrópolis: Vozes (ET (1986) *Introducing Liberation Theology*. London and Maryknoll: Burns & Oates and Orbis).

Booth, W. C. (1983) *The Rhetoric of Fiction*, 2nd edn. Chicago: University of Chicago Press.

Bornkamm, G. (1948) 'Die Sturmstillung im Matthäusevangelium', *Wort und Dienst. Jahrbuch der Theologischen Schule Bethel* 1, 49–54 (ET 'The Stilling of the Storm in Matthew', in G. Bornkamm et al., eds (1963) *Tradition and Interpretation in Matthew*. London and Philadelphia: SCM and Westminster Press, 52–7).

Boswell, J. (1980) *Christianity, Social Tolerance and Homosexuality*. Chicago: University of Chicago Press.

Bouma-Prediger, S. (2001) *For the Beauty of the Earth: A Christian Vision for Creation Care*. Grand Rapids: Baker Academic.

Brandon, S. G. F. (1967) *Jesus and the Zealots*. New York: Scribner.

Brooten, B. J. (1985) 'Paul's Views on the Nature of Women and Female Homoeroticism', in C. Atkinson, C. Buchanan and M. Miles, eds, *Immaculate and Powerful*. Boston: Beacon, 61–87.

Brooten, B. J. (1996) *Love Between Women: Early Christian Responses to Female Homoeroticism*. Chicago: University of Chicago Press.

Brown, M. (2004) *Blackening of the Bible: The Aims of African American Biblical Scholarship*. Harrisburg, PA: Trinity Press International.

Bultmann, R. (1921) *Die Geschichte der synoptischen Tradition*. Göttingen: Vandenhoeck & Ruprecht (ET (1963) *The History of the Synoptic Tradition*. Oxford and New York: Blackwell and Harper & Row).

Burer, M. H. and D. B. Wallace (2001) 'Was Junia Really an Apostle? A Reexamination of Rom. 16.7', *New Testament Studies* 47, 76–91.

Butler, J. (1990) *Gender Trouble*. London and New York: Routledge.

Byrne, B. (2000) 'Creation Groaning: An Earth Bible Reading of Romans 8.18–22', in N. C. Habel, ed., *Readings from the Perspective of Earth*, Earth Bible 1. Sheffield: Sheffield Academic, 187–203.

Byron, G. L. (2002) *Symbolic Blackness and Ethnic Difference in Early Christian Literature*. London and New York: Routledge.

Callahan, A. D. (2006) *The Talking Book: African Americans and the Bible*. New Haven: Yale University Press.

Calloud, J. (1976) *Structural Analysis of Narrative*, Semeia Studies. Philadelphia and Missoula: Fortress and Scholars Press.

Campbell, B. L. (1998) *Honor, Shame, and the Rhetoric of I Peter*. Atlanta: Scholars Press.

Carr, D. (1994) 'A Biblical Basis for Dalit Theology', in J. Massey, ed., *Indigenous People, Dalits: Dalit Issues in Today's Theological Debates*. Delhi: ISPCK, 231–49.

Carter, W. (2000) *Matthew and the Margins: A Sociopolitical and Religious Reading*. Maryknoll: Orbis.

Cassidy, R. (1987) *Society and Politics in the Acts of the Apostles*. Maryknoll: Orbis.

Castelli, E. (1991) *Imitating Paul: A Discourse of Power*. Louisville: Westminster John Knox.

Chakkarai, V. (1930) *Jesus the Avatar*, 2nd edn. Madras: Christian Literature Society for India.

Chatman, S. (1978) *Story and Discourse: Narrative Structure in Fiction and Film*. Ithaca: Cornell University Press.

Childs, B. S. (1984) *The New Testament as Canon: An Introduction*. London and Valley Forge: SCM and Trinity Press International.

Chilton, B. (1994) *A Feast of Meanings: Eucharistic Theologies from Jesus through Johannine Circles*. Leiden and New York: E. J. Brill.

Chilton, B. (2000) *Rabbi Jesus: An Intimate Biography*. New York: Doubleday.

Chilton, B. (2004) *Rabbi Paul: An Intellectual Biography*. New York: Doubleday.

Chilton, B. and J. Neusner (2007) *In Quest of the Historical Pharisees*. Waco: Baylor University Press.

References

Classen, C. J. (2000) *Rhetorical Criticism of the New Testament*. Tübingen: Mohr.

Clevenot, M. (1985) *Materialist Approaches to the Bible*. Maryknoll: Orbis.

Collins, J. J. (2005) *The Bible after Babel: Historical Criticism in a Postmodern Age*. Grand Rapids: Eerdmans.

Cone, J. H. (1969) *Black Theology and Black Power*. Maryknoll: Orbis.

Conradie, E. (2004) 'Towards an Ecological Biblical Hermeneutic: A Review Essay on the Earth Bible Project', *Scriptura* 85, 123–35.

Conzelmann, H. (1954) *Die Mitte Der Zeit: Studien Zur Theologie Des Lukas*, Beiträge Zur Historischen Theologie 17. Tübingen: Mohr (ET (1960) *The Theology of St Luke*. London: Faber; (1961) New York: Harper).

Craffert, P. (2007) *The Life of a Galilean Shaman: Jesus of Nazareth in Anthropological-Historical Perspective*. Eugene: Cascade.

Croatto, J. S. (1987) *Biblical Hermeneutics: Toward a Theory of Reading as the Production of Meaning*. New York: Orbis.

Crossan, J. D. (1976) *Raid on the Articulate: Comic Eschatology in Jesus and Borges*. New York: Harper & Row.

Crossan, J. D. (1980) *Cliffs of Fall: Paradox and Polyvalence in the Parables of Jesus*. New York: Seabury Press.

Crossan, J. D. (1991) *The Historical Jesus: The Life of a Mediterranean Jewish Peasant*. Edinburgh: T&T Clark.

D'Angelo, M. R. (1990) 'Women in Luke–Acts: A Redactional View', *Journal of Biblical Literature* 109/3, 441–61.

Danker, F. W., rev. and ed. (2000) *A Greek–English Lexicon of the New Testament and other Early Christian Literature*, 3rd edn. Chicago: University of Chicago Press.

Davies, W. D. and D. C. Allison (1991) *A Critical and Exegetical Commentary on the Gospel according to Saint Matthew*, vol. 2. London and New York: T&T Clark.

Davis, E. F. and R. B. Hays (2003) *The Art of Reading Scripture*. Grand Rapids: Eerdmans.

Day, L. and C. Pressler, eds (2006) *Engaging the Bible in a Gendered World: An Introduction to Feminist Biblical Interpretation in Honor of Katharine Dobb Sakenfeld*. Louisville and London: Westminster John Knox.

De La Torre, M. (2002) *Reading the Bible from the Margins*. Maryknoll: Orbis.

de Waard, J. and E. A. Nida (1986) *From One Language to Another: Functional Equivalence in Bible Translating*. Nashville: Nelson.

Deissmann, A. (1895) *Bibelstudien: Beiträge, Zumeist aus den Papyri und Inschriften, zur Geschichte der Sprache, des Schrifttums und der Religion des hellenistischen Judentums und des Urchristentums*. Marburg: N.G. Elwert (ET (1901) *Bible Studies. Contributions chiefly from papyri and inscriptions to the history of the language, the literature, and the religion of Hellenistic Judaism and primitive Christianity*. Edinburgh: T&T Clark).

Deissmann, A. (1908) *Licht vom Osten*. Tübingen: Mohr (ET (1910) *Light from the Ancient East*. London: Hodder & Stoughton).

Dibelius, M. (1919) *Die Formgeschichte des Evangeliums*. Tübingen: Mohr (Siebeck) (ET (1934) *From Tradition to Gospel*. London: Nicholson & Watson; (1965) New York: Scribner.

Downey, J. K., ed. (1999) *Love's Strategy: The Political Theology of Johann Baptist Metz*. Harrisburg, PA: Trinity Press International.

Dube, M. W. (2000) *Postcolonial Feminist Interpretation of the Bible*. St Louis: Chalice.

Dungan, D. L. (1999) *A History of the Synoptic Problem: The Canon, the Text, the Composition and the Interpretation of the Gospels*. New York: Doubleday.

Dunn, J. D. G. (2003) *Jesus Remembered*. Grand Rapids: Eerdmans.

Dunnill, J. (1992) *Covenant and Sacrifice in the Letter to the Hebrews*, Society for New Testament Studies Monograph Series 75. Cambridge: Cambridge University Press.

Eco, U. (1976) *A Theory of Semiotics*, Advances in Semiotics. Bloomington: Indiana University Press.

Edwards, G. (1972) *Jesus and the Politics of Violence*. New York: Harper & Row.

Ehrensperger, K. (2007) *Paul and the Dynamics of Power: Communication and Interaction in the Early Christ-Movement*. London and New York: T&T Clark International.

Ehrman, B. D. (1993) *The Orthodox Corruption of Scripture*. New York and Oxford: Oxford University Press.

Ehrman, B. D. (2005) *Misquoting Jesus*. San Francisco: HarperSanFrancisco (in the USA) and (2006) *Whose Word is it Anyway?* London: Continuum.

Ekblad, B. (2005) *Reading the Bible with the Damned*. Louisville: Westminster John Knox.

Elliott, J. H. (1990) *A Home for the Homeless: A Social-Scientific Criticism of I Peter, Its Situation and Strategy*. Philadelphia: Fortress.

Elliott, J. H. (1993) *What is Social-Scientific Criticism?* Minneapolis: Fortress.

Elliott, K. and I. Moir (2003) *Manuscripts and the Text of the New Testament*. London and New York: T&T Clark.

Elliott, N. (1994) *Liberating Paul: The Justice of God and the Politics of the Apostle*. Maryknoll: Orbis.

Epp, E. J. (2005) *Junia: The First Woman Apostle*. Minneapolis: Fortress.

Erasmus, D. (1516) *Novum Instrumentum omne, diligenter ab Erasmo Roterodamo recognitum et emendatum*. Basel: Johann Froben.

Evans, C. A. (2005) *Ancient Texts for New Testament Studies: A Guide to the Background Literature*. Peabody, MA: Hendrickson.

Evans, C. E. (1990) *Saint Luke*. London and Philadelphia: SCM and Trinity Press International.

Evans, J. (1981) 'Black Theology and Black Feminism', *Journal of Religious Thought* 38, 43–54.

Farmer, W. R. (1964) *The Synoptic Problem: A Critical Analysis*. New York: Macmillan.

Farrer, A. M. (1955) 'On Dispensing with Q', in D. E. Nineham, ed., *Studies in the Gospels: Essays in Memory of R. H. Lightfoot*. Oxford: Blackwell, 55–88.

Fatum, L. (1995) 'Image of God and Glory of Man: Women in the Pauline Congregations', in K. Elisabeth Børresen, ed., *The Image of God: Gender Models in Judaeo-Christian Tradition*. Minneapolis: Fortress, 50–133.

Feiler, P. F. (1983) 'The Stilling of the Storm in Matthew: A Response to Gunter Bornkamm', *Journal of the Evangelical Theological Society* 26, 399–406.

Felder, C. H., ed. (1991) *Stony the Road We Trod: African American Biblical Interpretation*. Minneapolis: Fortress.

Fetterley, J. (1978) *The Resisting Reader: A Feminist Approach to American Fiction*. Bloomington and London: Indiana University Press.

Fish, S. E. (1972) *Self-Consuming Artifacts: The Experience of Seventeenth-Century Literature*. Berkeley: University of California Press.

Fish, S. E. (1980) *Is There a Text in This Class? The Authority of Interpretive Communities*. Cambridge, MA: Harvard University Press.

Fishbane, M. (1985) *Biblical Interpretation in Ancient Israel*. Oxford and New York: Oxford University Press.

Foskett, M. F. and J. K.-J. Kuan, eds (2006) *Ways of Being, Ways of Reading: Asian American Biblical Interpretation*. St Louis: Chalice.

Fowl, S. E. (1996) *The Theological Interpretation of Scripture: Classic and Contemporary Readings*. Oxford and Malden, MA: Blackwell.

Fowl, S. E. (2000) *Engaging Scripture*. Oxford and Malden, MA: Blackwell.

Fowler, R. M. (1991) *Let the Reader Understand: Reader-Response Criticism and the Gospel of Mark*. Harrisburg, PA: Trinity Press International.

Frostin, P. (1988) *Liberation Theology in Tanzania and South Africa: A First World Interpretation*. Lund: Lund University Press.

Gabler, J. P. (1787) *Oratio: De iusto discrimine theologiae Biblicae et dogmaticae regundisque recte utriusque finibus*. Altdorf (ET (1980) J. Sandy-Wunsch and L. Eldredge, 'J.-P. Gabler and the Distinction between Biblical and Dogmatic Theology: Translation, Commentary and Discussion of his Originality', *Scottish Journal of Theology* 33, 133–58).

Gadamer, H.-G. (1960) *Wahrheit und Methode: Grundzüge einer philosophischen Hermeneutik*. Tübingen: Mohr (ET (1975) *Truth and Method*. London and New York: Sheed & Ward).

Gager, J. G. (1975) *Kingdom and Community: The Social World of Early Christianity*. Englewood Cliffs: Prentice-Hall.

Genette, G. (1980) *Narrative Discourse: An Essay in Method*. Ithaca: Cornell University Press.

Goodacre, M. (1998) 'Fatigue in the Synoptics', *New Testament Studies* 44, 45–58.

Goodacre, M. (2001) *The Synoptic Problem: A Way Through the Maze*. London and New York: T&T Clark.

Goodacre, M. (2002) *The Case Against Q*. London and Harrisburg, PA: SCM and Trinity Press International.

Gottwald, N. K. (1979) *The Tribes of Yahweh: A Sociology of the Religion of Liberated Israel, 1250–1050 B.C.* Maryknoll: Orbis.

Gottwald, N. K. and R. A. Horsley, eds (1993) *The Bible and Liberation: Political and Social Hermeneutics.* Maryknoll: Orbis.

Goulder, M. D. (1963) 'The Composition of the Lord's Prayer', *Journal of Theological Studies* 14, 32–45.

Greimas, A. J. and J. Courtés (1982) *Semiotics and Language: An Analytical Dictionary.* ET, Bloomington: Indiana University Press.

Greimas, A. J. and J. Courtés (1986) *Sémiotique: Dictionnaire raisonné de la théorie du langage,* vol. 2. Paris: Larousse.

Griesbach, J. J. (1789–90) *Commentatio qua Marci Evangelium totum e Matthaei et Lucae commentariis decerptum esse monstratur,* 2 vols. Jena: C. Heinrich Cuno.

Griesbach, J. J. (1978) 'A Demonstration that Mark was Written after Matthew and Luke', in *J. J. Griesbach: Synoptic and Text-Critical Studies.* Cambridge and New York: Cambridge University Press, 103–35.

Guest, D., R. E. Goss, M. West and T. Bohache (2006) *The Queer Bible Commentary.* London: SCM.

Gutiérrez, G. (1971) *Teología de la Liberación. Perspectivas.* Salamanca: Ediciones Sígueme (ET (1988) *A Theology of Liberation: History, Politics and Salvation.* London: SCM).

Habel, N. C., ed. (2000) *Readings from the Perspective of Earth,* Earth Bible 1. Sheffield: Sheffield Academic Press.

Habel, N. C. and V. Balabanski, eds (2002) *The Earth Story in the New Testament,* Earth Bible 5. Sheffield: Sheffield Academic Press.

Hanks, T. (2000) *The Subversive Gospel: A New Testament Commentary of Liberation.* Cleveland: Pilgrim Press.

Hayward, C. and S. R. Hiat (1978) 'The Church Ponders Evermore the Trivialization of Women', *Christianity and Crisis,* 26 June.

Heil, J. P. (1981) *Jesus Walking on the Sea: Meaning and Gospel Functions of Matt 14:22–33, Mark 6:45–52 and John 6:15b-21,* Analecta Biblica 87. Rome: Biblical Institute Press.

Heil, J. P. (1992) *The Gospel of Mark as Model for Action: A Reader-Response Commentary.* New York: Paulist Press.

Hennelly, A., ed. (1990) *Liberation Theology: A Documentary History.* Maryknoll: Orbis.

Herzog, W. (1994) *Parables as Subversive Speech: Jesus as Pedagogue of the Oppressed.* Maryknoll: Orbis.

Hills, E. F. (1984) *The King James Version Defended!* Des Moines: Christian Research Press.

Hjelmslev, L. (1961) *Prolegomena to a Theory of Language.* ET, Madison: University of Wisconsin Press.

Holland, N. N. (1975) 'Unity Identity Text Self', *PMLA* 90, 813–22.

Holtzmann, H. J. (1863) *Die synoptischen Evangelien: Ihr Ursprung und geschichtliche Charakter.* Leipzig: Engelmann.

Hooker, M. D. (1993) *The Gospel according to St Mark.* Peabody: Hendrickson.

Hopkins, K. (2002) 'Rome, Taxes, Rents and Trade', in W. Scheidel, ed., *The Ancient Economy*. Edinburgh: Edinburgh University Press, 190–232.

Hornsby, T. J. (2001) 'Paul and the Remedies of Idolatry: Reading Romans 1.18–24 with Romans 7', in A. K. M. Adam, ed., *Postmodern Interpretations of the Bible*. St Louis: Chalice.

Horrell, D. G. (1996) *The Social Ethos of the Corinthian Correspondence: Interests and Ideology from 1 Corinthians to 1 Clement*. Edinburgh: T&T Clark.

Horrell, D. G., ed. (1999) *Social-Scientific Approaches to New Testament Interpretation*. Edinburgh: T&T Clark.

Horrell, D. G., C. Hunt and C. Southgate (2008) 'Appeals to the Bible in Ecotheology and Environmental Ethics', *Studies in Christian Ethics* 21/2.

Horsley, R. (1989) *Sociology and the Jesus Movement*. New York: Crossroad.

Horsley, R. and J. Hanson (1985) *Bandits, Prophets and Messiahs: Popular Movements at the Time of Jesus*. New York: Seabury-Winston.

Howard-Brook, W. and A. Gwyther (1999) *Unveiling Empire: Reading Revelation Then and Now*. Maryknoll: Orbis.

Hunt, C., D. C. Horrell and C. Southgate (forthcoming) 'An Environmental Mantra? Ecological Interest in Romans 8.19–23 and a Modest Proposal for its Narrative Interpretation', *Journal of Theological Studies*.

Iser, W. (1972) *Der implizite Leser. Kommunikationsformen des Romans von Bunyan bis Beckett*. Munich: W. Fink (ET (1974) *The Implied Reader: Patterns of Communication in Prose Fiction from Bunyan to Beckett*. Baltimore: Johns Hopkins University Press).

Iser, W. (1976) *Der Akt des Lesens: Theorie ästhetischer Wirkung*. Munich: W. Fink (ET (1978) *The Act of Reading. A Theory of Aesthetic Response*. Baltimore: Johns Hopkins University Press).

Jefferson, T. (1904) *The Life and Morals of Jesus of Nazareth*. Chicago: University of Chicago Press.

Jeremias, J. (1969) *Jerusalem in the Time of Jesus: An Investigation into Economic and Social Conditions during the New Testament Period*. London and Philadelphia: SCM and Fortress.

Jeremias, J. (1971) *New Testament Theology I: The Proclamation of Jesus*. London and Philadelphia: SCM and Fortress.

Jobling, D., P. Day and G. Sheppard, eds (1991) *The Bible and the Politics of Exegesis*. Cleveland, Ohio: Pilgrim.

Jobling, D., T. Pippin and R. Schleifer, eds (2001) *The Postmodern Bible Reader*. Oxford and Malden, MA: Blackwell, 58–77.

Johnson, E. E. (1996) 'Divine Initiative and Human Response', in S. E. Fowl, ed., *The Theological Interpretation of Scripture: Classic and Contemporary Readings*. Oxford and Malden, MA: Blackwell, 356–70.

Jones, T. P. (2007) *Misquoting Truth: A Guide to the Fallacies of Bart Ehrman's Misquoting Jesus*. Downers Grove: IVP.

Joy, D. (2005) 'Markan Subalterns/The Crowd and Their Strategies of Resistance: A Postcolonial Critique', *Black Theology* 3/1, 55–74.

The Kairos Document: A Theological Comment on the Political Crisis in South Africa (1985). London: Catholic Institute for International Relations.

Katz, D. S. (2004) *God's Last Words: Reading the English Bible from the Reformation to Fundamentalism*. New Haven: Yale University Press.

Kee, H. C. (1993) *The Bible in the Twenty-First Century: Symposium Papers*. New York: American Bible Society.

Kee, H. C. (2005) *The Beginnings of Christianity: An Introduction to the New Testament*. New York: T&T Clark.

Kennedy, G. A. (1984) *New Testament Interpretation through Rhetorical Criticism*. Chapel Hill: University of North Carolina Press.

Kern, P. H. (1998) *Rhetoric and Galatians: Assessing an Approach to Paul's Epistle*. Cambridge and New York: Cambridge University Press.

Kilpatrick, G. D. (1946) *The Origin and Purpose of the Gospel according to St Matthew*. Oxford: Clarendon Press.

Kim, J. K. (2004) *Woman and Nation: An Intercontextual Reading of the Gospel of John*. Leiden: Brill.

Kim, S. H. (2006) 'Rupturing the Empire: Reading the Poor Widow as a Postcolonial Female Subject (Mark 12:41–44)', *lectio dificilior* (online) available at <http://www.lectio.unibe.ch/06_1/kim_rupturing.htm>

King, K. (2006) 'Canonization and Marginalization: Mary of Magdala', in R. S. Sugirtharajah, ed., *The Postcolonial Biblical Reader*. Oxford and Malden, MA: Blackwell.

Kinukawa, H. (1994) *Women and Jesus in Mark: A Japanese Feminist Perspective*. Maryknoll: Orbis.

Klausner, J. and H. Danby (1925) *Jesus of Nazareth: His Life, Times and Teaching*. London and New York: George Allen & Unwin.

Kloppenborg, J. S. (2000) *Excavating Q: The History and Setting of the Sayings Gospel*. Edinburgh and Minneapolis: T&T Clark and Fortress.

Kovacs, J. L., C. Rowland and R. Callow (2004) *Revelation: The Apocalypse of Jesus Christ*. Oxford and Malden, MA: Blackwell.

Kristeva, J. (1974) *La Révolution Du Langage Poétique: L'Avant-Garde À La Fin Du XIXe Siècle, Lautréamont Et Mallarmé*. Paris: Éditions du Seuil (ET (1984) *Revolution in Poetic Language*. New York: Columbia University Press).

Kuan, J. K.-J. (1999) 'Asian Biblical Interpretation', in *Dictionary of Biblical Interpretation*, vol. 1, ed. J. H. Hayes. Nashville: Abingdon, 70–7.

Kuefler, M. (2006) *The Boswell Thesis: Essays on Christianity, Social Tolerance, and Homosexuality*. Chicago: University of Chicago Press.

Kwok, P.-l. (1995) *Discovering the Bible in the Non-Biblical World*. Maryknoll: Orbis.

Lachmann, K. (1831) *Novum Testamentum Graece*. Berlin: G. Reimer.

Lausberg, H. (1998) *Literary Rhetoric*. Leiden: Brill.

Leitch, V. B. (1988) *American Literary Criticism from the Thirties to the Eighties*. New York: Columbia University Press.

Levine, A. J., ed. (2001–6) *Feminist Companion to the New Testament and Early Christian Writings*. Sheffield, London and Edinburgh: Sheffield Academic Press, Continuum and T&T Clark.

Lévi-Strauss, C. (1958) *Anthropologie Structurale*. Paris: Plon (ET (1963) *Structural Anthropology*. New York: Basic Books).

Lévi-Strauss, C. (1964) *Le Cru et Le Cuit*. Paris: Plon (ET (1969) *The Raw and the Cooked*. New York: Harper & Row).

Lévi-Strauss, C. (1968) 'The Structural Study of Myth', in *Structural Anthropology*. London: Allen Lane, 206–31.

Longenecker, R. N. (1990) *Galatians*. Dallas: Word Books.

Luz, U. (1985–97) *Das Evangelium nach Matthäus*. Zurich: Neukirchener Verlag (ET (2001–7) *Matthew: A Commentary*, 3 vols, Hermeneia. Minneapolis: Fortress).

Luz, U. (1994) *Matthew in History: Interpretation, Influence, and Effects*. Minneapolis: Fortress.

McGovern, A. (1989) *Liberation Theology and Its Critics*. Maryknoll: Orbis.

McKnight, E. V. (1969) *What Is Form Criticism?* Philadelphia: Fortress.

Malbon, E. Struthers (1986) *Narrative Space and Mythic Meaning in Mark*. San Francisco: Harper & Row.

Malbon, E. Struthers (1989) 'The Jewish Leaders in the Gospel of Mark: A Literary Study of Markan Characterization', *Journal of Biblical Literature* 108/2, 259–81.

Malbon, E. Struthers (1992) 'Narrative Criticism: How does the Story Mean?' in J. C. Anderson and S. D. Moore, eds, *Mark and Method: New Approaches in Biblical Studies*. Minneapolis: Fortress, 23–49.

Malbon, E. Struthers (1993) 'Echoes and Foreshadowings in Mark 4—8: Reading and Rereading', *Journal of Biblical Literature* 112/2, 211–30.

Malbon, E. Struthers (2000) *In the Company of Jesus: Characters in Mark's Gospel*. Louisville: Westminster John Knox.

Malina, B. J. (2000) *The New Testament World: Insights from Cultural Anthropology*, 3rd edn rev. Louisville: Westminster John Knox.

Malina, B. J. and J. J. Pilch (2006) *Social Science Commentary on the Letters of Paul*. Minneapolis: Fortress.

Malina, B. J. and R. Rohrbaugh (1992) *Social-Science Commentary on the Synoptic Gospels*. Minneapolis: Fortress.

Malina, B. J. and R. Rohrbaugh (1998–) Social Science Commentary series. Minneapolis: Fortress.

Marshall, C. (2001) *Beyond Retribution: A N.T. Vision for Justice, Crime and Punishment*. Grand Rapids: Eerdmans.

Marshall, I. H. (1978) *Gospel of Luke: A Commentary on the Greek Text*, New International Greek Testament Commentary. Grand Rapids: Eerdmans.

Martin, C. J. (1991) 'The *Haustafeln* (Household Codes) in African American Biblical Interpretation: "Free Slaves" and "Subordinate Women"', in C. H. Felder, ed., *Stony the Road We Trod: African American Biblical Interpretation*. Minneapolis: Fortress.

Martin, D. B. (1996) 'Arsenokoites and Malakos: Meanings and Consequences', in R. P. Brawley, ed., *Biblical Ethics and Homosexuality: Listening to Scripture*. Louisville: Westminster John Knox; also now available in D. Martin (2006) *Sex and the Single Savior: Gender and Sexuality in Biblical Interpretation*. Louisville: Westminster John Knox, 37–50.

Martin, D. B. (2006) *Sex and the Single Savior: Gender and Sexuality in Biblical Interpretation*. Louisville: Westminster John Knox.

Marxsen, W. (1969) *Mark the Evangelist: Studies on the Redaction History of the Gospel*. Nashville: Abingdon.

Meeks, W. (1974) 'The Image of the Androgyne: Some Uses of a Symbol in Earliest Christianity', *History of Religion* 13, 165–208.

Meeks, W. (1983) *The First Urban Christians*. New Haven: Yale University Press.

Metzger, B. M. (1971) *A Textual Commentary on the Greek New Testament: A Companion Volume to the United Bible Societies' Greek New Testament (3rd edn)*. London and New York: United Bible Societies.

Metzger, B. M. (1977) *The Early Versions of the New Testament: Their Origin, Transmission, and Limitations*. Oxford: Clarendon.

Metzger, B. M. and B. D. Ehrman (2005) *The Text of the New Testament: Its Transmission, Corruption, and Restoration*, 4th edn. Oxford and New York: Oxford University Press.

Miranda, J. (1974) *Marx and the Bible: A Critique of the Philosophy of Oppression*. Maryknoll: Orbis.

Moore, S. D. (1989) *Literary Criticism and the Gospels: The Theoretical Challenge*. London and New York: Yale University Press.

Moore, S. D. (1992) *Mark and Luke in Poststructuralist Perspectives: Jesus Begins to Write*. New Haven: Yale University Press.

Moore, S. D. and J. C. Anderson, eds (2003) *New Testament Masculinities*. Atlanta: Society of Biblical Literature.

Moore, S. D. and F. Segovia, eds (2005) *Postcolonial Biblical Criticism: Interdisciplinary Intersections*. London and New York: T&T Clark International.

Morris, C. W. (1938) *Foundations of the Theory of Signs*. Chicago: University of Chicago Press.

Mosala, I. J. (1986) 'The Use of the Bible in Black Theology', in I. J. Mosala and B. Tlhagale, eds, *The Unquestionable Right to be Free: Essays in Black Theology*. Johannesburg: Skotaville, 175–99.

Mosala, I. J. (1989) *Biblical Hermeneutics and Black Theology in South Africa*. Grand Rapids: Eerdmans.

Moule, C. F. D. (1962) *The British of the New Testament*. London: A&C Black.

Müller, M. and H. Tronier (2002) *The New Testament as Reception*. London and New York: Sheffield Academic Press.

Myers, C. (1988) *Binding the Strong Man: A Political Reading of Mark's Story of Jesus*. Maryknoll: Orbis.

Nanos, M. D. (2002) *The Galatians Debate: Contemporary Issues in Rhetorical and Historical Interpretation*. Peabody: Hendrickson.

Nestle, E. (1898) *Novum Testamentum Graece: cum apparatu critico*. Stuttgart: Privilegierte Württembergische Bibelanstalt.

Newman, B. M. (1996) *Creating and Crafting the Contemporary English Version: A New Approach to Bible Translation*. New York: American Bible Society.

Newsom, C. A. and S. H. Ringe, eds (1992) *Women's Bible Commentary*. London: SPCK.

Ngũgĩ wa Thiong'o (1986) *Decolonising the Mind: The Politics of Language in African Literature*. London and Portsmouth, NH: Currey and Heinemann.

Nida, E. A. and W. D. Reyburn (1981) *Meaning across Cultures: A Study on Bible Translating*, American Society of Missiology Series 4. Maryknoll: Orbis.

Nida, E. A. and C. R. Taber (1969) *The Theory and Practice of Translation*. Leiden: Brill.

Nissinen, M. (1998) *Homoeroticism in the Biblical World: A Historical Perspective*. Minneapolis: Fortress.

Nolan, A. (1978) *Jesus Before Christianity*. Maryknoll: Orbis.

Nolan, A. (1988) *God in South Africa: The Challenge of the Gospel*. Cape Town: David Philip.

Oakman, D. (1986) *Jesus and the Economic Questions of His Day*. Lewiston: Edwin Mellen.

Osiek, C., M. Y. MacDonald and J. H. Tulloch (2006) *A Woman's Place: House Churches in Earliest Christianity*. Minneapolis: Fortress.

Ottermann, M. (2007) ' "How Could He Ever Do That to Her?" Or, How the Woman who Anointed Jesus became a Victim of Luke's Redactional and Theological Principles', in G. O. West, ed., *Reading Other-wise: Socially Engaged Biblical Scholars Reading with their Local Communities*, Semeia Studies. Atlanta: Society of Biblical Literature, 103–16.

Owen, H. (1764) *Observations on the Four Gospels*. London: T. Payne.

Parker, D. C. (1997) *The Living Text of the Gospels*. Cambridge and New York: Cambridge University Press.

Parris, D. P. (2006) *Reading the Bible with Giants: How 2000 Years of Biblical Interpretation Can Shed New Light on Old Texts*. London and Grand Rapids: Paternoster and Eerdmans.

Patte, D. (1980) *Religious Dimensions of Biblical Texts: Greimas's Structural Semiotics and Biblical Exegesis*, Society of Biblical Literature, Semeia Studies. Atlanta: Scholars Press.

Patte, D. (1983) *Paul's Faith and the Power of the Gospel: A Structural Introduction to the Pauline Letters*. Philadelphia: Fortress.

Patte, D. (1987) *The Gospel according to Matthew: A Structural Commentary on Matthew's Faith*. Philadelphia: Fortress.

Patte, D. (1990) *Structural Exegesis for New Testament Critics*, Guides to Biblical Scholarship: New Testament Series. Minneapolis: Fortress.

Peirce, C. S. (1998) *The Essential Peirce, Selected Philosophical Writings, Volume 2 (1893–1913)*, Peirce Edition Project, eds. Bloomington and Indianapolis: Indiana University Press.

Pelikan, J. (1971–89) *The Christian Tradition: A History of the Development of Doctrine*, 5 vols. Chicago: University of Chicago Press.

Petersen, N. R. (1978a) ' "Point of View" in Mark's Narrative', *Semeia* 12, 97–121.

Petersen, N. R. (1978b) *Literary Criticism for New Testament Critics*. Philadelphia: Fortress.

Petersen, W. L. (1997) '*Oude egw se [kata]krinw*, John 8:11, The Protevangelium Iacobi, and the History of the Pericope Adulterae', in T. Baarda et al., eds, *Sayings of Jesus: Canonical and Non-canonical: Essays in Honour of Tjitze Baarda*. Leiden: Brill, 191–221.

Pilch, J. J. (2000) *Healing in the New Testament: Insights from Medical and Mediterranean Anthropology*. Minneapolis: Fortress.

Pippin, T. (1999) *Apocalyptic Bodies*. London: Routledge.

Powell, M. A. (1990) *What is Narrative Criticism?* Guides to Biblical Scholarship. Minneapolis: Fortress.

Powell, M. A. (2001) *Chasing the Eastern Star: Adventures in Biblical Reader-Response Criticism*. Louisville: Westminster John Knox.

Reed, J. L. (2000) *Archaeology and the Galilean Jesus: A Re-Examination of the Evidence*. Harrisburg: Trinity Press International.

Resseguie, J. L. (2005) *Narrative Criticism of the New Testament: An Introduction*. Grand Rapids: Baker Academic.

Rhoads, D. (2004) *Reading Mark, Engaging the Gospel*. Minneapolis: Fortress.

Rhoads, D., J. Dewey and D. Michie (1999) *Mark as Story: An Introduction to the Narrative of a Gospel*, 2nd edn. Philadelphia: Fortress.

Ringe, S. (1985) *Jesus, Liberation and the Biblical Jubilee*. Philadelphia: Fortress.

Robbins, V. (1996) *Exploring the Texture of Texts: A Guide to Socio-Rhetorical Interpretation*. Harrisburg: Trinity Press International.

Roberts, A. and J. Donaldson, eds (1886) *The Ante-Nicene Fathers*, vol. 7. Edinburgh: T&T Clark.

Robinson, J. A. T. (1979) *Wrestling with Romans*. London and Philadelphia: SCM and Westminster.

Robinson, J. M., P. Hoffmann and J. S. Kloppenborg, eds (2000) *The Critical Edition of Q: Synopsis Including the Gospels of Matthew and Luke, Mark and Thomas, with English, German and French translations of Q and Thomas*. Philadelphia: Fortress.

Rogers, J. B. (2006) *Jesus, the Bible, and Homosexuality: Explode the Myths, Heal the Church*. Louisville: Westminster John Knox.

Rohrbaugh, R. L. (2007) 'What Did Jesus Know (About Himself) and When Did He Know It?' in R. L. Rohrbaugh, *The New Testament in Cross-Cultural Perspective*. Eugene: Cascade, 61–76.

Rowland, C. C. (1979) 'The Visions of God in Apocalyptic Literature', *Journal for the Study of Judaism* 10, 137–54.

Rowland, C. C. and M. Corner (1990) *Liberating Exegesis: The Challenge of Liberation Theology to Biblical Studies*. London: SPCK; (1989) Louisville: Westminster John Knox.

Roy, R. (1820) *An Appeal to the Christian Public, in Defence of the 'Precepts of Jesus'*. Calcutta: [s.n.].

Said, E. (1978) *Orientalism*. London and New York: Routledge and Pantheon.

Samartha, S. J. (1987) *The Search for New Hermeneutics in Asian Christian Theology*. Madras: Christian Literature Society for India.

Samartha, S. J. (1994) 'Religion, Language, and Reality: Towards a Relational Hermeneutics', *Biblical Interpretation* 2/3, 340–62.

Samuel, S. (2007) *A Postcolonial Reading of Mark's Story of Jesus*. New York: T&T Clark International.

Sanday, W. and A. C. Headlam (1895) *Romans*, International Critical Commentaries. Edinburgh: T&T Clark.

Sanders, E. P. (1985) *Jesus and Judaism*. London and Philadelphia: SCM and Trinity Press International.

Sanders, E. P. and M. Davies (1989) *Studying the Synoptic Gospels*. London and Philadelphia: SCM and Trinity Press International.

Sanders, J. A. (1972) *Torah and Canon*. Philadelphia: Fortress.

Sanders, J. A. (1975) 'From Isaiah 61 to Luke 4', in Jacob Neusner, ed., *Christianity, Judaism and Other Greco-Roman Cults: Studies for Morton Smith at Sixty*. Leiden: Brill, Part I, 75–106.

Sanders, J. A. (1984) *Canon and Community: A Guide to Canonical Criticism*, Guides to Biblical Scholarship. Philadelphia: Fortress.

Sanders, J. A. (1993) 'From Isaiah 61 to Luke 4', in C. A. Evans and J. A. Sanders, eds, *Luke and Scripture*. Minneapolis: Fortress, 46–69.

Sanders, J. A. (2006) 'The Canonical Process', in Steven T. Katz, ed., *The Cambridge History of Judaism*, vol. 4: *The Late Roman–Rabbinic Period*. Cambridge: Cambridge University Press, 230–43.

Sandy-Wunsch, J. and L. Eldredge (1980) 'J.-P. Gabler and the Distinction between Biblical and Dogmatic Theology: Translation, Commentary and Discussion of his Originality', *Scottish Journal of Theology* 33, 133–58.

Saussure, F. de (1916) *Cours de linguistique générale*. Lausanne: Payot (ET (1983) *Course in General Linguistics*. London: Duckworth).

Sawyer, D. F. (2007) *God, Gender and the Bible*. London: Routledge.

Sawyer, J. F. (2006) *The Blackwell Companion to Bible and Culture*. Oxford: Blackwell.

Scanzoni, L. and V. R. Mollenkott (1978) *Is the Homosexual My Neighbor? Another Christian View*. San Francisco: Harper & Row.

Schmidt, K. L. (1919) *Der Rahmen der Geschichte Jesu: literarkritische Untersuchungen zur ältesten Jesus überlieferung*. Berlin: Trowitzsch.

Schottroff, L., S. Schroer and M.-T. Wacker (1998) *Feminist Interpretation: The Bible in Women's Perspective*. Minneapolis: Fortress.

Schottroff, L. and W. Stegemann (1986) *Jesus and the Hope of the Poor*. Maryknoll: Orbis.

Schüssler Fiorenza, E. (1983) *In Memory of Her: A Feminist Theological Reconstruction of Christian Origins*. New York: Crossroad.

Schüssler Fiorenza, E. (1984) *Bread not Stone: The Challenge of Feminist Biblical Interpretation*. Boston: Beacon Press.

Schüssler Fiorenza, E. (1986) 'Missionaries, Apostles, Coworkers: Romans 16 and the Reconstruction of Women's Early Christian History', *Word & World* 6/4, 420–33.

Schüssler Fiorenza, E. (2001) *Wisdom Ways: Introducing Feminist Biblical Interpretation*. Maryknoll: Orbis.

Schweitzer, A. (1906) *Von Reimarus zu Wrede. Eine Geschichte der Leben-Jesu-Forschung*. Tübingen: Mohr (ET (1954) *The Quest of the Historical Jesus*. London: A&C Black).

Scroggs, R. (1983) *The New Testament and Homosexuality*. Philadelphia: Fortress.

Segovia, Fernando F. (2000) *Decolonizing Biblical Studies: A View from the Margins*. Maryknoll: Orbis.

Segovia, F. and M. A. Tolbert (1998) *Teaching the Bible: The Discourses and Politics of Biblical Pedagogy*. Maryknoll: Orbis.

Semler, J. S. (1779) *Beantwortung der Fragmente eines Ungenannten insbesondere vom Zweck Jesu und seiner Jünger*. Halle: Verlag des Erziehungsinstituts.

Shelley, P. B. (1960) *The Complete Poetical Works of Percy Bysshe Shelley*. Oxford: Oxford University Press.

Singgih, E. G. (1995) 'Let Me Not be Put to Shame: Towards an Indonesian Hermeneutics', *Asia Journal of Theology* 9/1, 71–85.

Smith, S. H. (1996) *A Lion with Wings: A Narrative-Critical Approach to Mark's Gospel*. Sheffield: Sheffield Academic Press.

Stanton, E. C. and the National American Woman Suffrage Association Collection (1895) *The Woman's Bible*. New York: European Publishing.

Stanton, G. (1992) *A Gospel for a New People: Studies in Matthew*. Edinburgh and New York: T&T Clark.

Stegemann, E. and W. Stegemann (1999) *The Jesus Movement: A Social History of Its First Century*. Philadelphia: Fortress.

Stegemann, W., B. Malina and G. Theissen, eds (2002) *The Social Setting of Jesus and the Gospels*. Minneapolis: Fortress.

Stendahl, K. (1966) *The Bible and the Role of Women*. Philadelphia: Fortress.

Stendahl, K. (1976) *Paul among Jews and Gentiles, and other essays*. Philadelphia: Fortress.

Stendahl, K. (1995) *Final Account: Paul's Letter to the Romans*. Minneapolis: Fortress.

Streeter, B. H. (1924) *The Four Gospels: A Study of Origins*. London: Macmillan.

Sugirtharajah, R. S. (1998) *Asian Biblical Hermeneutics and Postcolonialism: Contesting the Interpretations*. Maryknoll: Orbis.

Sugirtharajah, R. S. (2002) *Postcolonial Criticism and Biblical Interpretation*. Oxford and New York: Oxford University Press.

Sugirtharajah, R. S., ed. (1991) *Voices from the Margin: Interpreting the Bible in the Third World*. London and Maryknoll: SPCK and Orbis.

Sugirtharajah, R. S., ed. (1998) *The Postcolonial Bible*. Sheffield: Sheffield Academic Press.

Swartley, W. (2006) *Covenant of Peace: The Missing Peace in New Testament Theology and Ethics*. Grand Rapids: Eerdmans.

Tamez, E. (2007) *Struggles for Power in Early Christianity: A Study in the First Letter to Timothy*. Maryknoll: Orbis.

Tannehill, R. (1977) 'The Disciples in Mark: The Function of a Narrative Role', *Journal of Religion* 57, 386–405.

Tannehill, R. (1986–90) *The Narrative Unity of Luke–Acts*, vols 1–2. Minneapolis: Fortress.

Theissen, G. (1978) *The First Followers of Jesus: A Sociological Analysis of the Earliest Christianity*. London: SCM (*The Sociology of Early Palestinian Christianity*. Philadelphia: Fortress).

Theissen, G. (1982) *The Social Setting of Pauline Christianity*. Edinburgh and Philadelphia: T&T Clark and Fortress.

Thorley, J. (1996) 'Junia, a Woman Apostle', *Novum Testamentum* 38/1, 18–29.

Tischendorf, C. (1869–72) *Novum Testamentum Graece: ad antiquissimos testos denuo recensuit*. Leipzig: Giesecke & Devrient.

Trible, P. (1984) *Texts of Terror: Literary-Feminist Readings of Biblical Narratives*. Philadelphia: Fortress.

Tuckett, C. (1987) *Reading the New Testament: Methods of Interpretation*. London: SPCK.

Vaage, L. E., ed. (1997) *Subversive Scriptures: Revolutionary Readings of the Christian Bible in Latin America*. Valley Forge: Trinity Press International.

Van Tilborg, S. (1972) 'A Form Criticism of the Lord's Prayer', *Novum Testamentum* 14/2, 94–105.

Vanhoozer, K. J., ed. (2006) *Dictionary for Theological Interpretation of the Bible*. London and Grand Rapids: SPCK and Baker Academic.

Wall, R. W. and E. E. Lemcio (1992) *The New Testament as Canon: A Reader in Canonical Criticism*. Sheffield: Sheffield Academic Press.

Walsh, B. J. and S. C. Keesmaat (2004) *Colossians Remixed: Subverting the Empire*. Downers Grove: Intervarsity.

Weaver, D. (2001) *The Nonviolent Atonement*. Grand Rapids: Eerdmans.

Webber, R. C. (1996) *Reader Response Analysis of the Epistle of James*. London and San Francisco: International Scholars.

Wellhausen, J. (1905) *Einleitung in die drei ersten Evangelien*. Berlin: G. Reimer.

West, C. (1984) 'Religion and the Left: An Introduction', *Monthly Review* 36, 9–19.

West, G. O. (1995) *Biblical Hermeneutics of Liberation: Modes of Reading the Bible in the South African Context*. Maryknoll and Pietermaritzburg: Orbis and Cluster.

West, G. O. (2003) *The Academy of the Poor: Towards a Dialogical Reading of the Bible*. Pietermaritzburg: Cluster.

West, G. O., ed. (2007) *Reading Other-wise: Socially Engaged Biblical Scholars Reading with their Local Communities*, Semeia Studies. Atlanta: Society of Biblical Literature.

West, G. O. and M. W. Dube, eds (1996) '*Reading with*': *African Overtures*, Semeia 73. Atlanta: Society of Biblical Literature.

West, G. O. and M. W. Dube, eds (2000) *The Bible in Africa: Transactions, Trajectories, and Trends*. Leiden: Brill.

White, L., Jr (1967) 'The Historical Roots of our Ecologic Crisis', *Science* 155, 1203–7, and reprinted in R. J. Berry, ed. (2000) *The Care of Creation*. Leicester: IVP, 31–42.

Williams, D. (1993) *Sisters in the Wilderness: The Challenges of Womanist God-Talk*. Maryknoll: Orbis.

Williams, J. F. (1996) 'Discipleship and Minor Characters in Mark's Gospel', *Bibliotheca Sacra* 153, 332–43.

Wilson, N. (1995) *Our Tribe: Queer Folks, God, Jesus and the Bible*. San Francisco: HarperSanFrancisco.

Wimbush, V. (2003) *The Bible and African Americans: A Brief History*. Minneapolis: Fortress.

Wimbush, V., ed. (2000) *African Americans and the Bible: Sacred Texts and Social Textures*. New York and London: Continuum.

Wink, W. (1984) *Naming the Powers: The Language of Power in the New Testament*. Minneapolis: Fortress.

Witherington III, B. (1995) *Conflict and Community in Corinth: A Socio-rhetorical Commentary on 1 and 2 Corinthians*. Grand Rapids: Eerdmans.

Wrede, W. (1897) *Über Aufgabe und Methode der sogenannten neutestamentlichen Theologie*. Göttingen: Vandenhoeck & Ruprecht (ET (1973) *The Nature of New Testament Theology*. London: SCM).

Yamaguchi, S. (2002) *Mary and Martha: Women in the World of Jesus*. Maryknoll: Orbis.

Yeo, K.-k. (1998) *What Has Jerusalem to Do with Beijing? Biblical Interpretation from a Chinese Perspective*. Harrisburg: Trinity Press International.

Yeo, K.-k. (2002) *Chairman Mao Meets the Apostle Paul: Christianity, Communism, and the Hope of China*. Grand Rapids: Brazos.

Yoder, J. H. (1972) *The Politics of Jesus*. Grand Rapids: Eerdmans.

Ziesler, J. A. (1989) *Paul's Letter to the Romans*. London and Philadelphia: SCM and Trinity Press International.

Further reading

1 Historical criticism

Barton, J. (2002) *The Biblical World*. London and New York: Routledge.
Chilton, B. (1994) *A Feast of Meanings: Eucharistic Theologies from Jesus through Johannine Circles*. Leiden and New York: Brill.
Chilton, B. (2000) *Rabbi Jesus: An Intimate Biography*. New York: Doubleday.
Chilton, B. (2004) *Rabbi Paul: An Intellectual Biography*. New York: Doubleday.
Kee, H. C. (2005) *The Beginnings of Christianity: An Introduction to the New Testament*. New York: T&T Clark.

2 Social science criticism

Blasi, A., Jean Duhaime and Paul-Andre Turcotte (2002) *Handbook of Early Christianity: Social Science Approaches*. Walnut Creek, CA: Alta Mira.
Craffert, P. (2007) *The Life of a Galilean Shaman: Jesus of Nazareth in Anthopological-Historical Perspective*. Eugene, OR: Cascade.
Elliott, J. H. (1993) *What is Social-Scientific Criticism?* Minneapolis: Fortress.
Horrell, D. G., ed. (1999) *Social-Scientific Approaches to New Testament Interpretation*. Edinburgh: T&T Clark.
Malina, B. J. (2000) *The New Testament World: Insights from Cultural Anthropology*, 3rd edn, rev. Louisville: Westminster John Knox.

3 Form criticism

Bauckham, R. (2006) *Jesus and the Eyewitnesses: The Gospels as Eyewitness Testimony*. Grand Rapids: Eerdmans.
Dunn, J. D. G. (2003) *Jesus Remembered*. Grand Rapids: Eerdmans.
Kloppenborg, J. S. (2000) *Excavating Q: The History and Setting of the Sayings Gospel*. Edinburgh: T&T Clark.
McKnight, E. V. (1969) *What Is Form Criticism?* Philadelphia: Fortress.

4 Source criticism

Dungan, D. L. (1999) *A History of the Synoptic Problem: The Canon, the Text, the Composition and the Interpretation of the Gospels*. New York: Doubleday.
Goodacre, M. (2002) *The Case Against Q*. Harrisburg: Trinity Press International.
Robinson, J. M., P. Hoffmann and J. S. Kloppenborg, eds (2000) *The Critical Edition of Q: Synopsis Including the Gospels of Matthew and Luke, Mark and Thomas, with English, German and French Translations of Q and Thomas*. Philadelphia: Fortress.
Sanders, E. P. and M. Davies (1989) *Studying the Synoptic Gospels*. London and Philadelphia: SCM and Trinity Press International.

5 Redaction criticism

Bauckham, R. (1998) *Gospels for All Christians: Rethinking the Gospel Audience.* Edinburgh and New York: T&T Clark.

Goodacre, M. (2001) *The Synoptic Problem: A Way Through the Maze.* London and New York: T&T Clark.

Stanton, G. (1992) *A Gospel for a New People: Studies in Matthew.* Edinburgh and New York: T&T Clark.

Tuckett, C. (1987) *Reading the New Testament: Methods of Interpretation.* London: SPCK.

6 Textual criticism

Ehrman, B. D. (1993) *The Orthodox Corruption of Scripture.* New York and Oxford: Oxford University Press.

Ehrman, B. D. (2005) *Misquoting Jesus.* San Francisco: HarperSanFrancisco (in the USA); and published (2006) as *Whose Word is it Anyway?* London: Continuum.

Elliott, J. K. and I. Moir (2003) *Manuscripts and the Text of the New Testament.* London and New York: T&T Clark.

Jones, T. P. (2007) *Misquoting Truth: A Guide to the Fallacies of Bart Ehrman's Misquoting Jesus.* Downers Grove: IVP.

Metzger, B. M. and B. D. Ehrman (2005) *The Text of the New Testament: Its Transmission, Corruption, and Restoration,* 4th edn. Oxford and New York: Oxford University Press.

Parker, D. C. (1997) *The Living Text of the Gospels.* Cambridge and New York: Cambridge University Press.

7 Translation theory

de Waard, J. and E. A. Nida (1986) *From One Language to Another: Functional Equivalence in Bible Translating.* Nashville: Nelson.

Katz, D. S. (2004) *God's Last Words: Reading the English Bible from the Reformation to Fundamentalism.* New Haven: Yale University Press.

Newman, B. M. (1996) *Creating and Crafting the Contemporary English Version: A New Approach to Bible Translation.* New York: American Bible Society.

Nida, E. A. and W. D. Reyburn (1981) *Meaning across Cultures: A Study on Bible Translating,* American Society of Missiology Series 4. Maryknoll: Orbis.

Parris, D. P. (2006) *Reading the Bible with Giants: How 2000 Years of Biblical Interpretation Can Shed New Light on Old Texts.* London: Paternoster.

8 Canonical criticism

Evans, C. A. (2005) *Ancient Texts for New Testament Studies: A Guide to the Background Literature.* Peabody, MA: Hendrickson.

Sanders, J. A. (1993) 'From Isaiah 61 to Luke 4', in Craig A. Evans and James A. Sanders, eds, *Luke and Scripture.* Minneapolis: Fortress, 46–69.

Sanders, J. A. (2006) 'The Canonical Process', in Steven T. Katz, ed., *The Cambridge History of Judaism*, vol. 4: *The Late Roman–Rabbinic Period*. Cambridge: Cambridge University Press, 230–43.

Wall, R. W. and E. E. Lemcio (1992) *The New Testament as Canon: A Reader in Canonical Criticism*. Sheffield: Sheffield Academic Press.

9 Rhetorical criticism

Anderson, R. D. (1996) *Ancient Rhetorical Theory and Paul*, Contributions to Biblical Exegesis and Theology 18. Kampen: Kok Pharos.

Campbell, B. L. (1998) *Honor, Shame, and the Rhetoric of I Peter*. Atlanta: Scholars Press.

Classen, C. J. (2000) *Rhetorical Criticism of the New Testament*. Tübingen: Mohr.

Nanos, M. D. (2002) *The Galatians Debate: Contemporary Issues in Rhetorical and Historical Interpretation*. Peabody, MA: Hendrickson.

Witherington III, B. (1995) *Conflict and Community in Corinth: A Socio-rhetorical Commentary on 1 and 2 Corinthians*. Grand Rapids: Eerdmans.

Witherington III, B. (2008) *New Testament Rhetoric: A Handbook*. Eugene: Wipf and Stock/Cascade.

10 Narrative criticism

Malbon, E. Struthers (2000) *In the Company of Jesus: Characters in Mark's Gospel*. Louisville: Westminster John Knox.

Moore, S. D. (1989) *Literary Criticism and the Gospels: The Theoretical Challenge*. New Haven and London: Yale University Press.

Powell, M. A. (1990) *What is Narrative Criticism?* Guides to Biblical Scholarship. Minneapolis: Fortress.

Resseguie, J. L. (2005) *Narrative Criticism of the New Testament: An Introduction*. Grand Rapids: Baker Academic.

Rhoads, D., J. Dewey and D. Michie (1999) *Mark as Story: An Introduction to the Narrative of a Gospel*, 2nd edn. Philadelphia: Fortress.

Smith, S. H. (1996) *A Lion with Wings: A Narrative-Critical Approach to Mark's Gospel*. Sheffield: Sheffield Academic Press.

11 Structural criticism

Calloud, J. (1976) *Structural Analysis of Narrative*, Semeia Studies. Philadelphia and Missoula: Fortress Press and Scholars Press.

Dunnill, J. (1992) *Covenant and Sacrifice in the Letter to the Hebrews*, Society for New Testament Monograph Series 75. Cambridge: Cambridge University Press.

Malbon, E. Struthers (1986) *Narrative Space and Mythic Meaning in Mark*. San Francisco: Harper & Row.

Patte, D. (1983) *Paul's Faith and the Power of the Gospel: A Structural Introduction to the Pauline Letters*. Philadelphia: Fortress.

Patte, D. (1987) *The Gospel according to Matthew: A Structural Commentary on Matthew's Faith*. Philadelphia: Fortress.

Patte, D. (1990) *Structural Exegesis for New Testament Critics*, Guides to Biblical Scholarship: New Testament Series. Minneapolis: Fortress.

12   Poststructural criticism

Aichele, G. (1997) *Sign, Text, Scripture: Semiotics and the Bible*. Sheffield: Sheffield Academic.

Castelli, E. (1991) *Imitating Paul: A Discourse of Power*. Louisville: Westminster John Knox.

Crossan, J. D. (1980) *Cliffs of Fall: Paradox and Polyvalence in the Parables of Jesus*. New York: Seabury Press.

Moore, S. D. (1992) *Mark and Luke in Poststructuralist Perspectives: Jesus Begins to Write*. New Haven: Yale University Press.

13   Reception history

Beuken, W. and S. Freyne (1995) *The Bible and Cultural Heritage*. London: SCM.

Kovacs, J. L., C. C. Rowland and R. Callow (2004) *Revelation: The Apocalypse of Jesus Christ*. Oxford and Malden, MA: Blackwell.

Luz, U. (1994) *Matthew in History: Interpretation, Influence, and Effects*. Minneapolis: Fortress.

Müller, M. and H. Tronier (2002) *The New Testament as Reception*. Sheffield: Sheffield Academic.

Sawyer, J. F. (2006) *The Blackwell Companion to Bible and Culture*. Oxford: Blackwell.

14   Theological interpretation

Adam, A. K. M. (2006) *Faithful Interpretation*. Minneapolis: Fortress.

Adam, A. K. M., S. Fowl, K. Vanhoozer and F. Watson (2006) *Reading Scripture With the Church*. Grand Rapids: Baker Academic.

Bockmuehl, M. (2006) *Seeing the Word: Refocusing New Testament Study*. Grand Rapids: Baker Academic.

Davis, E. F. and R. B. Hays (2003) *The Art of Reading Scripture*. Grand Rapids: Eerdmans.

Fowl, S. (2000) *Engaging Scripture*. Oxford and Malden, MA: Blackwell.

Vanhoozer, K. J., ed. (2006) *Dictionary for Theological Interpretation of the Bible*. London and Grand Rapids: SPCK and Baker Academic.

15   Reader-response criticism

Fowler, R. M. (1991) *Let the Reader Understand: Reader-Response Criticism and the Gospel of Mark*. Harrisburg, PA: Trinity Press International.

Heil, J. P. (1992) *The Gospel of Mark as Model for Action: A Reader-Response Commentary*. New York: Paulist Press.

Powell, M. A. (2001) *Chasing the Eastern Star: Adventures in Biblical Reader-Response Criticism*. Louisville: Westminster John Knox.
Webber, R. C. (1996) *Reader Response Analysis of the Epistle of James*. London and San Francisco: International Scholars.

16 Feminist criticism

Day L. and C. Pressler, eds (2006), *Engaging the Bible in a Gendered World: An Introduction to Feminist Biblical Interpretation in Honor of Katharine Dobb Sakenfeld*. Louisville and London: Westminster John Knox.
Ehrensperger, K. (2007) *Paul and the Dynamics of Power: Communication and Interaction in the Early Christ-Movement*. London and New York: T&T Clark International.
Moore, S. D. and J. C. Anderson, eds (2003) *New Testament Masculinities*. Atlanta, GA: Society of Biblical Literature.
Schottroff, L., S. Schroer and M.-T. Wacker (1998) *Feminist Interpretation: The Bible in Women's Perspective*. Minneapolis: Fortress.
Schüssler Fiorenza, E. (2001) *Wisdom Ways: Introducing Feminist Biblical Interpretation*. Maryknoll: Orbis.

17 Queer criticism

Butler, J. (1990) *Gender Trouble*. London and New York: Routledge.
Guest, D., R. E. Goss, M. West and T. Bohache (2006) *The Queer Bible Commentary*. London: SCM.
Hornsby, T. J. (2001) 'Paul and the Remedies of Idolatry: Reading Romans 1.18–24 with Romans 7', in A. K. M. Adam, ed., *Postmodern Interpretations of the Bible*. St Louis: Chalice.
Martin, D. B. (2006) *Sex and the Single Savior: Gender and Sexuality in Biblical Interpretation*. Louisville: Westminster John Knox.
Nissinen, M. (1998) *Homoeroticism in the Biblical World: A Historical Perspective*. Minneapolis: Fortress.

18 Liberation criticism

Hanks, T. (2000) *The Subversive Gospel: A New Testament Commentary of Liberation*. Cleveland: Pilgrim Press.
Rowland, C. and M. Corner (1990) *Liberating Exegesis: The Challenge of Liberation Theology to Biblical Studies*. London: SPCK; (1989) Louisville: Westminster John Knox.
Vaage, L. E., ed. (1997) *Subversive Scriptures: Revolutionary Readings of the Christian Bible in Latin America*. Valley Forge: Trinity Press International.
West, G. O. (1995) *Biblical Hermeneutics of Liberation: Modes of Reading the Bible in the South African Context*. Maryknoll and Pietermaritzburg: Orbis and Cluster.

West, G. O., ed. (2007) *Reading Other-wise: Socially Engaged Biblical Scholars Reading with their Local Communities*, Semeia Studies. Atlanta: Society of Biblical Literature.

19   Sociopolitical criticism

Hennelly, A., ed. (1990) *Liberation Theology: A Documentary History*. Maryknoll: Orbis.

Myers, C. (1988) *Binding the Strong Man: A Political Reading of Mark's Story of Jesus*. Maryknoll: Orbis.

Rowland, C. and M. Corner (1989) *Liberating Exegesis: The Challenge of Liberation Theology to Biblical Studies*. London: SPCK.

Schottroff, L. and W. Stegemann (1986) *Jesus and the Hope of the Poor*, trans. M. O'Connell. Maryknoll: Orbis.

Swartley, W. (2006) *Covenant of Peace: The Missing Peace in New Testament Theology and Ethics*. Grand Rapids: Eerdmans.

Tamez, E. (2007) *Struggles for Power in Early Christianity: A Study in the First Letter to Timothy*. Maryknoll: Orbis.

Wink, W. (1984) *Naming the Powers: The Language of Power in the New Testament*. Minneapolis: Fortress.

20   Black criticism

Blount, B. K. (1995) *Cultural Interpretation: Reorienting New Testament Criticism*. Minneapolis: Augsburg/Fortress.

Blount, B. K. (2001) *Then the Whisper Put on Flesh: New Testament Ethics in an African Context*. Nashville: Abingdon.

Brown, M. (2004) *Blackening of the Bible: The Aims of African American Biblical Scholarship*. Harrisburg, PA: Trinity Press International.

West, G. and M. Dube, eds (2000) *The Bible in Africa: Transactions, Trajectories, and Trends*. Leiden: Brill.

Williams, D. (1993) *Sisters in the Wilderness: The Challenges of Womanist God-Talk*. Maryknoll: Orbis.

Wimbush, V., ed. (2000) *African Americans and the Bible: Sacred Texts and Social Textures*. New York and London: Continuum.

21   Postcolonial criticism

Dube, M. W. (2000) *Postcolonial Feminist Interpretation of the Bible*. St Louis: Chalice.

Moore, S. D. and F. Segovia, eds (2005) *Postcolonial Biblical Criticism: Interdisciplinary Intersections*. London and New York: T&T Clark International.

Samuel, S. (2007) *A Postcolonial Reading of Mark's Story of Jesus*. New York: T&T Clark International.

Sugirtharajah, R. S. (2002) *Postcolonial Criticism and Biblical Interpretation*. Oxford and New York: Oxford University Press.

Sugirtharajah, R. S., ed. (1998) *The Postcolonial Bible*. Sheffield: Sheffield Academic Press.

22 Asian criticism

Abesamis, C. H. (1990) 'Some Paradigms in Re-reading the Bible in a Third-World Setting', *Mission Studies* 7/1, 21–34.

'Asian Women Doing Theology' (2004) *In God's Image* 21/4 (special thematic issue).

Kuan, J. Kah-Jin (1999) 'Asian Biblical Interpretation', in *Dictionary of Biblical Interpretation*, vol. 1, ed. J. H. Hayes. Nashville: Abingdon, 70–7.

Singgih, E. G. (1995) 'Let Me Not be Put to Shame: Towards an Indonesian Hermeneutics', *Asia Journal of Theology* 9/1, 71–85.

Sugirtharajah, R. S. (1998) *Asian Biblical Hermeneutics and Postcolonialism: Contesting the Interpretations*. Maryknoll: Orbis.

23 Ecological criticism

Berry, R. J., ed. (2000) *The Care of Creation*. Leicester: IVP.

Bouma-Prediger, S. (2001) *For the Beauty of the Earth: A Christian Vision for Creation Care*. Grand Rapids: Baker Academic.

Conradie, E. (2004) 'Towards an Ecological Biblical Hermeneutic: A Review Essay on the Earth Bible Project', *Scriptura* 85, 123–35.

Habel, N. C., ed. (2000) *Readings from the Perspective of Earth*, Earth Bible 1. Sheffield: Sheffield Academic Press.

Habel, N. C. and V. Balabanski, eds (2002) *The Earth Story in the New Testament*, Earth Bible 5. Sheffield: Sheffield Academic Press.

Horrell, D. G., C. Hunt and C. Southgate (2008) 'Appeals to the Bible in Ecotheology and Environmental Ethics', *Studies in Christian Ethics* 21/2.

Hunt, C., D. G. Horrell and C. Southgate (forthcoming) 'An Environmental Mantra? Ecological Interest in Romans 8.19–23 and a Modest Proposal for its Narrative Interpretation', *Journal of Theological Studies*.

Index of biblical and ancient texts

225

Index of modern authors

227